T0244359

Praise for Michael Ray Richardson

"Michael Ray Richardson deserves to have his flowers as one of the great guards to ever play in the NBA. That's what George Gervin says about it."

—George Gervin, NBA Top 75 player

"Pressure makes pipes explode. But pressure also makes diamonds. And Michael Ray Richardson is a diamond."

—Nancy Lieberman, Basketball Hall of Famer

"He was like a Magic Johnson but with a better outside shot."

—Spencer Haywood, Basketball Hall of Famer

"Michael was just a hell of a player, in the NBA and in Italy. He had the best hands, getting all these steals. Defensively, he was just awesome."

—Bob McAdoo, NBA Top 75 player

"Michael was fearless. He would go into the other team's locker room before the game. No lie. Whether it was Magic Johnson, whether it was Isiah Thomas, he'd go into the locker room and tell them, 'I'm going to bust your ass tonight!'"

—Otis Birdsong, four-time NBA All-Star

"Intimidation is part of being a successful basketball player and Sugar was the best."

—Michael Cooper, Basketball Hall of Famer

"What I remember most about Sugar Ray is that the level of trash-talking between him, Larry Bird and Kevin McHale always elevated the competition."

—Robert Parish, NBA Top 75 player

"A great player and a good man!"

—Tyrone "Muggsy" Bogues, NBA icon

"Michael Ray Richardson captured my imagination as a young person. He was ahead of his time on the court and his story demands to be heard. It's not a happy story, in the traditional sense, but it contains the joy of someone who found himself when others believed him to be lost."

—Dave Zirin, sports editor, *The Nation*

BANNED

BANNED

HOW I SQUANDERED AN ALL-STAR NBA CAREER BEFORE FINDING MY REDEMPTION

MICHAEL "SUGAR" RAY RICHARDSON
WITH JAKE UITTI

FOREWORDS BY GEORGE "ICEMAN" GERVIN
AND NANCY LIEBERMAN

SPORTS
PUBLISHING

Sports Publishing books may be purchased in bulk at special discounts for sales promotion, corporate gifts, fund-raising, or educational purposes. Special editions can also be created to specifications. For details, contact the Special Sales Department, Sports Publishing, 307 West 36th Street, 11th Floor, New York, NY 10018 or sportspubbooks@skyhorsepublishing.com.

Sports Publishing® is a registered trademark of Skyhorse Publishing, Inc.®, a Delaware corporation.

Visit our website at www.sportspubbooks.com.

10 9 8 7 6 5 4 3 2 1

Library of Congress Cataloging-in-Publication Data is available on file.

Jacket design by Brian Peterson
Front jacket photographs: Getty Images

Print ISBN: 978-1-68358-490-2
Ebook ISBN: 978-1-68358-491-9

Printed in the United States of America

For my mother and my family
—Michael

For Coco and Emi
—Jake

CONTENTS

FOREWORD

BY GEORGE "ICEMAN" GERVIN

WHEN I was with the San Antonio Spurs, and we played New York, Michael Ray and Ray Williams were with the Knicks. They were two dogs, man. You had to come ready for them to play hard. They were both tough to deal with on the defensive end—Mike especially. He would challenge you every time. He had good anticipation and he'd reach for the ball and take it from you if you weren't on your game. It was fun playing against him, in a way, because he was so tough—especially at the Garden.

Mike, with his size, was one of them special guys back then. He was that *good* size. He was six-five, six-six and was just as quick and could move like a six-one, six-two guard. Of course, you had to have a big guard to play me! I'm six-eight. So when we played against one another, he won some and I won some. I was known as a scorer then, but Mike made me work really hard, even if I wound up and got my numbers on those nights.

Walt Frazier, Pearl Monroe, those guys played in New York, too, but Mike was three or four inches taller than them. To be that tall and play that position is really special. A lot of us, and I'm including Mike, don't get our due today for what we were able to accomplish back then. But if you talk to people like me and other greats from that era, all we talk about is each other. It's a respect we keep for that time in our lives.

The NBA has to sell the game today, I understand that, but when you start looking at analytics—you can't take the numbers away. You start putting ours into the computers and you quickly see that our era was filled with greatness. If you compared us with guys from today, you'd find yourself talking more and more about us. As veterans, we have to be comfortable with what we did in our yesterdays, because if we harp on it too much, we'd go blue in the face!

But on the defensive side, there aren't a whole lot of guys who could play like Mike. He could guard *anybody*, including all the greats. Mike is part of that greatness, too. Trust me. I'm one of the best scorers of all time, and I'm telling you he's part of that greatness, especially when you talk defensively. I always mention him because of how hard he played me. But Mike could shoot the ball, too. He could score. I'm a Mike fan, man—and we ain't talking MJ!

When people bring up Michael Ray being banned from the NBA—you know, life is tough. And sometimes we get on the wrong road and we get stuck. But as long as we're able to get off that road and tell our story—that's the point. That's part of Mike's greatness. We all know what it's like in some way or another. We all had our issues—who hasn't? But look at the great career he had even before leaving the NBA. Four All-Stars and leading the league in steals and assists.

Mike's ups and downs are something to mention, but they ain't nothing to talk about, if you know what I mean. Because who would be the one to cast the first stone? That's how I look at it. That's what I love about Mike as a man . . . even though he could never really hold a sentence together because of his stutter! He always pushed through every day. That's what makes him special to a guy like me.

If you're reading this, you've chosen the right guy and the right story. If you want to know about one of the great players from his era, someone who was capable of doing what he did at the size that he was, the specialness and excitement he brought to the game, then keep reading Michael Ray's book. It's a story about redemption. And that's everything! Because we all get knocked down. Tell me somebody who ain't been knocked down? It's about *getting up*.

I'm going to say it: there are fools out there who try to make his addiction and ban from the NBA the main story of his career. But they're wrong. Today, Mike is on his own two feet. He's happy, he's got family. And he's able to tell you *his* story. Nobody will tell you his story better than he can. That's the beauty of it. Now, if he wasn't here because of some of the choices he made, then that's different.

But if you want to hear the story about what happened in his life, it's all here. Michael Ray Richardson deserves to have his flowers as one of the great guards to ever play in the NBA. That's what George Gervin says about it.

—George Gervin, NBA Top 75 player
(Gervin and Richardson faced each other in
19 regular-season games.)

FOREWORD

BY NANCY LIEBERMAN

MICHAEL and I first met in 1986. I was at home in Dallas, wondering if I'd ever get to play again, because the women's league (WABA) had just folded. I was working out and playing when I got a phone call from this guy, Andy Eckman, who said, "Would you like to play in the USBL? It's a men's league." And I said yes. So I go up there and my first year is fantastic. I had such a great time. In my second, my team, the Springfield Fame, had folded, and so I ended up playing for Dean Meminger and the Long Island Knights. My teammate there was Michael Ray Richardson.

Everyone knows, I'm a big Knicks fan. I'm a New York basketball fan. So I knew Michael had the three-strike rule with Commissioner Stern. Today, Michael and I are like a married couple, and I'm sure our stories will vary, but how I remember it is Dean Meminger said, "Nancy, you need to room with him." And I'm like, "What?" They were testing me. And I was like, "Okay, I don't really care." Michael and I became roommates on the road. I remember being in the lobby of hotels and girls would be waiting for him. I'd say, "He came with me, he's leaving with me."

We'd go up to our room and I just loved being around him. We hit it off right away. I was very protective of him. Michael is a very, very special guy. You know his talent on the court. He was a four-time NBA All-Star. But I remember one game we were playing at home and the 5-foot-3 Tyrone Bogues was on the other team. Geoff Huston and Michael were in the huddle and Dean goes, "Okay Sugar, you're guarding Bogues." And Michael goes, "I ain't guarding him!" But I was listening—nobody wanted to guard Muggsy, he was so quick and talented.

I looked at the coach and said, "I'll guard him." Dean put me in the game. I looked at Geoff Huston and said, "If you don't want to play, I'll play. I don't care who I play against!" And Michael supported me. Michael is very, very loyal. A couple times that year, people on the other teams would try to mess with me. There was this guy who threw an elbow in my chest, as if to say, *Why are you even here?* It was Othell Wilson, who played at Virginia with Ralph Sampson. It was on a side out of bounds play. He did that to me, so I just started throwing my hands.

Then everybody jumped in. But Michael jumped in front and knocked Othell down. Michael had his forearm under his chin on his chest, saying, "Don't touch my baby. You leave her alone." While I'm behind all the guys, like, "Yeah! Don't touch me! Michael is going to kick your ass!" At the time, we were probably two of the most prominent names in the league. I'd had a crappy childhood and so I identify with people who got into trouble. I'm like Big Mike from *The Blind Side*. I have protective instincts.

For Michael, I had protective instincts. I wasn't going to let some chick waltz into his life just because of who he was or that he might have had some money. That's who I am as a person. I was like that with Sugar. I was like that with Muhammad Ali. And Kobe. And I'm like that with Deion Sanders. I was very protective of other people who I love and respect. Some people say, "That's my dog." But I'm not anybody's *dog*. I'm a wolf. And wolves eat dogs. I'm a wolf and I don't want anybody to hurt my guys!

I'm a tough little girl from New York and I wanted to learn the game from Michael. Like I said, I didn't have a place to play. People were saying I was the best basketball player in the world, yet I couldn't show my hard work or my skillset. I'd get by somebody in the USBL and a seven-footer would block my shot. I needed Michael to teach me what I didn't know. Because he was such an elite player and that was very, very important to me. Michael was willing to share what he knew. We would go into the gym and he would teach me what I needed to know.

But my job, as far as I saw it, was to get Sugar back to the league. The NBA. In my eyes, this guy didn't belong in the USBL, sitting next to me. Everybody thought, "Oh my god, this guy was a drug addict." But he wasn't like that. Michael is such a great human being and that's why David Stern loved him. That's why everybody you know doesn't have a bad thing to say about Michael Ray Richardson. We all go through stuff in life, and he paid the piper. And look how long he played. Then his coaching career! Michael has excelled at everything he's ever wanted to do.

I'd like to close with this: Pressure makes pipes explode. But pressure also makes diamonds. And Michael Ray Richardson is a diamond.

—Nancy Lieberman, Basketball Hall of Famer

PREFACE

BY OTIS BIRDSONG

I **FIRST** met Michael when we played against each other when I was with the Kansas City Kings. He was in New York playing for the Knicks. He and Ray Williams were a heck of a backcourt. It was a great matchup going against them with my teammate Phil Ford, our starting point guard. I remember we had some good battles against Sugar and Ray. I don't remember any trash talking when we played against each other, though, because Ray guarded me and Michael had Ford.

But Michael was blazing fast with the ball. He could really attack the basket. He had great hands and great anticipation on defense. He gambled a lot, but he always came up with the steal. He was great at help defense and was a great individual defender, too. Even though he didn't guard me when I was in Kansas City, I still tease him all the time. My sons went and found our stats when we played against each other back then, so I show him when I had 30 or 35 points!

I tell him, "Michael, you must have been guarding me that night!" And he says, "N-no, no, no that was Ray guarding you!" We laugh about it all the time. When we were teammates in New Jersey, though, it was amazing. One of the New York–area magazines had us on the cover. They called us "Rhythm & Blues." I guess because we made sweet music together. He was one of the greatest competitors I ever played with. He could have been in the Hall of Fame.

Michael was fearless. He would go into the other team's locker room before the game. No lie. Whether it was Magic Johnson, whether it was Isiah Thomas, he'd go into the locker room and tell them, "I'm going to bust your ass tonight!" He was just fearless on the court. Michael didn't fear anyone, and that's very rare. He was respectful about it, I guess, but normally you don't tell your opponent you're going to bust his ass before the game . . . unless you're Larry Bird!

The 1983–84 season was a great year for us. Stan Albeck did a tremendous job with the entire team. Our chemistry was so good. Buck Williams was playing out of his mind, as was Darryl Dawkins, Darwin Cook, and Mike Gminski. In the playoffs that year, we beat the defending champion Philadelphia 76ers. For some reason, Sugar and I always matched up well against Andrew Toney and Maurice Cheeks. Michael was just too big and too quick for Cheeks.

It was a nightmare matchup for Maurice guarding Michael. And I always played well against Andrew Toney. We just had a phenomenal series. We both played great. But Michael—I hate to use this word, but he really just *destroyed* Maurice Cheeks.* They had no answers for him. Michael had a tremendous series. I remember we won the first two games at their place, then they came to New Jersey and won the next two against us.

---

* Michael Ray Richardson averaged 20.6 points per game in the Eastern Conference First Round, while averaging 12 points per game during the season.

For the fifth game, Dr. J said in the newspaper that the Nets shouldn't even make the two-hour trip up to Philly because no team would beat them three straight at home, especially in the playoffs. Ha! I remember Michael and I both had 24 points that night and we won the series. What was crazy though was that we beat the defending champions on a Thursday night, but we had to turn around and play a Sunday afternoon game in Milwaukee.

Because we were on such a high, though, we won that first game in Milwaukee. In the second game, we were close with about a minute left. But a bad call hurt us. A referee whistled Michael for traveling (a self-pass), saying he touched a loose ball when he didn't. If not for that, we would have had the ball and they would have had to foul us, but they called traveling. We could have won those first two games in Milwaukee. Instead, we lost the series in six games.

When Michael was banned from the NBA, from a team perspective, it was devastating. You lose a talent like that, your point guard, your cog who makes everything go, that's a big blow. He's still my favorite point guard I played with. We had some good players to help fill in, but they were no Michael Ray Richardson. For me, as far as him being my friend and backcourt mate, it was crushing. He was my guy. We hung out together; we didn't live that far from each other.

From a basketball perspective it was bad but, from a friendship perspective, it was tougher. He was banned from the league. I know he loved playing the game and he was good at it. For him not to be able to be in the NBA was hard. But he and I stayed in touch, even when he went overseas. He always told me that after he was banned, a lot of guys, a lot of his friends, they didn't want to deal with him anymore. But we stayed in touch.

When Sugar came back from overseas, it was easy for us to pick up again. Today, he and I work closely together as business partners. He's a hilarious guy! He works hard, too. But the key thing about Michael is his loyalty. He tells me all the time, if he has a nickel, half of it is mine. That's the way we roll. We have a good time, but no clubbing! We're not out in these streets! He doesn't drink. Just good ol' fashion fun.

The fascinating thing is, when Michael went to rehab or when he'd disappear while going on those binges, he didn't ever contact me. He never called and said, "Bird, I need help. Bird, come get me. Bird, I'm doing this or that." I can only imagine that he felt despondent, sad, because he let people down, let his family down. But he never contacted me when he was on those binges. In fact, I never saw him use anything, ever. I never saw him sniff cocaine or smoke a joint. He never did that in front of me. He knew I didn't do it, so he never did it around me. He never said, "Bird, I'm going into the city, I need you to ride with me. Let's pick something up." I just never saw him do anything like that. And I did see other guys do it. I saw some guys smoking the pipe and I didn't know what the hell they were doing the first time I saw that. I even saw teammates sniff cocaine in front of me. They'd even offer it to me, and I'd say, "No, all I do is drink beer, brother." But Michael never brought that stuff around me.

What people don't know about Sugar is that he's a family man. I've never seen someone, especially a man, talk to his kids as often as he does. He talks to his kids, who are overseas, every day and is in touch with his kids in the States, too. He really cares about each of them.

One more thing: Michael was a great minor-league basketball coach. He won five championships. I was the president and GM of an NBA developmental league team while Michael was coaching in the minor leagues. At the time, I already had a coach, so I couldn't hire him. Later, when were in Oklahoma, we worked together. But at one point they were putting an NBA developmental team in Colorado. When I heard that, I told him, "Man, wouldn't that be a great story of redemption? For you to be the first person banned from the league, now you're a champion coach and you could come home back to your home state of Colorado and coach in the D-League. What a story." I got in contact with David Stern to see if he could get Michael an interview. The disappointing thing was that the Colorado team only gave him, like, a ten-miniute interview over the phone.

They didn't even have the decency to at least let him come in and sit down and talk face-to-face. It was a token interview. I'm not saying the NBA does this as a whole and I don't know who interviewed him then and didn't hire him. But over the years, I've seen different pockets of people hold Michael's past against him. I've talked to him about it. They even question me, like, what am I doing, working events with him and running camps? *How does it look to the parents?*

There are still people who hold that against him more than thirty years later. They don't know that he wasn't the only player doing drugs. Sure, he was the first to get kicked out. But Michael wasn't the only player in the NBA to go to rehab. How can you hold that stuff from thirty years ago against him today? He's not the same person. Michael has been sober now for more than *three* decades. He's one of my best friends, and I'm honored to call him a brother.

—Otis Birdsong, four-time NBA All-Star

INTRODUCTION

WHENEVER my name is brought up in basketball circles, so too are my troubles with drugs. It's inevitable and has been for decades. But while that part of my life, being addicted to cocaine and losing my NBA career as a result, is certainly the most salacious part of my life, it is not who I am. At worst, it's who I was *for a period of time*. There's a saying: *We are not our worst days*. Of course, while we all know that human beings make mistakes, we sometimes don't let each other forget them. It's human nature, I suppose. But that's why I wanted to write this book. To tell my story—completely and truthfully.

From Lubbock, Texas, to Denver, Colorado, to New York City, Oakland, California, New Jersey, Israel, Europe, and beyond, I have played the game of basketball at a high level and in several countries. Other than my mother, the warrior, the sport of basketball was my only love. But then everything changed for me. I went from living a straight-edge life, one who never partied, to one controlled by drugs. I blame no one but myself for the choices and poor decisions in my past. But again, that's not who I am at my core—and it's *certainly* not who I am here, today.

Now, I am a father, grandfather, teacher, camp counselor, husband, sibling, and son. I'm also a former four-time NBA All-Star, league leader in assists, three-time league leader in steals, and big-time college player from the University of Montana.

But the moment in my career that stands out to me the most is my choice in 1988 to go to Italy. Making *that* decision saved my life and extended my playing career into my late forties. I am proud of so much of what I've done in my life, what I've overcome—both internally and externally—that I no longer let the bad times—from my mistakes to my infamous stutter—override the good ones.

I've been sober for more than three decades. I learned my lesson, thanks in part to former NBA commissioner and friend David Stern. I got clean and have remained so for more than half my life. This is my story about all of that. No stone unturned. From country bumpkin to NBA star to becoming the first player to be banned from the league for drugs to becoming the first to be *reinstated* back to the NBA. From All-Star to coach to motivational speaker and camp counselor. This is also a story about hitting rock bottom and the recovery that followed. After all, when the ball hits the floor, it must bounce back up.

This book is me, unfiltered. As a four-time All-Star, two-time All-Defensive first team player, and Comeback Player of the Year recipient, steals and assists leader, and an international sports celebrity, this is my truth, word for word. I never thought drugs would get to me, but I learned that it could happen to anybody. I know that now. I made my bed and have had to sleep in it all these years. Finally, I'm now ready to tell my story, after decades of hard work, soul searching, and living. Gratefully, I've come out clearheaded and on the other side. Thank you for reading and thank you for caring.

—Michael Ray Richardson
Lawton, Oklahoma, 2024

1

BEATING THE CHAMPS

DURING the 1984 NBA playoffs, my team, the New Jersey Nets, had a theme song, "Ain't No Stoppin' Us Now," by McFadden & Whitehead. And we proved that line in the opening round series against the defending champion Philadelphia 76ers. That team was stacked, from former MVP Moses Malone to the basketball god that was Julius Erving. The Sixers also had Mo Cheeks, Andrew Toney, and Bobby Jones. Hall of Famers left and right.

But we had their number.

Even though I missed about half the season for my well-publicized issues with cocaine, the team had gone 3–3 against Philly that year, winning the final two matchups. And even though they were the defending champs, we weren't scared of their roster or their history. We simply matched up well against them. Julius and his older legs had a problem guarding our twenty-four-year-old small forward Albert King. And Philly's guards couldn't check me and Otis Birdsong. We were bigger, faster, stronger.

BANNED

Going into the series, we knew all the pressure was on them. They were the defending champs and wanted to repeat. But they had to go through us first. Our roster included two-time All-Star Buck Williams and Darryl "Chocolate Thunder" Dawkins up front, along with me, King, and four-time All-Star Otis Birdsong on the wing. Philadelphia finished 52–30 that season, while we were 45–37. So they had home-court advantage. They must have thought we'd be walk-overs.

In Game One, we beat them 116–101. Buck had 25 points and 16 rebounds. I had 18 points, nine assists, and six boards. Otis scored 24 and King had 16. In the next game—well, we won it again in dominating fashion, 116–102. I scored 32 with nine more assists and seven rebounds. Dawkins, playing his former team, added 22 points and King had 15. Though Moses scored 25 and Andrew Toney had 22 for Philly, the rest of the team couldn't muster what they needed to get over the hump. No stoppin' us now!

We'd found something that worked. Instead of letting Mo Cheeks and Andrew Toney pressure me and Otis as we brought the ball up, we had Albert King bring it up because we knew Julius wasn't going to take him full court. When Albert got past half court, he'd just pass it to me and I'd get the offense going. Coach Stan Albeck was a genius for that one. Before Game Two, he told us, "Keep it close and we'll win in the fourth." Stan was right again. Philly ran out of gas.

On the back of the bus going home to New Jersey after winning the first two, I remember Dawkins drinking a six-pack of Heineken in about five minutes. Laughing all the way, he'd chug a can and then smash it and go for the next. Back on our home court a couple days later, the Sixers hit back and took Games

2

Three and Four. We were riding high and took them for granted. Though Philly was an older team, they dug into their reserves. They were still the defending champions. They still had pride. And we didn't play aggressively like we should have.

Now everything was tied at two apiece and we were heading back to Philadelphia for the deciding fifth game. That's when Julius Erving sealed the series for us by saying the wrong thing.

Don't get me wrong, Dr. J is a basketball deity. He was my hero growing up. But that's why what he said then was so helpful to us. After Game Four, he was being interviewed by some reporters. He told them that we might as well mail in the stat sheet because we weren't going to win in Philly.

Challenge accepted. Julius had said Game Five was already over, that we had no shot. That we could never beat them three times in one series on their floor. When we got up the next morning and filed onto the bus in Jersey to head to Philly, Stan brought the newspapers with him to show us. "Julius Erving Says Mail in Stat Sheets." All we thought was that we were going to *our* home court. Philly belonged to *us*. And we felt no pressure.

Going into the deciding game, I wanted to tear the six-foot Maurice Cheeks a new asshole. And I did. We threw a haymaker in the first quarter, going up 31–25, but Philly came back in the second, outscoring us 28–19. While they led 53–50 at the half, we still knew it was our game. Then in the third and fourth, we brought it home. I scored 24, dished six assists, six boards, *and* six steals. Otis got 24 and Buck had 17 and 16. Despite Dr. J and Moses notching double-doubles, we won the game and the series!

It was the biggest moment in Nets franchise history since the team had come over to the NBA from the ramshackle ABA a decade prior. The irony was that the Nets were Dr. J's old team. As a kid, I'd had dreams of playing against him. When I woke up each morning, I would run down to the kitchen and tell my mother and my sisters that I'd dunked on "The Doctor" while I was sleeping. Now, I'd beaten him on an honest-to-God NBA floor. What could be better?

The series win was a sign of great things to come—that's what everyone hoped. But after all I'd been through—the rehabs, the drug houses, the stints gone missing—no one was going to hold their breath for my future. Not even me. I'd seen too much and knew what I was capable of, both good and bad. Little did I know what the next few months would have in store for me, let alone the next few decades. All I knew was that we'd just won big. But was it too good to be true?

2

A FAMILY MOVING NORTH

MY mother Luddie Hicks, the warrior, gave birth to me on a kitchen table in a small home in Lubbock, Texas. It was April 11, 1955, and I'm sure I screamed my little round head off. Years later, she told me that I wasn't born in a hospital because, back then, for whatever reason, it was common enough for some babies to be birthed in the home.

Located in northwest Texas about six hours from both Dallas and San Antonio, Lubbock was a horrible place to live if you were Black. My mother and the rest of our family sought to move from the area as soon as we could. It was, in a word, a *shithole* where, just before we left, my grandfather was beaten badly by three white men and robbed as he was leaving his job at a cleaners. To find a better life, mom left for Denver, Colorado. There, she looked for a job and, when she found one, taking a position with the Colorado General Hospital kitchen staff, our family followed north. Hospitals were okay for work, but I guess not for giving birth.

Lubbock, in the panhandle of the state, was small. And I was, too. I was just five years old when mom left for Colorado with a tiny hope in her heart. The rest of us—me and my siblings and my mother's parents—stayed behind, waiting for any good news. My father, Billy Jack Richardson, was hardly ever around the family. He was in the military, stationed far away—in New Mexico, if I remember right. He was in and out of our lives and I was never very close with him. Truth be told, I think when it came to my mother, he was mostly just a sperm donor.

His mother lived outside Lubbock in the country on a pig farm. Before we left for Denver, she had us come out there to visit and help feed the pigs. I remember crap was everywhere. A mess of pigs playing in their own slop. I didn't like her farm. It was disgusting—the biological smells, the cakes of squishy mud and rancid feces, the pigs gleefully spinning around in all of the mess. My dad's mom also ran a small nearby café for local field workers. The café wasn't all that much better than the farm. I'm a neat and tidy guy. The kind of person who squares a tissue box at a right angle on the countertop. So, pigs? Nope, not for me.

A month into mom's job search is when my grandfather was beaten. Fearing more violence and cursing Lubbock, we left for Denver several months earlier than we'd initially planned. But while my mother had forged a road ahead for us, don't get it confused: despite her hard work for our family, she wasn't all sunshine and daisies. She could put a whoopin' on your ass good. When I was around six years old, I remember she threw me a birthday party She served cantaloupe and watermelon to the guests. When she gave me a piece, I tried the watermelon and I didn't like it.

So what did I do? I took that slice of watermelon around to the back of the house and threw it in the grass. Then I took out my willie and peed on it. To this day, I have no idea why that was my reaction, other than I just didn't like the taste of it. I still don't like the taste of watermelon. But what did I get for that decision? When my mother turned the corner and saw me, I got the whooping of my life. And while it hurt like hell, deep down, I understand why. My mother, a single Black parent, needed to instill discipline in her kids. She knew it better than anyone. Instinct in a cold, unforgiving world.

* * *

I grew up with a tightly knit family. I have six siblings and am the third eldest. My brother Billy was born first. Then Harold, who unfortunately passed away just a few years ago. Then me, followed by my sisters Dorothy, Ineda, and Sherry. Lastly, there's Troy, who has a different father than the rest of us. All in all, we were a normal family just trying to make it through the days. We were content, all things considered. And mom made sure we were all fed (I particularly liked fried pork chop sandwiches!), clothed, and good to one another.

After we moved to Denver, mom married a man named Johnny. He worked a desk job for the local government in Denver and became something of a father figure to me. Truth be told, he was one of my first surrogate fathers (and he was Troy's actual father). The need for a father figure and that positive affirmation is important for young kids, and it was especially important for me. In some ways, it still is today. It's probably a hole that I've been trying to fill all my life, on the court and off. With my dad all but gone, I needed that direction. I craved it. But life was good in Denver, civilized. Much better than it was in Lubbock.

As much as I could, I spent time outdoors, whether playing marbles or baseball with the neighborhood kids, dribbling a basketball in the backyard, or walking to a nearby court. Our family lived in a small home on 32nd Street attached to a church in a lower-income part of east Denver. It was a modest red brick house with a stone front porch. The backyard had a little fence around it and there was a tall tree in front that still stands today. I used to sit on that stoop with my mother and watch the traffic pass like seconds off a lazy clock. It was also the "punishment porch" when mom made us stand out there alone, for everyone to see.

Normally, the house connected to the church would be the place where the preacher lived, but for some reason they were renting it out and we got it. It was a six-bedroom home and a cozy place for all of us to live. It had a small yard but was on a main street, so we didn't play in the yard much. Instead, we went a block or two to the well-kept Cole Junior High, where I'd dribble and shoot on their hoops (to avoid mom yelling at me for dribbling in her house again). I'd play with friends like Rodney Long, Dennis Reed, Larry Benford, and Sam Combs. Some called where we lived a "ghetto" of Denver, but it never felt bad to us. Life was peaceful.

I have a lot of good memories from this time (everything but the snow). As I got older, another place we'd play at was the Red Shield Community Center, a Salvation Army on 29th and High Street. We'd play there after school let out and during the summers. They had good winter and summer leagues, and the place was open early to late, from nine to nine. That community center kept me and a lot of other kids out of trouble. The facility is still there to this day, located at 2915 High Street. I owe a lot of my love for the game to the Red Shield Center. It was a home away from home and a place where I could learn the game early in my life.

* * *

I first picked up the game of basketball when I was in sixth grade at Mitchell Elementary School. The principal of the school, Donald Wilson, also served as the basketball coach. One day at recess, while I was outside, I grabbed a basketball and started to play around with it on the court. I immediately felt a connection to it. Dribbling it, shooting it. Mr. Wilson must have seen me out there and he came up to me and asked if I wanted to play on the elementary school team. I told him "Yeah!" and, just like that, my career had begun. The game came naturally to me, its speed and fluidity. My obsession grew.

To this day, I remember the first morning I ever touched a basketball. We could grab a baseball, football, or basketball, but for whatever reason, I picked up that orange orb. It was a magnet. As I played more, I watched the game on television, following the NBA during its once-a-week broadcasts. I also loved watching the ABA and wanted nothing more than to be the god-like Julius "Dr. J" Erving. But if not him, then the smooth George "Iceman" Gervin. Those men could *fly*. Today, people don't know how good they truly were because there isn't enough old film of them. But in their ABA prime, they were everything.

I wasn't especially tall growing up. Early in high school, I was *maybe* six feet. As I'd taken more and more to basketball, I found my niche playing guard. I could handle the ball and I was fast out there on the court. I also found I was a suffocating defender. But when I turned seventeen during my senior year of high school, I grew even more. The coach started to play me at small forward, expecting me to score, but I still handled the ball a lot. By the time the season ended, I was 6-foot-5. That's when I began to dream about playing in college. The game made me feel free. Like, one day, I could be the king of the world.

* * *

I was a well-behaved student in middle school, all things considered. I liked school enough and I was a good student. My sense of discipline was, well, beaten into me from my mother, and I knew if I didn't bring home good grades, then I wouldn't be allowed to play outside. And I wanted to play basketball so badly that I made sure to get the marks I needed to in order to make her happy. (Though I always had trouble with spelling!) As a result, I remember a lot of Bs and C-pluses on my report cards. But even though I was a good kid, that didn't mean I didn't make my fair share of mistakes and hear about it from her.

Since my mother had to be at work at the hospital most days by 4 a.m., we had to wake ourselves up in the morning to go to school. We'd get up and we only had one ironing board to iron our clothes for the day. My siblings and I would fight over it. And I was late to school because of it at least once a week. Every Friday, the school sent home slips if you were late, and every Friday I got whooped by my mother for it. Sometimes a mother doesn't even need an excuse. That's how strict she could be with us. And how much she cared about our schooling. If I got in trouble, she'd holler, "MICHAELRAY!" And I knew I was in for it.

* * *

It's the strangest thing, and I don't know how it happened. At some point during my life, the world began to spell my name MICHEAL. If you look on websites, in news stories, it's too often spelled -EAL and not MICHAEL, as it's traditionally written. I guess people started writing it that way at some point and never stopped. No one ever asked me about it, either. But I wanted to set the record straight. My name is Michael. My son's name is Michael. And it's Michael on our birth certificates, just as it was on my early basketball trading cards! My mother, the warrior, named me what she wanted to name me, and I'm going to honor her wishes. That's for sure.

* * *

Every week, one of us kids had to do the chores, which meant tidy her room, make her bed, wash the dishes, and take out the trash cans. We rotated weeks. The chores were something we all had to do so that she could come home to a good clean house after working so much. If my mother could cook and clean every day in that hospital, I could pass my classes and help tidy up around the house. I remember sitting on the end of the bed one day and telling her that we'd be rich when I grew up. That I'd buy her a house where she could rest her feet. I wanted to go pro just to fulfill that promise to her.

* * *

BANNED

Because my mother worked so much in Lubbock and then in Denver to support us, me and my siblings were raised by her parents at home. Mom would tell us kids that she was the mother *and* the father of our family. And she was right. But while she was away at work, our maternal grandparents, Dorothy and Anderson Blaylock, took care us. Today, people don't give enough respect to older people. But our elders are the ones with the knowledge. You can learn a lot from them. If they want to teach you something, listen. You'll learn and hear valuable lessons every time.

That's why it was such a scare to us when those men jumped my grandfather. We couldn't risk that happening again, or worse. So, we rushed up to Denver. Born in Greenville, Texas, some four hundred miles east of Lubbock, my mother always talked about leaving the state forever. Living in the south wasn't good for Black people and especially for a Black woman. There was hardly any financial opportunity for her. All the work there was cleaning other people's houses. Little dignity and no upward mobility. That was the standard contract.

You'd work all week and make forty dollars. Just barely enough to get to the next one. She tried to get other jobs. My mother didn't have a lazy bone or bit of marrow in her body. But whatever it was she could find in Lubbock, her pay always came out to some forty dollars a week. That wasn't money at all. That was a kind of indentured servitude. Or slavery, really. My mother had a high school education, and she had a lot of common sense. But what did that all get her? Just forty dollars a week in Lubbock— and *Whitey on the Moon*, as poet Gil Scott-Heron might say.

In Denver, mom found a better life. Along with hospital work, some nights, she also bar tended in a local dive. Most of her free time, when there was any, she spent with Johnny. She didn't spend a lot of time watching my basketball games, or any sports at all, really. But that didn't bother me. I knew she was busy. Meanwhile, I played in a lot of games growing up. There were the middle school teams during the week. And on the weekends, we would play in leagues at Clayton College. The gym was nine blocks from my house. I'd wake up early on Saturdays and walk down there with a crew.

As I got older, I began to notice I was better than the other kids. Every time we played pickup, I was the first guy chosen. So, I knew I was good, and that other guys thought so, too. In a lot of the tournaments I played in as a young kid, I was awarded small plastic trophies. I amassed a ton of those over the years. My bedroom was filled with them, which made my mom proud. It was also something that distinguished me from my siblings and the other local kids. While I knew they didn't put any food on the table, they were points of pride. Something I wanted to bring home for my mother to admire.

* * *

Being good at basketball gave me a lot of confidence. And I needed it. Growing up without my father, I found myself constantly looking for approval. It didn't help, too, that when I talked, I had a bad stutter. Even today, when I speak, it often takes me a lot to get the words out. I trip up on the beginnings of them and I have a small lisp. As you can imagine, as a kid, I used to get teased for it. Laughed at when I spoke in class. People called me "Mumbles." But the way I thought about it was kids were always getting teased for things. It seemed normal. We gave each other nicknames and we rough on each other equally.

The insults didn't always get to me. But deep down, they could hurt. Mom told me to laugh *with* them, so it wouldn't feel so bad. But I hated to be different because of the way I talked. And I hated when people couldn't understand me. So, in eighth grade, I began taking speech therapy classes and my stutter improved some. I learned tricks to help my tongue catch up with my brain. While I was self-conscious and even embarrassed as a kid, as I got older, I grew out of those worries. Even today, I stutter noticeably, but I don't get hung up on it. I can only be who I am. And I'm fine with that. None of us are perfect and no one shoots 100 percent from the floor.

While it's ultimately unknown *why* people stutter, it's thought to be the outcome of several things, including genetics and neurological factors. Some studies show it comes down to a single chromosome in your DNA. While it starts in childhood, few adults grow up to be afflicted. I am one of those few, for whatever reason. Along with Thomas Jefferson and Charles Darwin. The stuttering 1 percent of the population. It can be exacerbated by trauma, stress, and anxiety, too. Lord knows I've had my helpings of those pies by now.

Thankfully, my stuttering doesn't bother me today. Even if it is a little like Smiley from Spike's *Do the Right Thing*. But the thing is that it probably pushed me to overcompensate in other areas in my life. Gave me a fire in my belly. I knew what it was like to feel bad, and I wanted to flip it. And instead constantly feel what it was like to feel good. Growing up, I was always very competitive. I hated to lose. I just had to win when I played cards, dominoes, or sports like baseball and football. But especially playing basketball. Winning felt good and I wanted to feel that all the time. Never the feeling of being the loser. I decided that wasn't for me.

* * *

After junior high came high school. There, I'd have three years to prove to myself and anyone else watching that I could play basketball at the next level. In high school, it's a big leap. There are tournaments and scouts and big-time coaches looking at you. As a kid coming up in Denver, this all felt foreign. The world of agents and recruiters was still far away. But I was beginning to smell it from around the corner. If I worked on my game obsessively, I just might have a chance to go to college and get a scholarship. To make something of myself, get an education, and maybe go pro. To make a *name*. I rolled that idea in my mind over and over again.

As one of six kids who grew up without a father in a home where our mother was often gone, getting attention was both hard to come by and something I wanted. What's more, I could really focus in on something if I put my mind to it. Basketball was that thing for me. And more precisely, succeeding at basketball was where I had my sights set. To shoot better than anyone, to play defense better than anyone, to assist and rebound better than anyone. It was all that I could think about at school and then in the summers. You need a goal as a young person to keep yourself steady.

If I was going to make it out of my modest Denver neighborhood and our small church home, if I was to play on courts bigger than the Red Shield Community Center, it would be through hard work and focus. I looked at the game of basketball as my best and perhaps my only chance to help my family achieve more than we had. Like I said, I was *obsessed*. As high school came, I wondered if I would make the varsity team or if I would have to play junior varsity and move up. I wondered if I would one day bring home a state championship. As it turned out, I would get my shot at it sooner than later.

3

HIGH SCHOOL AND BEYOND

IN high school, I was shy. In fact, for much of my life I've considered myself shy. I had a gap in my teeth and spoke funny. During lunchtime, I would go off by myself to this place near the school called Chris's, which was this little trailer that the owner turned into a hamburger joint. Damn, I can still taste those dripping burgers right now! When I tell you that place was packed at lunch, you can believe me. Chili-cheese-smothered burgers. The best chili and cheese I ever had. I wish I could have one of those suckers right now.

Another place I frequented in those days, which is still there to this day, was a Mexican restaurant called Curtis Park Creamery. Every time I go home to Denver these days, I try and stop by there. It's been passed down over three generations. I knew the original owner and he gave it to his kids and now the grandkids are running it. That's a beautiful thing. When I go in there today, I see my picture up on the wall from my playing days. Every time I'm in the Curtis Park Creamery, those guys take good care of me. Shout out to them! Their beans are perfectly cooked, and their burritos and quesadillas are the definition of delicious.

Though I remember those early days sitting by myself at Chris's or Curtis Park Creamery, as I got more playing time with the basketball team in high school, my popularity grew around the classrooms. The varsity games were jam packed. Standing room only. That helps a guy's reputation! Not only did I get more friends and become more popular as I worked my way up the ranks, but I also eventually found a serious girlfriend. Her name was Renee Davenport, and she was my high school sweetheart. We got so close that we stayed together even when I went off to college. I would come back to visit her whenever I could and she would come up to visit me, too. The good ol' days. Renee and I would have a child together and get married. But, I don't mean to get ahead of myself.

* * *

In the fall of 1971, I enrolled in Denver's Manual High School. The three-year school, located off Franklin and 28th Street in the center of Colorado, spanned sophomore to senior. As a sophomore, I tried out, made, and started on the junior varsity team. That was a good initiation for what was to come. I got to lead the team and acclimate myself to a new level of the game with my peers.

During my junior year, I moved up. The varsity squad was so good that it won the Colorado state championship. Thanks to a growth spurt over the summer, the coaches began to notice me. But while I suited up for the team, I only got a few minutes here and there. Instead of taking a role in winning the trophy, I had to watch mostly from the sidelines and wait my turn for a bigger role the following season.

But it was in junior year when I first dunked a basketball . . . and I made sure everyone knew about it after the fact. I was now 6-foot-2. I had definitely shot up substantially since my sophomore year. I decided to try something new, something I'd always wanted to pull off. We were at practice in the gym after school one day, and I just went up and slammed the thing home. Well, truth be told, I barely got it over and through the rim. (We used to call those "rub dunks.") But it was a dunk all the same. I'd finally done it! *Yes,* I thought, *I'd actually dunked! Oh boy, I can really fly!* You couldn't tell me anything after that one. When I went home that evening, I made sure to alert everyone within earshot. "I dunked the ball, I dunked the ball at p-practice!" It was unbelievable. But I also knew it was only the beginning.

Today, I still get questions about why I didn't play more during my first two years in high school. What it came down to was our coach, the great Floyd Theard, and his philosophy. Like many, Coach Floyd didn't believe in playing young guys. As a sophomore, I was so skinny that my socks wouldn't stay up on my legs. Coach Floyd prized experience, so I sat on the bench and learned from watching the upperclassmen. Earlier in his life, Coach Floyd had been in the pros on the ABA's Denver Rockets during the 1969–70 season. He'd also represented the USA playing in two World University Games under coaches John Kundla, John Bennington, and John McLendon. His teams won gold in 1965 and 1967. In his first season as the head coach at Manual, our varsity team won the championship. I knew he knew what he was doing.

Prior to my senior year, to get better, I played at the Red Shield Community Center in summer leagues, and I routinely scored 30 points in those games—often talking smack. "You can't handle me!" Back then I had to be home by nine at night and in bed by ten, and most of the days I stayed at the Red Shield the whole time. Wishing to be Julius Erving. It kept me off the streets and allowed me to focus on the growth of my game. The place also had billiards tables and so when we weren't playing basketball on the indoor courts, we shot pool. Anything to keep us occupied. We played a little cards, too. Kids need places like that, and playing there not only helped me improve my game but kept me on the straight and narrow. All that work at the community center made me believe that my senior year could be special and, except for a big letdown at the end of the season, I was right.

By the start of my senior year, I'd grown another three inches. At 6-foot-5 and around 185 pounds, I knew I was big enough to make an impact on the varsity. It had been a process to gain confidence. In Denver, I was playing against older guys at the community center and the summer leagues and not only holding my own but even showing out at times. My mind soon began to wonder, *What could be next? Could I play in college, go pro?* I needed someone to tell me where I stood. And That's around the time I first met Larry Harvey Brown. It happened thanks to Coach Floyd, as the two of them knew each other through the ABA. I found out that sometimes I was even a topic of their conversation. *Maybe Larry Brown will draft me one day*, I dreamed.

Brown, who had taken a job in 1974 as the head coach of the Denver Rockets ABA team (soon to be renamed the Nuggets), was a defensive-minded signal-caller, which is why he worked so well in Detroit later with guys like Ben Wallace. I've always loved defense.* It was always a top priority. Why? Well, growing up, I was taught by coaches that if I wanted to make the next level (and the next level after that), I had to play it. So I concentrated on being a great defender. If your shot isn't falling, you can always rely on playing defense well until it comes back. There's always going to be guys out for their points. But if you defend, you can stand out. It was hard work but I wanted to play defense and I knew Coach Brown liked that. And one day he told me so. He told me to "keep working, just keep on working and things will work out." That was enough.

It was a blessing to have the Denver ABA team in the city at that time. Their players were regulars at summer leagues and pro-ams around the city. And one of the Rockets players I spent some time with during my high school years was a guy named Ralph Simpson. We're still good friends to this day. Ralph was a 6-foot-5 shooting guard from Michigan State who played in Denver from 1970 until 1976. He played again for the team in 1977–78. An All-Star five years in a row, Ralph could *score*. He averaged more than 27 points and nearly five assists in 1971–72, my first year in high school. Al Smith, who led the ABA in assists in 1973–74, was another friend of mine.

It felt good to have their validation, along with Coach Brown's. The guys gave me tips on how to make the pros. What the other coaches looked for, what drills to do, how to stay in shape. I soaked it all in, single minded on making it to the next level. Spencer Haywood was another icon in Denver, playing for the team for a season. He won *both* MVP and ROY honors in 1969–70, he also led the league in games (84), minutes (45.3),

---

* In the NBA, Richardson led the league in steals three seasons.

rebounds (19.5), and points (30) after bringing home a gold medal for the US in the '68 Olympics.

Spencer was something special. He would later take the NBA to the Supreme Court and win, earning players the right to enter the league before finishing four years of college. He was a good example for someone like me. Truly, having professional basketball in my backyard was invaluable. For a guy without a father, it was important for me to see grown Black men achieve and do so in a white world. It gave me and my friends hope. I'll always appreciate those Denver teams for that reason. They're cherished. Amazingly, out of everyone I grew up with, everyone who watched those guys play every day, I was the one to play professional ball.

Later on, during my college days, I'd come home during the summers and play in the Denver leagues and pro-ams. I would see Coach Brown around there, too. Back then, the game was more of an inside-out game. The focus was on centers, like Moses Malone or Kareem Abdul-Jabbar. When I played in the pros, the only time we shot a three was at the end of the shot clock. The league was much more physical. If I played today, I'd average at least 10 free throws a game** given how many times the refs blow their whistles. Playing against the Denver ABA guys in high school, I knew that to hang in the pros you had to be tough. And I played tough against them, which told me that I could make it in the league one day.

* * *

** Editor's note: Richardson averaged 3.4 free-throw attempts per game during his NBA career.

When I was in high school, I used to work at the Denver Coliseum, selling popcorn in the stands. *Popcorn! Get'cher popcorn here!* I was that guy. But I would also get to see all the ABA games and watch the players from the stands for free as I slang my bags of snacks. Then after the games, I would sneak back into the locker rooms to meet the players. Back then, security wasn't anything like it is today. It was lax and, as a popcorn salesman, I could pretend like I belonged backed there. In the locker room, I would introduce myself to all the players and coaches.

Even though basketball was my focus while in school, I made sure to always have a job. It was important to me to keep the structure and keep myself busy. My mother, the warrior, told me if I wanted anything for myself, I had to earn it. At one point when I was about thirteen, I was working for Firestone Tires, where I would do oil changes and replace flats. I also worked at the Gates Rubber Company during the summer in high school, where I drove a forklift to load up big semi-trucks. Later in high school, my mom got me a job at Colorado General Hospital. My job there was to scrub the hot pots the kitchen staff used to cook the meals for the patients and staff.

With so many siblings (six) and so few parents (one), I knew that there was only so much my mother could do. That's why I knew that, if I wanted something, it had to come from my own pocket. Another job I had was throwing newspapers with two of my friends, Larry Biffert and Dennis Reed. When I was a sophomore, we used to go around the streets of our Denver neighborhood tossing newspapers onto subscribers' front doors. Growing up in the city, though, during much of the year, snow piles up high. It gives off a feeling like you could get lost in it if you aren't careful.

As you could imagine, weather conditions made it much more difficult to land those newspapers on the front porches around snowbanks that high. Not to mention the bitter cold and poor visibility. Larry, Dennis, and I would wake up around two o'clock in the morning and go outside onto the porch. There, big boxes of newspapers would be waiting for us. We'd then bring them into the house and fold them up and put rubber bands around them. If it was raining or snowing—which was almost all the time—we'd put them all in bags and get them in a pile, ready to be tossed home to home.

We'd get in the back of Larry's car (he was a year older and had a license), and he'd drive really slowly on those almost always icy roads as we tossed out the papers from the back trunk to the addresses we'd already memorized by heart. But after about a year, I quit the newspaper gig. The constant Denver snow was too much for me. But along with my mother pushing me, another reason I liked work was because I enjoyed numbers. I've always been good with them, and in high school, I liked playing around with them in math class. Reading was never much my thing; speaking has always been hard; and I don't like science. But I always took challenging math classes. Working these jobs and taking math classes helped me later on get a handle on my contracts, salaries, taxes, and budgets during my years in the NBA. Mom was right to put me to work!

* * *

During my senior year, I thought I'd finally *made it* as a basketball player. I was a starter on the team finally, playing the small forward position. Still a great defender and a good scorer,

I notched about 10 points per game and was most definitely the team leader. We were good, too. Strong enough to make the state tournament postseason and go all the way to the finals. I remember like it was yesterday. In the 1974 finals, we matched up against Bear Creek, a predominantly white high school. As soon as I knew they were our opponent, I was worried. Not for any skill reason, but because of possible "home cooking."

Manual, which is a traditional basketball powerhouse that today boasts twelve state titles (tied for most in the state), was predominantly Black when I was a senior. We're talking 80 percent, at least. Compared to us, playing Bear Creek was like David versus Goliath. What did Wilt Chamberlain say? *No one roots for Goliath.* Well, that's right. Against Bear Creek, we were ready for their lineup—that's not what worried me. What did was what the referees would have in store for us. Now, I know it's loser talk to blame the refs. But I can tell you, the white Bear Creek team got a favorable whistle that game. That's just how it was.

Up until that game, we hadn't lost all year thanks to my leadership and the play of teammates like Wayne Johnson, Phil Taylor and Sam Combs. We were *undefeated*, 23–0. The state finals were the culmination of a great season and of my high school career. I'd sat on the bench, waiting my turn behind some bigger players, even though at times I believed I was superior. Now we were ready to make history ourselves. But the game ended up like the movie *Hoosiers*, with David coming out on top. Maybe that's how the scriptwriters would have put it down on the page, anyway. Everything *was* already written.

Either way, we lost to Bear Creek, 62–59. It was that close. The win remains their school's only state championship. My senior year team was comprised of a lot of guys I played with as far back as middle school, and we were collectively crushed. Undefeated until the season's final game. We cried for days. Of course, we'd wanted to win, and we'd wanted to be undefeated. But to go out like we did on shoddy calls, it didn't feel like we lost as much as it was taken from us. In the end, I made first-team all-tournament, but it was little consolation.

The 1974 state championship game had been played at the city's famed Denver Coliseum. One of the guys sitting in the stands that day, I can only imagine, was Coach Larry Brown. That was the same year he'd taken over the head coaching job with the Rockets, soon to be renamed the Nuggets. A basketball junkie, Brown was likely in the stands scouting out the next local star to draft. Today, the accomplished coach is the sole individual to win both an NCAA and NBA championship (with the University of Kansas in 1988 and the Detroit Pistons in 2004, respectively). After taking the Denver job, Brown remained in the city with the franchise as it transitioned to the NBA. Later, he took a head coaching job with the New Jersey Nets near his childhood hometown of New York City (and later coached the Knicks for one season). The basketball world is a small one.

The game against Bear Creek was a back-and-forth affair and, despite a lot of foul calls, we should have won. But, at the end of the day, we didn't play well, and I personally didn't play as good as I was capable of. If it was indeed that close, I should have pulled it out for us. I'll put the defeat on my shoulders. Ultimately, it was on me, our best player, the team's leading scorer and rebounder. But, shit, those tough calls and prejudiced refs didn't help our cause. After that, coach Floyd left Manual for an assistant's job at the University of Iowa. The era was over. I'd done what I could, making all-city and all-state.

After we lost in the finals, I had to figure out what the next chapter of my life would look like. I knew I wanted to play in college, and at a Division I school. During my senior year, a few scouts began to look at me and regard my game. That is the benefit of going undefeated, after all. My teammate Phil Taylor was 6-foot-10 and because he was so big, scouts took notice of both our school as a whole and of me specifically. Phil was getting a lot of offers and I had a few myself. Two in particular were from Colorado State and Iowa State, but they said I'd have to sit on the bench my freshman year, so I wasn't excited about either of them.

One place that interested me was the University of Montana. It was a good school and a place that promised me playing time, even a starting role. With that, I knew I'd have a chance to make a name for myself on the next level if I played my cards right. The Grizzlies went 19–8 during my senior high school season and their coach, Jud Heathcote, had a great reputation. After the state tournament game, Montana's assistant coach Jim Brandenburg (who sadly just passed away) paid me a visit in Denver. He spent time with me and my mother in our home and after we talked, he offered me the chance to visit the Montana campus. The following week, I flew up and stayed the weekend and see the pastoral, albeit all-white campus and play in a few pickup games, impressing with my quick hands on defense and knack for getting to the rim.

I also had the opportunity to meet Jim's wife and their kids and to talk with Coach Heathcote face to face. He said liked big guards, especially ones who were strong leaders. He said again that I'd have the chance to play big minutes for him as a freshman. There were already some good players on the team, too, like Ken McKenzie and Eric Hays. But the team needed a point guard. He told me all of this over dinner and afterwards, I was sold. The following Monday, I signed my letter of intent to attend the University of Montana. I was now a Grizzly. It was one of the best decisions of my life. It all went well, a chance at the next level. That was all I needed. *Michael*, I told myself, *this is just the beginning.*

4

THE UNIVERSITY
OF MONTANA GRIZZLIES

WHEN I was thirteen years old, I went down to visit my father and grandmother in Lubbock. My dad and I never had a close relationship; it was never the best of times, but we did keep in touch here and there. Even so, my mother wanted me to visit him on occasion. She wanted me to get away from Colorado, see my grandmother, and keep up at least a minimal relationship with her ex. So I went down to visit them in Texas at my grandmother's café and pig farm, the messy place she ran by herself since my grandfather had passed away long ago.

My grandmother wanted me to work in the café one morning, taking the customers' orders, bringing them their meals, and cleaning the plates off. But I didn't want to do that. Instead, my grandmother made me go out on a farmer's truck at seven in the morning. There were dozens of us loaded onto several trucks, and they took us out to this cotton field. Everyone got a croker (burlap) sack, and we put them on our backs and were guided to these long rows of cotton in the fields. Long, long rows. And I went down my never-ending row and plucked the cotton and tossed it in the tweed sack over my shoulder.

It took all day to fill up that sack. And at the end of the day, the farmers gave each of us seventy-five cents. The trucks that had dropped us off came back and picked us up. That night, I was too tired to know what hit me. They did this every day, and people did it every day to make a tiny bit of money. My grandmother made me do it again the next day, too. I got up at six thirty in the morning, got home around five in the evening. I did this for three days in a row. On the fourth, as I walked down that relentless unending row, I heard one of the other kids yell, "Snake, snake!" I dropped my croker sack and ran. That was my last day for me in that fucking field!

* * *

For my first three years at the University of Montana, I was the only Black player on the team—and one of only a few on campus. A lot of people ask me if the transition was a "culture shock," but it really wasn't. Even though I'd come from an almost all-Black high school in Denver and was now at an almost all-white at the University of Montana, it didn't bother me. I wasn't raised to worry about skin color. I always focused on a person's character. Still, it took a little time to get used to the open space and the quiet, but not the people.

But I was definitely lonely at first. Early on in school, I felt shy. All I did was go to class and back to the dorm. That's it. On weekends, I'd sometimes drive the 1,800-mile round trip home to visit mom. I'd stay for a few days, and then drive back Sunday. It was nuts, but it was better than being alone.

In October, once the basketball season started, I went to practice, class, and the dorm. It wasn't an especially social time for me. Like I said, there weren't even any other Black guys on the team until my senior year. And while race wasn't especially important to me, it can be nice to be around people—at least some—who look like you and know how you were raised.

The whole campus was white, as a matter of fact. And I don't just mean ethnically. At the University of Montana, the campus was practically always covered in snow. First Denver, and now here!

Later into the year, I became friendly with a handful of guys on the football team, some Black and Samoan players, including a fellow named Greg Anderson, who was from Chicago and played cornerback. I also hung around with a guy named Rich Jordan, who was from Tacoma, Washington. I went to a few keg parties but didn't partake. I just hung around. I didn't have my first beer until sophomore year, and even then I knew it wasn't for me. The good thing was, though, things began to slowly ease up for me. I began to find my rhythm on campus, and those eighteen-hour trips back home weren't as necessary.

The only real problem was my roommate. The guy sharing my dorm with me was messy. My first year, I lived in Miller's Hall and my roommate was a farm boy who used to dip. That's when a guy puts a big pinch of tobacco in his lip. And he'd spit that tobacco stuff in cups and leave them all over the place. Our room was small; we each had a little bed and a little desk on our own sides. He was the type of guy to wear filthy socks day after day. Our first week together, I told him I had a problem. I'm a neat freak, I know. But leaving dip spit and your clothes everywhere isn't normal. I knew that, growing up, you had to take care of what you had. I learned that because we didn't have much to start with. If you have little and let it go to crap, then you've got even less. He had to clean his shit up or that problem would get worse. I was clean and he was dirty, and I wasn't going to allow it.

Thankfully, he got the message quick and cleaned up his space. Later, when his parents came down to visit, they said, "How did you get him to clean his room?"

* * *

One time, when I was a junior and living off campus, it snowed so much that they closed the university for a week. Do you know how much snow has to fall in Montana for the university to close? It snowed so much that you couldn't even open your front door. Growing up in Denver, though, you get used to it. At times in high school after practice in the evenings, we just stayed in the gyms because the snow was so high. After one game, we came outside, and it had snowed so bad that we just camped out in the locker room.

When it comes to snow, you have to do what you have to do. You're at its mercy. Then, you hope, someone comes by in some big heavy truck to plow it away and you're free to get on with your day. One time much later, when I was coaching in Albany, it snowed so bad that we had to sleep in the arena overnight. I slept in my office. The fans had gone but the coaches and the players were still in the building as the stuff piled up outside. That was one of the biggest snowstorms upstate New York had seen in a long time.

But I've always been adaptable. I just rolled with what cards came my way.

* * *

My coach as a freshman was Jud Heathcote. On the floor, he was a nut. Off the floor, he was one of the funniest men you'd ever want to meet. I remember one game my freshman season, we were pitted against our cross-state rivals, Montana State. I was playing erratically, still learning the college game, and I had a few early turnovers. Jud called a timeout. Now, for those that don't know, Jud was bowlegged. Well, he came out to meet me at half-court, walking side-to-side, and just punched me in my stomach.

"You can't play like a fucking freshman!" he shouted. Then *bam*! Right in the gut. After that timeout, if you were open and I had the ball, sorry, you weren't getting it. I was taking it to the hole and scoring. I wasn't getting suckered again. But that was Jud and those were the times. In contrast, his lead assistant, Jim Brandenburg, was kind and calm. After Jud ripped you a new one, Jim would come from behind and massage everything out. He'd say, "Coach didn't really mean that; he's just trying to help you."

Back home in Denver, a lot of my friends who I'd played with in high school came back home, quitting school one by one. It was hard for me up at the University of Montana, but my mother would tell me, "Don't be like them. Don't you come back home. Please don't come back home." And I'd tell her, "Mom, I'm not coming back home." She'd list of names of people who came back, who'd given up. I said, "M-mama, I'm not coming back home."

She wanted me to get my education. To set myself up for the future. I wanted to keep my promise to her, that I wouldn't quit. I was on a mission. If I stuck it out, *maybe* I could make the pros.

* * *

We had a great season my freshman year. We won the Big Sky Conference, and the school made its debut appearance in the famed NCAA tournament. Our record in 1974–75 was 21–8, which was the most wins the school had since joining the Big Sky in the 1960s. We played Utah State in the first round and won, 69–63, with me notching 13 points. Heading to the West Regional Semifinal, our next opponent was UCLA, with legendary head coach John Wooden. Can you picture it? The tiny University of Montana making its debut in the Big Dance going up against UCLA, with all its history and stars?

Going into the game, Coach Heathcote's plan was to hold the ball and make sure we only got the best of shots. We knew we would have trouble scoring upwards of 80 or 90 points against anyone. so defense and ballhandling were key—my specialties. Against a team that went 28–3 on the season and outscored opponents by more than 300 points, we only trailed by a single point at the half, 34–33.

It was just as tight in the second half, but they outscored us 33–31. In the end, we lost 67–64—not bad for our David vs. Goliath match-up. For the Bruins, Richard Washington and Pete Trgovich each scored 16. For us, Ken McKenzie scored 20 with 10 rebounds and Eric Hays scored 32. I had two points, four steals (guarding their top players), two assists, and four rebounds in 35 minutes off the bench.

All things considered, it was a masterful coaching job by Jud, but we fell just short. We would then play UNLV in the regional third-place game but lost, 75–67. UCLA would beat Arizona State next and go on to win the whole thing that year, giving Wooden his tenth and final championship. Little did I know, it would be the only time I'd make the Big Dance in my four years in Montana. Now my freshman season was over. In the offseason, I dedicated myself to going to class, learning and working on my game. I had tunnel vision. After the year, I went home and played in as many summer leagues as I could. I saw my mom. I saw my sweetheart, Renee. And then I went back to work the following fall.

* * *

I'd driven to school as a freshman in a little red Volkswagen. The tires had those gangster white walls and spoke wheels. But the whole gas tank took four dollars to fill. It rumbled a little as I drove to school again for my sophomore year. The University of Montana campus is laid back. And so was assistant coach Jim Brandenburg. I used to go over to his home and eat dinner all the time. His wife, Jan, would invite me over so that I wouldn't be homesick. I became very close with their family, including his three kids. Until his passing in 2023, we talked at least once a week. I'll always be thankful for those dinners.

My sophomore season with the Grizzlies, I was ready for a bigger role. I'd worked hard in the summer, took care of myself. Improving is about playing all the time. Rain, sleet, snow. Like a postal worker. I still didn't drink or party. Basketball and the NBA were my only focuses. I'd averaged just 7.5 points and

3.6 rebounds in my opening season. But that would be the last time over the next three years that I'd be under 18 points and 6 rebounds. On campus, I was treated well, and I had friends. Some might think that even though there were only thirty Black students on campus *total*, it would be hard to make friends. But it was easy for me.

I've always been a curious person. I remember in high school, I used to go horseback riding up the Colorado mountains. In college, I hunted bear and moose. And as far as the town of Missoula where the university was, it was a nice college oasis. Bozeman, the rival town, is full of bull riding and rodeos. But Missoula has little coffee shops. Still, the state itself is one for cowboys. I remember going to what people called a night club with a few teammates during my freshman year. It was more of a saloon, truth be told. People rode their horses and tied them to a pole at the front door like it was the 1800s. And that was just fine by me.

Along with stepping into a bigger role on the court, there was another big change in my life. As a freshman, I lived on campus and Renee stayed back in Denver, working as a nurse. But as my sophomore year began, she got pregnant. So, she moved up to Missoula to stay with me. We lived together in off-campus married student housing. She wanted to be with me in Montana for the year so that we could prepare for the new child. But she had plans to go back to Denver with the baby and continue with her nursing career.

Renee and I met in high school when I was a junior and she was a sophomore. A friend of mine named Hot Rod used to date her cousin, Barbara. After Renee and I were introduced, we began seeing each other. She is half-Black and half-Latina, very short and very pretty. She is also a bright person. Her father was a mechanic who fixed semi-truck engines and he didn't like me. I don't blame him, though. I towered over his daughter, was a popular basketball player, and had a smile that was too cute for my own good. Not to mention, Renee was a light-skinned Black girl and I'm dark-skinned. Colorism is a real thing in the Black community.

When Renee and I began to date, I lived in a low-income housing area and her family lived across in a better part of town. Her father didn't approve of us seeing each other. He thought I would drag her down. He used to call me "Darkie." He even called me over to the house one tie and said, "I don't want you guys seeing each other." I said, "Okay, that's fine." But he ended up buying her a brand new Ford—a red Maverick. I'll never forget it. She couldn't yet drive it. Her sister Linda would take her to visit me on *the wrong side of the tracks*. She'd drop Renee off there for a few hours and probably take that red truck out for a joyride.

After my sophomore season, I made the all-conference team. It was the first of three straight All-Big Sky Conference acknowledgements for me. That season, we finished 13–12 overall and 7–7 in the conference, but didn't make the inaugural Big Sky Conference tournament, where Boise State beat Weber State in the finals. In my first season as a full-time starter, I averaged 18.2 points, 6.3 boards and 3.8 assists. It wasn't a banner year for us, though we had our moments. The year was a success for me, though, because I'd taken another step forward.

While I hadn't been the key contributor I'd wanted as a freshman, coming off the bench in the tournament, my time had now come. It was an important step in my evolution as a big-time player. And as a person, there was another important evolution: fatherhood. Renee had our child, Tosha, during my junior year. As of this writing, Tosha is forty-eight years old, and the eldest of my five children. Today, I have three girls and two boys: Tosha, Corey, Tamara, Kimberly, and Michael Amir Richardson Jr., a professional soccer player who just played in the Olympics and earned a bronze medal. Family has always been very important to me, as long as I can remember.

* * *

After my sophomore season, I was invited to try out for the 1976 Olympic basketball team. Four years earlier, the United States lost to Russia in the most controversial ending ever. And for the '76 team, the US brought in UNC's Dean Smith to coach. While I knew the roster was likely decided upon even before the tryouts began, it was still an honor to be in the mix. The committee brought in some fifty to sixty guys, and they were going to keep about a dozen. Along with me and Otis Birdsong, there was Darrell Griffith and Bo Ellis trying out, too. But in the end, the team picked seven ACC players and four from UNC, including Mitch Kupchak and Phil Ford.

So while it would have been an honor to play for my country in the Olympics, this just meant that I'd have a bit more free time—not a lot, but more than if I was playing Olympic ball. Summers between school years, I did two things: work a job and work on my game. After my freshman year, I went home to play in the summer leagues and see mom. Summers after that, I stayed on campus and worked a job. The university's boosters were always able to help me find something. One time, I worked at a dairy company. I got up at three in the morning, put a protective uniform on from head to toe, and worked in a freezer, loading up delivery trucks. For those of a certain age, there used to be milkmen going house to house. Well, I got *them* their milk for delivery.

Another summer, I drove a forklift in a Montana sawmill, moving big tree trunks around. Then, my senior year, I had a job at a car dealership. Something a bit cushier than manual labor. But when I was home in Denver for a week or two here and there, I played in summer leagues populated with former ABA players, along with up-and-coming high school and college players. I played in the Denver pro-ams, banging against pros like David Thompson, Bobby Jones, and Ralph Simpson. The summers were all about work: making money and honing my game.

On campus later, though, I got another stomach punch from Coach Heathcote—this time metaphorically. One afternoon, coach called me into his office and told me he was leaving the school and taking a job as the head coach at Michigan State. The news brought tears to my eyes. "Coach, so what I heard on the radio is true?" And Jud said it was. I said, "Coach, you can't leave me! You've been like a father to me." He just said, "Michael, I've been on you to go to class all the time, that's what a coach does, not a father." And all I could say was, "You have to remember, I don't have a father!"

Just told me I'd be okay and that I just had to keep working. But I was heartbroken. I loved Coach Heathcote. Renee knew it, too. "Michael bonded with him," she said later. And she was right. In the end, I assumed Coach Heathcote was leaving to make more money. And I thought about following him, but I didn't want to lose a year of eligibility transferring and I knew that if I stayed, I'd have a chance to stand out on our team. I'd be the man as a junior and that might not be the case with the Michigan State Spartans. I begged Jud, a father figure, not to go, but his mind was made up.

Coach Heathcote would go on to coach Magic Johnson in a win against Larry Bird and his Indiana State Sycamores in the most famous college basketball game ever played. That 1979 championship is still talked about today; the grainy video highlights still shown on TV. It's one of the many strange ways me and Magic have been linked over the years. Big point guards, same college coach, both left the game early against our wills. Now with Jud gone, though, Jim took over the role of head coach. Thankfully, he and I already had a great relationship, and staying to play for him was the best thing I could have done.

* * *

During my junior year, I had a big scare off the court. One night, I went to a dance club with Sam, a friend of mine I'd gone to high school with. He later transferred to the University of Montana, though he wasn't a ballplayer. Anyway, at some point, these six girls walked into the club, and me and Sam started talking to them. As the night progressed, I was hitting it off with this one girl and she and I ended up going home together to my place. The two of us went to the bedroom (while Sam was in the other room). She and I had sex and then, once we'd finished, she left and drove home.

The next morning, though, I got a call from Jim saying, "Michael Ray? You raped somebody?" I said, "Coach, what are you talking about?" He told me there was a girl saying that I raped her. What I later found out was that after we had sex and the girl left, her friends found out what she'd done with me and started teasing her. "You fucked a nigger! You fucked a nigger!" But not knowing that yet, in the moment my head was spinning. Coach asked me, "Would you be able to take a lie detector test? You and Sam?" I said, "Fuck yes."

What made the whole thing worse is that I had to wait a whole week to take that fucking lie detector test. Do you know what a string of days can do to your imagination when you're waiting to take a lie detector test to decide whether you, a Black man, raped a college-aged white girl? I couldn't sleep the whole week. *They're trying to frame me*, I thought over and over. Finally, the investigator made it to the university from distant Seattle that Friday, and me and Sam took the tests individually. I took mine first.

They put all these wires on my fingers and chest, and they asked me questions. When everything was over and they took the wires off me, they told me to leave the room and not to look at Sam. Just walk straight ahead. The whole thing was so fucking weird. I walked out, looking straight ahead. And then Sam went in there. After he took the test, we got in our car together and went home. Five minutes after we got home, coach called and told us what the investigator from Seattle said. We were innocent.

Coach Brandenburg said the Seattle investigator added, "Those guys didn't rape that girl; they both passed the test with flying colors." Then the investigator, I was told, called the girl to take the test. But she declined. When that happened, the police asked if I wanted to file charges against her. That whole week was the scariest moment of my life up to that point. If I wasn't on the basketball team, if the lie detector hadn't been available—or even *invented*—what might have happened? I ended up not filing charges. I just wanted to put it all behind me.

Some hearing this story might ask, "What about your daughter and her mother?" The answer is that I just wasn't a one-woman guy. While I loved them both, we had an arrangement. While it may not have been perfect and while I probably should have been more settled down, I wasn't. For whatever reason, that just wasn't my way. Maybe I'd gotten it from my own father. He wasn't around, so why did I have to be all the time? It would take me a long time to learn to be a better dad and partner. But after that bogus rape accusation, I learned to distrust people.

Thankfully, that was the only bad experience I had at Montana. And it was just one stupid girl and her friends. It had nothing to do with the school, my team, or the town, I'm happy to say. Today, I hope that girl and her friends feel a special kind of shame for what they tried to do to me. But I won't linger on this subject any longer. My time in college was wonderful otherwise. People opened their homes to me, and I'm forever grateful. I even liked the classes. While I majored in physical education, I worked on a math minor. Good for a guy that would soon be in the NBA with a big contract.

* * *

During my junior season, I averaged 19.2 points, 8.6 rebounds, and 3.6 assists. But as a team we had a poor year, the lowest in my tenure at the school. *Officially*, we finished 7–19 and 6–8 in the conference. What happened was that the school had signed a guy named Lee Johnson out of Omaha, Nebraska. The story we were told was that he'd gone to summer school to build up his grades, and so coach was able to get him to play for us. Apparently, that wasn't the whole story, because our team got into hot water because of him.

College basketball is cutthroat and, might I add, hypocritical. Once the other coaches caught wind of us signing Lee, they began complaining to the NCAA. People looked into his grades and said something wasn't right with his summer school transcript. Making a devastating decision, the NCAA took away *eleven* wins from us, including a blowout we earned on the road against Long Beach State. Really, for the season, we'd ended up 18–8. But the NCAA cut us down to 7–19. Lee ended up leaving campus later and enrolling in a Texas junior college.

Amazingly, in 1979, Lee was the 17th overall pick in the NBA draft, selected by the Houston Rockets. He was 6-foot-11 but only weighed about 200 pounds. Lee could jump out of the gym, but he only lasted 12 games in the league. He went on to play professionally overseas, where he suited up for more than a dozen years. Lee and I even became good friends after our time together in college. What's even crazier is that he became the general manager of a team in France . . . and he signed me to his roster. That year we won the league championship. Basketball is incredible.

* * *

As the years passed, I became the big jock on campus. I had a lot of friends. People liked me, and I brought pride to the school as someone who could dominate at both ends of the court. For fun, I used to go to this bar called Stockman's. The place is still there, actually. I met a lot of ladies at that place. And we had a lot of fun. As for guys I hung around with, I remember these two brothers, Benny and Steve. Two hometown Missoula basketball stars. We became really good friends. Benny and Steve would take me out elk and bear hunting through the Montana woods.

In the state, outdoor life is prized above all else but God and family. Especially back then. Now Missoula is bigger, more sprawling. But in the late 1970s, it was the wilderness. And Benny and Steve helped me take it all in. They'd let me borrow their shotguns and rifles and we'd carry them out into the woods and hunt from sunup to sundown. It was a fun break from basketball. But as my senior year approached, I started to itch for the new challenge of being the veteran leader. And afterward, if all went according to plan, maybe I'd get a shot to try out for the NBA. My dream!

* * *

During my senior year, I remember we were playing a game in Flagstaff, Arizona, up in the mountains. Ahead of the game in the locker room, someone came in and told me, "Willis Reed will be at the game. He's coming to see you play." The Knicks must have been playing the Suns then. Still, that was a big deal and a big gesture from Willis. If know you the area, you know it's hard to get to. You have to fly down, rent a car, then drive for two hours to get to the campus. That meant Reed, a two-time champion and one of the greatest Knicks ever (who was going into his second season as the team's head coach), really wanted to see me play. Well, that night I had a triple-double and we won the game.

Ever since that contest, people were telling me that I would go pro. That I'd be a top pick in the NBA. Probably taken in the beginning of the second round.

* * *

I had an unbelievable senior season. We wowed fans in the 9,000-capacity Dahlberg Arena, including the students in the "Zoo" section. It was the year I'd been hoping for since I picked up a basketball all those years ago. That season, the only opposing player to really work me was Portland State's Freeman Williams Jr. Even though we beat his team 79–71, Freeman dominated. I mean, he *averaged* 35.9 points his senior season!

That year also marked another milestone. For the first time in my collegiate career, my mother was coming up to visit and watch me play in a game. I was so excited for her to see me but, as luck would have it, I sprained my ankle the week she arrived.

Distraught, I was on crutches the whole week. And that Saturday night, we were set to play our biggest rivals, Montana State. My ankle was swollen like crazy. I was icing it and rubbing stuff into it that trainers gave to horses. All I wanted was to be healthy for the game—for the team and for my mom, who was coming up from Denver. The team's training staff was giving me treatment around the clock. Strangely, some of that stuff I rubbed on my ankle made my breath smell like garlic. After all their treatments, the swelling finally came down by the time my mom arrived on campus, I knew there was no way I was going to miss the game. I had to show out for the warrior.

Before the game, I got my ankle taped—wrapped tighter than a Christmas gift—and was able to lace up my sneakers. That was something I wasn't sure about, given all the swelling. But I was good to go. I wanted to make my mom proud.

I hit my first three shots and was on a roll from there. Once I started moving around and heating up, the pain in my ankle went away. I was running, jumping, dunking, getting around people, getting them to move where *I wanted* them to go. I scored 40 and we beat Montana State. I scored 40 and we beat Montana State, and for a long time that point total was the school's single-game scoring record. My name is in the record books for most field goals made in a game, too, with 18.

But the next morning? I could *not* walk. I had my feet in ice the entire day. However, I knew I'd shown my mother that her boy could play ball. Indeed, as a senior, I averaged 24.2 points and 6.9 rebounds over 27 games. We won the regular season Big Sky crown, going 20–8 overall and 12–2 in-conference, and we were the No. 1 seed going into the Big Sky tournament, which was held in our gym. But, sadly, we were upset by the perennial Big Sky powerhouse, Weber State. We lost 62–55 in overtime. We let it slip through our fingers in the waning seconds, missing a crucial late-game free throw (by me) in the last seconds.

What's frustrating is that we'd led 28–20 at the half. Even though I scored 25 points, I wish I had notched 26. It was *me* who missed a free throw with just 21 seconds left. Instead, I could only tie the game at 49–49. I'd hit four free throws in the extra period to give us a chance, but it was no matter. Thanks to that missed free throw, we didn't earn a coveted automatic bid to the NCAA Tournament and, just like that, my college career was over.

I graduated school an All-American honorable mention after leading the Big Sky in scoring, and was ready for the next chapter in my life. In my mind, it was NBA or bust!

Memory Lane: Tosha Richardson

When I think of my dad, what comes to mind is that, with him, there's never a dull moment! It's always the unexpected. Nothing is going to be sugarcoated. He's going to tell you exactly how he feels about everything—but he has a heart of gold. He'd truly give you the shirt off his back.

My father is a good all-around person, and believes in doing things the old-school way. Work hard and good things will come. So, when I think of him, that's what I always think about. He always says to us, "Nothing comes for free. You're always going to have to work for what you have in life."

Some of my favorite early memories with my dad were when he was in New Jersey. I remember playing with Buck Williams in the family room. My dad's teammates were just a bag of laughs all the time. They were always joking around. My father's relationship with the players on his teams had always been very good.

My father and I talk every day, and a lot of the times it's more than necessary! But it's so funny; he checks in with me about the kids, what I'm up to, and if I'm doing too much. He and I have always had a close relationship. My being the oldest, even though we haven't always lived together, because I was with my mom, we really stayed close.

I guess you could say that I'm his favorite, but don't tell my siblings that! Another favorite moment with him that I remember is being overseas, which you'll hear more about later. The people in Italy, they got crazy when they see him, calling out his name, like, "Shooo-gahhh! Shooo-gahhh!" That was always fun because they treated us like kings and queens.

5

THE 1978 NBA DRAFT

FOR my four-year career at the University of Montana, I averaged 17.1 points and 6.3 rebounds on 49 percent shooting in 107 total games. For that, I was named first-team All-Big Sky Conference for three straight years—my sophomore through senior seasons—and made the prestigious All-Big Sky Tournament team in 1978 (even though we'd lost in the conference finals). My senior year average of 24.2 points is still good for third all-time at Montana, and my total points remains in the top-20 in Big Sky history. All that is without the help of the 3-point line, which wouldn't become a part of the NCAA until I was already in the pros.

Though Montana wasn't known as a school that professional teams looked at for future talent, my collegiate accolades provided me the resume to get attention from NBA scouts. I had chance at the next level, which then helped me get invited to important tournaments outside Missoula. One such tournament was all the way in Hawaii. I hopped on several planes and flew out to the islands. My four-year term wasn't quite up yet at school, but I was able to take a week-long trip to better my prospects a few months ahead of graduation. It was nice in Hawaii, too. As soon as I stepped off the plane, they put flowers over me. The heat hit my face. I thought, *Is this what being a pro is all about?*

Everyone playing at the tournament—known as the Aloha Classic—was good and most were seniors like me. It was May, just weeks before the draft, and the coaches and NBA front office people wanted one more look at the young men who might soon populate their rosters. One of the big-time players there was Ron Brewer from Arkansas (who the Portland Trail Blazers would take with the seventh overall pick). Others included Phil Ford (taken second overall by the Kansas City Kings) and Reggie Theus (taken ninth by the Chicago Bulls). The moment I arrived in Honolulu, I checked right into my room and got comfortable, knowing the next few days would be busy, to say the least.

That second day, we were broken up into teams. Over the course of the week, we played in a bunch of scrimmages set up to see who the best players were—and I killed on both ends of the court. I did so well that by the end of the week, I'd made the all-tournament team. While anyone can score, my love of defense definitely helped my stock rise. Due to my performance at the tournament, scouts began to swarm all over me. They were telling me that they'd never seen a guy that could play the passing lanes as well as I could. That I was a great on-ball defender. At the time, I was one of the first tall point guards. Even before Magic Johnson hit the NBA in 1979, there I was, bringing the ball up at 6-foot-5.

Growing up, I'd been smaller for so long that I learned how to handle the ball like a guard. So when I shot up, I kept all those skills but now could also *see* over the defense and watch how the play unfolded. My vision and anticipation have always been my sharpest talents. I could pass and guess when an opponent was going to make a pass and where he was going with it. That kind of defense helps a team and, as they say, defense wins championships. People at the tourney noticed it, too. Not just scouts (as there were many), but agents as well.

Though Hawaii is surrounded by water, most of the sharks that weekend were on land. From the moment we began to scrimmage, all the agents were trying to get us players to sign with them. Coming to us with money, promises, girls, and sliding them all into our pockets. "Sign with me, sign with me." Promising you astronomical sums for your name on a simple piece of paper. Back then, "agents" didn't have to be certified with the league. Everyone and anyone could be an agent. So you can imagine the nefarious dealings that were going on. They would approach players when they were out at night partying, too. Under the influence. But I just went home after the games to sleep to avoid anyone trying to take advantage of me.

Even so, I would listen to any agent who wanted to talk. I would nod and take their money . . . but I wouldn't sign. When I eventually did sign with one, it was after I came back from Hawaii. I signed with a guy out of Houston—but don't let me get ahead of myself.

After Honolulu, I came back to the University of Montana and finished school. Outside of class, I played hoops with guys on campus on the blacktop court outside my old freshman dorm. Just staying ready in case my name was called. I knew I'd miss school when I had to leave. I was the university's best player and, might I say, a big man on campus. To say I had a lot of phone numbers was an understatement.

* * *

Draft day was one of the strangest of my life. I'd just graduated and was outside playing basketball at Montana on the blacktop outside the old freshman dorm—I know that today that seems impossible, given all the hoopla around the NBA draft, but it's true! Then, from inside the dorm, someone yelled out to me, "Yo, man! Willis Reed is looking for you!" I stopped what I was doing and said, "What?!" Apparently, Reed had called Coach and told him the New York Knicks were preparing to select me with the fourth pick in the first round *that day*. Coach Brandenburg lived down the street from the university and he'd got word to me now. To say I was full of excitement was a tremendous understatement!

In a flash, I ran down to Coach's house. Willis called up again and told me the good news. At that time, the NBA draft wasn't televised—no green room, no mock draft websites. So the team had to call directly to let the players know what was happening. There was a rumor that some within the Knicks organization wanted to draft Bird, but I guess with the clout Willis had with the franchise, they took me instead! It was a dream come true. I hung up the phone and called my mother and told her I was to be drafted by the New York Knicks. I'd never been to New York City before, but boy was I happy to be going. Here I'd been shooting around with friends at the University of Montana, and now I was a Knick. Part of the NBA. My dream had come true.

There had been a rumor that the Chicago Bulls were interested in me and that they'd take me then if I was still available to them. But Willis had shown a special notice in me ever since he saw me in Flagstaff. And afterward, I'd improved my stock in Hawaii, taking on the top talent in the country. I wondered if I'd go in the first round but never had a thought it could be true. Until now.

* * *

The 1978 draft was a historic one. Portland had two picks in the first round (first and seventh), and with their first selected Mychal Thompson (father of Klay) from the University of Minnesota. The mustached Phil Ford from the University of North Carolina went second to Kansas City. Bruiser Rick Robey from Kentucky went third to Indiana.

And I was fourth.

The pick that had landed me for New York had changed many times in trades that involved other guys, including Moses Malone, Mike Bantom, Phil Jackson, and Vinnie Johnson. Larry Bird went sixth to Boston (he would come out the following year), Reggie Theus from UNLV went ninth to Chicago. In the second round, Maurice Cheeks went 36th to Philly. Michael Cooper was picked 60th.

But all I cared about, in that moment, was my new home. After the draft, I flew back to Denver, still on cloud nine.

Once I got back, my eldest brother, Willie, threw me a draft party. We had a big shindig to celebrate. A bunch of family and friends came over to the house. It was really nice, a good way to remember where I'd come from. The Knicks selecting me was all over the local news in Missoula, New York, and Denver. It was amazing. I felt like a king! Before I'd been drafted, a lot of the guys I played summer leagues with were telling me I wasn't good enough. Well, I shut a lot them up on draft day.

I had a few days before I had to be with the Knicks, so in that free time I played in as many pro-am games as I could, against the likes of Ralph Simpson, David Thompson, and Al Smith. I knew I had to be as sharp as I could. In the best shape time would allow. Then, all of a sudden, just three days later, I was on a plane, and I touched down in New York. I flew there with my mother, while my wife and our daughter stayed behind in Denver. Renee didn't want to be part of the hustle and bustle just yet, but she did give me her blessing to travel to New York and do my best for the Knicks. I kissed baby Tosha goodbye and told Renee I'd see her soon. I almost couldn't believe I'd made it this far.

The plane landed at 11:30 at night on July 1. New York City wasn't nearly as lit up then as it is now. So when the team representatives picked us up, I couldn't see much of the area as we made our way through the city streets over to the hotel. Mom and I checked into our room that night and went right to sleep, exhausted from our flight and in preparation for the days ahead.

The next morning, when we went outside to check out our new surroundings, I kept looking for trees and grass. "W-where is the grass?" I muttered. "And where are all the trees?" It was a shock. All the people. *Whooshing* this way, *whooshing* that way. Moving so fast and not speaking to each other.

There wasn't any of that where I'd come from. In Denver and Montana, when people walk by, they say, "How you doing?" and all of that. But, all of a sudden, I'd gone from the smallest place to the biggest. In New York, everybody was in their own world. And it's not sociable. It was just a different attitude, but it was fine by me.

Besides, I was on top of the world because, after I was drafted by New York, I signed a four-year deal with the team worth about $900,000 ($800,000 over those years, with $100,000 deferred). At the time, the biggest deal in the NBA went to Bill Walton and Moses Malone for $1 million for a single year, but nearly $1 million over four as a rookie was fine by me. The de facto owner of the Knicks, Sonny Werblin, gave the contract to my agent, Sidney Slinker, and I put my name to it. All of a sudden, I'd gone to bed broke, and I woke up the next morning with money!

The night I signed the deal, I took my mother out to eat a big steak dinner in New York, and soon after bought her a new home in Denver for about $80,000. I had fulfilled my promise to her! Around that time, there was a rumor at the time that I bought myself a Rolls-Royce and that big bad Willis Reed made me return it but that was just a drummed-up news story. In truth, I had a friend who rented those cars out and I drove one around for a little while, but I never owned anything crazy like that my rookie season.

* * *

The morning after we arrived in New York, my mother and I visited Madison Square Garden with my agent to meet Coach Reed. I still have a photo of us from then that was printed in the paper. MSG was a massive place. I've always known it because of the Muhammad Ali fights. But now it was my home. I'd seen the Knicks win their rings in 1970 and 1973, and I knew it was a special place. As for the man who selected me, who was also the coach of the team, Willis was great. He was a laid-back players' coach. And he took me under his wing.

That year, the Knicks were at the tail end of their most successful decade ever (and it's still their most successful decade ever). New York had won two titles with the likes of Reed, Walt Frazier, Dave DeBusschere, and Bill Bradley. They'd also had Phil Jackson and Earl "The Pearl" Monroe as part of the franchise. Red Holzman had been the coach (or team general) and, as a result, a Knicks hero. The game of basketball has a long history in New York, a city full of people and short on space. And the years between 1970 and 1973 might have been its height. The New York media put that pressure on me as a high draft pick from the jump, and it wasn't always easy.

The city especially cares about point guards, those ballhandlers who initiate the offense, take care of the ball, and dish out assists with wizard-like skills. When Willis—who had retired as a player just three years prior in 1975—drafted me, I was positioned to be the next Walt "Clyde" Frazier. Born in Atlanta, the 6-foot-4 Frazier attended Southern Illinois and was drafted in 1967 by the Knicks with the fifth pick. He was known for his tight defense, scoring, and playmaking. He was a seven-time All-Star and two-time champ. He was traded by the Knicks to Cleveland the year before I arrived, and they wanted me to fill his talented shoes.

* * *

Before the season, the Knicks held training camp in Monmouth, New Jersey, at Monmouth College. Willis had me playing behind Jim Cleamons, a seventh-year, 6-foot-3 point guard from Ohio State. With career averages of eight points and four assists, I knew I was better than Jim. There was no way around it. But I was okay waiting my turn . . . for now. The other starting guard was Ray Williams, a second-year player out of Minnesota who could really score. Even though I had to be patient, I worked hard; the first to practice and last to leave. My mother's diligent work ethic rung in my rookie ears.

The season prior, the Knicks had gone 43–39 and lost in the Eastern Conference Semifinals to the Philadelphia 76ers. While without Frazier, the team still included marquee players like Spencer Haywood, Phil Jackson, Bob McAdoo, and "Pearl" Monroe. My rookie season, some of those veterans were still there including Spencer, McAdoo, and Pearl. But we started off slow, going 6–8 through our first 14 games. It seemed that New York's ownership thought we should be doing better so they fired Willis, which crushed me, and Holzman took over, having been gone from the team for just over a year. The man who had drafted me and brought me in was—*poof*—gone.

I don't think I would have survived that time had it not been for Pearl Monroe, also known as "Black Jesus" or just "Jesus." Every rookie has a "vet" that helps him through the early years, navigating the problems that might arise with your new life as a pro. And Pearl was that guy for me. He was a great mentor, someone who knew the NBA game and the street game. Someone who could do it one-on-one but also facilitate teammates and lead an offense. For me, the Philly-born Black Jesus was a guiding light. I was blessed to be around him for two seasons before he retired in 1980. A four-time All-Star and a future Hall of Famer.

Earl was one of those guys who could put the ball in the basket in his sleep if he wanted. We would sit on the bus together or after practice and he and I would just talk basketball, brainstorming about how to work together on the court. He had so much knowledge. Earl must have had fifteen operations during his career, and always told me to take care of myself. After games, I would come in and take a shower and leave, but Earl would be in the locker room for an hour, icing his legs and getting treatment. He'd say, "This is going to come to you, too, young fella!"

Reaching again for the old days, the Knicks brought back Holzman to coach again, which meant a change for me. For those first games with Willis, I came off the bench but was getting good minutes. In an early win at MSG against the Pacers, I scored 19, grabbed four rebounds, dished out four assists, and got two steals in 28 minutes. Two games later, in a loss to the Lakers, I scored 10 points and added two rebounds and a steal in just 14 minutes. And in a win against the SuperSonics two games after that, I had 13 points, nine rebounds, and three assists in 21 minutes. But when Red came in, I knew my minutes would dry up.

At first, Red, a former Coach of the Year, actually started me for a few games. But about a week into that, I was almost completely out of the rotation. Against the 6–13 Detroit Pistons on November 21, I played six minutes off the bench. The next game, in a loss at Boston, I played nine minutes off the bench. We were 24–30 at the All-Star break and, in the last game before the midseason mark, I didn't even get in the game. When they'd fired Willis, I woke up the next morning shocked, reading about it in the newspaper. Now, it seemed Red wasn't working out either.

What made the season worse was that management shipped out McAdoo and Haywood halfway through the year, with Bob heading to Boston and Spencer sent to New Orleans. They were two all-timers going out the door with not much coming back. The team kept Pearl around for one more season before he retired. After that, the big names from the past were all gone. It made me especially upset, though, because McAdoo was one of my best friends on the team. He and I would hang out after games, even stopping into the famed Studio 54 together. Not to drink or anything like that, just to hang out, dance a little and check out a lady or two. Bob knew where all the clubs were, even though he wasn't a drinker.

On the court, Bob was a million-dollar scorer with a great face-up game, and it was my job to get him the ball where he liked it. We'd talk about that in the clubs. He would tell me, as the disco music played, that he worked best when he got the ball on the baseline or in the high post. Sometimes I couldn't believe that I was in Studio 54 with the great Bob McAdoo talking hoops. What a life!

As for Spencer, he was another amazing veteran. I'd known him from Denver, when he was in the ABA. I used to hang out with him in the locker room after he was done playing and I was done selling popcorn and hot dogs. He'd give me tickets to future games and I'd tell him that one day I'd meet him in the pros. Back then, he was one of the best basketball players on the planet. Him and Julius Erving. And man, he could fly! When he was with the Knicks, though, he was a bit older, yet the consummate veteran. His game was slower, but he was still effective. Later, Spencer got in trouble for using drugs, but back then, that wasn't anything we talked about. I was on a mission, and drugs had nothing to do with it. That's why still, to this day, I can't believe I got sidetracked.

"You can do it," he'd tell me with his sweet, melodic vice. "You've just got to put the hard work in."

But the Knicks chose Red over three former league MVPs and future Hall of Famers.

Indeed, the Knicks had *just* hired Red and, thus, couldn't shit-can him again. Now I was caught up in the middle of it all, the rookie high draft pick. But since Red didn't believe in playing rookies, I went weeks without playing in games and when I did get in, I played a mere handful of minutes. But in practice? Hell, I was killing Jim Cleamons. I took it personal that I wasn't play-ing, and knew it was my job that Jim had ownership of. So every day at practice was like war. I'd show Red he was wrong for keep-ing me on the bench. I told him, "You'll regret not playing me, Red Holzman." I needed experience. If I was bad, let me get the mistakes out now.

But Red didn't draft me, and so he had no real allegiance to me. He didn't even play me at guard all the time, the position where I felt most comfortable. I guess some people are just stuck in their ways. Red was nearing sixty years old and, yes, he knew the game well. The game was also passing him by in real time. That's not an insult. It's just that things change. It's Father Time. He catches up with all of us. Red, who started coaching in the NBA in 1950s with the Milwaukee Hawks, was great in his era. But he wasn't the same when I was with the team at the dawn of the 1980s.

New York City is a hard place to be a professional athlete. That is true now and it was during my rookie year in 1978. Just ask Willis Reed. After he got fired and the team brought in Red, it was difficult for me to find any rhythm on the court (as nobody can really make an impact on the game when they're playing just two or three minutes at a time). And while I wanted to play, I knew that I still had a lot to learn. My problem on the court was trying to do too much. I was too fast. That was my sin on the hardwood that season. I turned the ball over too much. So much so that we began to hear boos from the fans. I didn't know if they were for me or for Red or the entire team, but it wasn't fun whether they were for me or not.

* * *

It only got worse for us after the All-Star break. We won only seven more games, a dismal streak that included losing our last eight, to finish 31–51. We were getting booed off the court almost every night. There was one game, I was so pissed at Red. He'd called me to get ready to get in with about two minutes before the half. There I was, waiting at the scorer's table to check in. But, unusually, there were no fouls or timeouts, no time stoppages, and I never got in. In the second half, Red didn't even look my direction. What was I supposed to do? How was I supposed to improve if I couldn't get on the court? He was yanking me around. I even thought about trying to get traded.

But there was nothing I could do. I couldn't talk to him. He would just tell me, "Wait until it's your turn." For a whole year? I remember telling people Red would pay for this. For my rookie season, I averaged 6.5 points, 1.4 steals, 3 assists, and 3.2 rebounds in just under 17 minutes per game in 72 contests. To say I was unsatisfied would be a big understatement. With the season over, I went home to Denver and played in every game within twenty square miles of the city. I vowed to be in the best damn shape of my life so that when I got back for my second season, if Red didn't play me, the team's owners would have to send him to the funny farm.

Memory Lane: Spencer Haywood

Michael Ray was a rotten ol' fucking rookie! In fact, all of them, all my rookies on that Knicks team, were just rotten to the core. And they were led by Sugar! Michael Ray, Toby Knight. They drove me fucking nuts. Why? Because they were rookies, and they didn't want to do what you asked them to do. Oh, I forgot Ray Williams. Man, poor Willis Reed. He was scratching his head, going, "Oh god." It was disgusting!

No, I'm just kidding, they were all good kids. But we gave them the nickname "Clockwork Orange," those crazy little fuckers. Those rookies. They even started wearing those fucking derby hats! But I would also say this: Michael Ray was like a Magic Johnson but with a better outside shot at that time. He grew up with me in Denver when I was in the ABA. He was in high school when I played there with the Rockets. He was my guy, I love him, that bad little fucker!

6

BECOMING AN ALL-STAR

YOU might be wondering why I haven't talked about my drug use yet. The simple answer is that, by this point in my life, I still hadn't tried any narcotics. If anything, basketball was my drug of choice. Even if I was a bit young and pigheaded at the time, the game was my passion in New York. A young man, though, I did also like to spend time with a few women when I could. But hard drugs? No way. That awful stuff wouldn't take ahold of me and my life for another year or two. For now, it was all basketball, and I was on a mission. First and foremost, it was my aim to earn the starting point guard job for the New York Knicks in my sophomore season.

The NBA at that time was packed with big names. At the top of the list were Julius Erving and Kareem Abdul-Jabbar. Then Bob McAdoo, Elvin Hayes, George Gervin, and many more. But the All-Stars didn't intimidate me like they might have others. I already knew that I belonged because I'd gone up against the Denver pros in my youth. I'd even met Dr. J. When I was in high school, I was at one of the Denver games and the cheerleaders were throwing mini red, white, and blue ABA basketballs into the stands. Well, I caught one and after the game, I went into the locker room and waited for Dr. J. When he arrived, he signed the ball for me.

On it, he wrote his name and added "Keep on truckin'," and I'll always remember that. I kept that ball into adulthood and when I played against Julius and his 76ers my rookie year for the first time, I showed him the mini ball. He got the biggest grin on his face. That was one of the best feelings of my life. He shook his head and couldn't believe it. Now, here I was, ahead of my second season in the league, playing for the New York Knicks. In a couple more years, I'd be a *veteran*. Going into the 1979–80 season, Red Holzman was still our coach. And before training camp, I was worried this year would be a repeat of the last one. I knew it was up to me to do everything I could to make sure that didn't happen. Let my play do the talking.

* * *

In the NBA, you quickly learn the *big* lesson: that the league is full of talent. Once you make a team, it's not about your skills anymore. It's about your *brain* and your ability to be *consistent*. After playing in college and coming to the pros, you notice the game slows down. It's more controlled. It becomes a mind game, and your job is to make it seem slower still. Everyone in the league, after all, is just as good as you are (more or less). Everyone is strong, athletic, and quick. So you have to outsmart them. You have to think and do before the other guy thinks and does. And as a player, that's where I shined.

I was born with great instincts. God-given talents. On the court, I used them to my advantage. I always made sure to know where the ball was because the ball is the only thing that can hurt you. My mind was always on it and my body was always positioned so that I could see and react to it. That's how I got so many steals in my career. I knew where the ball would be before it got there. (Though I *occasionally* did guess wrong.) But what I didn't quite anticipate was how Red would greet me in camp early on, since the guy would put me in for 30 seconds and then take me out or wait until garbage time to give me time as a rookie.

I didn't have a handle on him, other than to think he probably hated me as a player. I couldn't read the old NBA lifer. I could only guess that he was trying to trade me to a team in Siberia or Shanghai. Amazingly, though, my guesses were all wrong. In that first practice on that first day of Knicks training camp, Red came over to me and looked me in the eye. He put the basketball in my hand and told me, "You're our starting point guard." That's how everything began for me in my second season with New York. In that moment, Red gave me the confidence I'd needed. I'd earned my role, and it was time for my career to take off.

* * *

Truth be told, I didn't waste any time. That first month of the new year, I earned player of the week for the week of October 28. The week before that, Julius Erving had taken the award. It was the first time I'd received any form of acknowledgement in my playing career. It felt overwhelmingly good to be recognized by the league, and knew I was on my way. In New York, as my role progressed, my life off the court was also steady. My rookie year, I had been living with our backup shooting guard, Mike Glenn.

Mike had been a rookie the year before with the Buffalo Braves, and we got along well. He had an apartment in Flushing, Queens, and he asked if I wanted to move in to split the rent. I said sure, and all of a sudden, I had a place in the city. It worked out well between us because at that time, I didn't do much at night. I wasn't really going out. No parties, no drinking. Alcohol has never really interested me. I always saw people get stupid when they got drunk. They would fall over, and their speech would slur. They'd get that glazed look in their eyes. That wasn't for me. I had enough excitement in my life as an NBA player already. Besides, I told myself, it would only hurt my game and my chances at fame. People who drank got slower, gained weight. Why would that be good for me?

After all, I was just trying to get established in the NBA—and New York, for that matter. Because as the Frank Sinatra song goes, if you can make it in New York, you can make it anywhere.

Prior to Mike asking if I wanted to move in, I was going to live in a place in New Jersey. It was more isolated from Manhattan than Queens. But Mike was a good guy and I liked the idea of having someone to lean on. We used to catch the 7 train to Manhattan together for practice and on game days.

In fact, I remember one night when Mike and I were out late, which was something of a rare occasion. He and I were on the train on our way home when, just two stops before our final destination, about four or five of these big guys got on the train. For some reason, Mike and I could both feel their eyes on us as soon as they stepped foot from the platform to the car. We both knew, somehow, they were about to try and rob us. Two tall, Black visible NBA players. We must have stood out like sore thumbs. But since we'd felt their eyes on us before they even got foot on the train, Mike and I slipped out just before the doors closed behind us.

We kept closer attention of our surroundings after that. I never wanted to fight, but that doesn't mean I was never in them. For example, after my rookie season, I went home and played in all those Denver games. Well, guess what? All the guys in those leagues who *weren't* in the NBA wanted to prove they could hang or even outdo someone who was. The late '70s were an interesting time for a professional basketball player. The league was popular but not *so* popular. Today, pros are surrounded by security guards and wouldn't go near subway cars. But the past was different.

Back then? To be more of a civilian was common. So, these guys in Denver went at me. They played as hard as they could, wanting to show their girlfriends and mothers they could hang with an NBA star. The result of that, sometimes, was an impromptu bare-knuckle boxing brawl. The same thing even happens in NBA practices and training camps behind closed doors. People are trying to make careers and names for themselves. Some even as bruisers. Fights happen more often than people think. In a two-hour NBA training camp practice, one hour is spent on basketball and the other is often spent on fighting.

In the league, you can't let anybody punk you. You do what you have to do. If someone beneath you is coming at you (like I was for Cleamons), it's imperative to remember that it's your job to keep your spot and theirs to try and take it. That's in any league. In my time, people were going to try me. Poke and prod. Try to fuck with me. That's where the mental game comes into play most. If you let someone see they could push you off your game, you were done. Even in the pro games, if there wasn't fighting, per se, there was really rough play. So you had to do what it took to get an advantage on the floor: hustle, scuffle, or score.

I remember scrapping one time with the big 6-foot-9 bruiser named Maurice Lucas. I was in my second season and he was playing for the Nets. He'd been a six-time All-Star in the ABA and NBA and won the '77 title with Bill Walton (like me, another famous stutterer) in Portland. But he was a jerk when he played. In this one game at MSG, we were going back and forth with the Nets. It was a close one. During one play, I came down on offense and kicked the ball out for an assist. After I passed it, my momentum kept me running through the lane. As I stopped to make a U-turn to go back up the court, I felt this big *POP* in my chest.

Lucas, who would be my teammate a couple years later (the NBA is wild), had gotten me with his big forearm and knocked me down. All the air left my body. As I was gasping for breath, he looked down from above me and said, "Young fella, when you come in here, you better be looking around." You can't do the stuff Lucas did in the league today. When I got my breath back, I jumped up and we started jawing at each other back and forth. A few guys broke it up and, as I went back to our bench, a couple of my teammates told me that Lucas wasn't someone to mess with. But I didn't care. In the end we didn't throw punches. We kept the game going.

Later, when we were on the Knicks, Lucas would instruct me to let my man get past me and into the lane. "Let him come to the basket," he'd tell me. "I'm going to put him in the wood." And Lucas would put the guy into the floor—the "wood." Just like he'd done to me. People often like to take their shit out on others. Sometimes sports gives us a reason to do so. NBA players aren't boxers, but when I played, some of them certainly thought they were or could be—especially big guys like Lucas. The game gives us all different rewards. For some, it's glory. Others, it's a payday. For Lucas, it was hitting the shit out of people.

* * *

As my second season unfolded, I was in the best shape of my life. I'd now seen how the league worked and was set to show what I'd learned. I'd finally earned the trust of Red and I couldn't let him down.

During the season, Red would tell me, "You have to be me on the floor out there. Because I can't pass and I can't shoot the ball anymore. Don't be afraid to voice your opinion to the guys either because I'm behind you 100 percent." He also told me, "Remember, if you keep the big men happy, they'll work hard for you and make your life easy." As a coach, Red didn't say a ton to his players. But all he had to do was give you a look and you knew he meant business. You could see it in his expressive eyes. If he communicated anything, I made sure to take it all in from the two-time champion coach.

That year, I became only the third player in NBA history to lead the NBA in steals and assists in a single season. For the year, wearing my No. 20 jersey, I averaged 15.3 points, 3.2 steals, 10.1 assists, and 6.6 rebounds. My steals and assists numbers set

Knicks records. I'd rebound, push, and we'd score. I also made the All-Defensive first team.

I earned the praise I'd always wanted—from teammates like McAdoo, Ray Williams and Bill Cartwright to newspaper men like Harvey Araton from the *New York Post* and Filip Bondy for the *Daily News*, who wrote stories about my growth in the game. And I told Red, "See, I knew I could always play in this league!" Jeez, was I a brash young man. Always talking loudly about something. While I had cat-like reflexes, I wasn't shy like one anymore, that's for sure. In fact, sometimes when I was pissed with Red, I'd go to the press. I shake my head at it now, but I'd say back then, "That old man, he doesn't know what t-talent is!" I threatened to call my agent and demand a trade. All while Red was in the locker room watching. I really didn't care, I was hotheaded. But even if I was right, it wasn't always the best tactic.

* * *

On offense, I knew where my guys would be and who needed a shot. At the end of the day, I wanted to make everyone better. I was quick, slashing to the basket and I could have averaged more points. But basketball is a team game, though. One man can't do it all by himself. I don't care how good you are. A team needs everyone to do their job. When you're the point guard, at least in my era, you had the ball some 80 percent of the time. I could shoot anytime if I'd wanted. But to be an assist leader, you have to be a willing passer. You have to be comfortable passing shots for the sake of others. I also knew that if I wanted my power forwards and centers to play tough defense, rebound, and outlet the ball to me, then I'd have to keep them happy. That was my responsibility.

As a defender, I used my knack for anticipation to get into passing lanes and steal the ball. That season also marked the year the NBA adopted the 3-point line, which had grown in popularity due to the ABA. While no one took much advantage of it early on, I made sure to take them during the game when the shot clock was running down or at the end of quarters. I saw the value of hoisting them up in those moments even though I wasn't a knock-down shooter from outside. But with all my hard work on both ends of the court, I was rewarded for my efforts. I made my first All-Star team.

* * *

Earning Red's confidence, I averaged just over 37 minutes per game, which was more than double than the year prior. I also played in all 82 games. Back then, there was no such thing as load management. People wanted to play as much as possible. In that way, it's a different league today.*** Guys make so much money now that they can afford to sit out or even dog it at times. In a few years, star players will be making $100 million *a season*. That's a far cry from the seventies, when a big contract was $100,000 a year. When I was coming up, the NBA hadn't grown to the global export it is today, so we had to earn every dollar. And I didn't mind. I loved being on the court. Both sides of it.

***Editor's Note: For the 1979–80 season, there were 55 players that appeared in all 82 regular-season games. For the 2022–23 season, there were nine.

* * *

We finished the 1979–80 season with a record of 39–43, which was an eight-game improvement over the one prior. Unfortunately, we *just* missed the playoffs. We'd actually tied the Washington Bullets with the same record for the final spot, but lost the league's tiebreaker, and so Washington was let into the bracket and not us (they lost to Philly in the first round). But our team was headed in the right direction. We had some talented offensive players on the roster, like small forward Toby Knight, who could really score (until a knee injury ended his career). We also had rookie Bill Cartwright, a center who was also named an All-Star that season.

The athletic shooting guard Ray Williams could fill it up from anywhere, too, and my old roommate, Mike Glenn, who came off the bench, could shoot it from distance with the best of them. Our team chemistry came down to each of us knowing where the other liked to get the ball. We looked out for each other. We worked to set each other up. I wanted to find my teammates in their sweet spots. Bill liked the ball down on the block where he could turn to his left and shoot his little fadeaway. Toby's sweet spot was on the right side of the court, where he could turn over his left shoulder and score. Mike Glenn was an excellent spot-up shooter and he liked to get the ball at the foul line or foul line extended. With Ray, you could put the ball anywhere by the rim and he was just going to go up and get it.

This was also the last season for the legend Earl Monroe. While he wasn't the player he'd been as a young man, when they called him "Jesus" on the court, he was a good mentor, a great guy, and an NBA all-timer. I learned a lot watching the Hall of Famer, even before I made the league. What he could do with the ball was more wizardry than it was sport. But as with life, everything must change. And new iconic guards were coming into the league.

* * *

Here I'd like to add a quick note on some of the other guards in the league at the time. Over the course of my basketball life, I've had a lot in common with Magic Johnson. And that season, Magic's first in the league, fresh off winning a championship at Michigan State with my former coach, Jud Heathcote, Magic took his Los Angeles Lakers to the NBA Finals and won it all. Magic was the other big point guard in the NBA at that time. But he was taller than me, by some three inches. But I was quicker! Since we were both big, we were often compared to one another, so much so that some people called me the Magic of the East. And Magic has said, "Every time I saw him, he went right at me."

Sportswriter Peter Vecsey said I was the one guy Magic feared. As a big point guard, I used to love to kill all the little guards. One guy I enjoyed matching up against was Isiah Thomas. Don't get me wrong, he's a Hall of Famer and a champion—but I used to take it to him back in the day. Later in my career, when I was with the New Jersey Nets, I would go into the Detroit Pistons locker room before games and tell Isiah that I was going to bust his ass that night. He looked at me like I was crazy. Isiah is a legend in the game, but he's also only about six feet tall, so I had an advantage there. We had some big battles on both ends of the floor. Isiah respected me and I gave it back to him.

George Gervin was another guy whom I respected. He was maybe the best scorer in the league and is certainly one of the best of all time. His backcourt mate, James Silas, could fill it up, too. He was once the runner-up for MVP in the ABA. Otis Birdsong and Phil Ford were great teammates. Otis could get buckets and Phil was the consummate floor general. He would always make the right decision. I tried to take a little piece from all these guys. I wanted to be the best I could while also keeping my team happy.

With the Knicks, Ray Williams and I used to love to play against the Seattle SuperSonics, too, largely because their backcourt of Gus Williams and Dennis Johnson was so celebrated. Gus was also Ray's brother. We'd have some good games when we played against those guys, and they fed off their sibling rivalry. Truly, I loved playing with Ray. During that season, we were probably the best defensive backcourt in the entire league. We had little side bets on who would the most steals on a certain night. While I led the league, he wasn't too far behind. We had amazing eye contact. On offense, I would just toss him ally-oops and we'd get Madison Square Garden going. We felt like were the best one-two punch at guard perhaps in the entire NBA.

* * *

It takes a lot to make the NBA. A lot of work and sacrifices. So all I was trying to do that season was keep my head above water and play well. I got the starting job and now I needed to hold onto it. Sometimes, though, I would go out at night to blow off some steam or talk about the night's result with the guys. Ray Williams and I would go to this night club called Justine's near

MSG on West 38th Street. We'd go there and to this other night club called Leviticus on West 33rd Street. I'd also find myself at the infamous Studio 54 at times, surrounded by famous people like Yankees slugger Reggie Jackson, along with actors and artists.

But I wasn't there to party as much—I was to meet women. In truth, monogamy was never really important to me. It's not that I felt that way out of disrespect to any particular person. It was more out of a respect for myself and how I felt about relationships. So, I'd find gals at places like Justine's and other spots around town. It was great having a home court in the middle of the city. Leviticus was similar, it was a nice laid-back dance club, and I'd often go there with Hollis Copeland, Geoff Huston, and Ray.

At Studio 54 . . . man. That place was a *scene*. The first time I ever went was with my teammate Bob McAdoo. We were close my rookie year, and he sort of took me under his wing. He was the man. I love that guy to this day. When you arrive at Studio 54—which was maybe the hottest club in the world in the mid-1970s—there were some two hundred to three hundred people waiting *outside*. The bouncers had to pick you for you to get in. To be selected, you either had to be someone or know someone. Well, they let me and Bob in no problem.

Inside Studio 54 were three floors. The first was for the normal folks. The second was more prestigious. You might see a woman giving a blowjob or two guys kissing in a corner on the second floor. And the third, well, that was for the most special of people. You had to be *really* special to make it to the third. Everything was fair game on the third floor. Drugs, women, you name it. When I first started going there, I mostly hung out on the second floor. Eventually, I met the owners, thanks to Bob, and was allowed to roam the place after that. The height of the club's popularity coincided with my peak on the Knicks. So I started hanging out there more over time.

With my growing success and popularity, an affinity for hanging out at night began to grow inside of me. I enjoyed chasing women. A few times during my rookie year, I woke up Mike Glenn at one or two in the morning to see if he wanted to go out to dance clubs. I got restless. Sometimes, I'd drive one of my sports cars. At times, flying fast through the city felt like the way to travel! I was so brash that I even kept my car parked outside Studio 54, paying someone to watch it. And I never got a ticket. Occasionally, I could be found at other hotspots like Plato's Retreat or the Cotton Club. Over time, I began making a name for myself in these places.

* * *

Summers meant working on my game during those first early years. "I've never seen you so focused," my wife Renee told me. Each summer, I got better than the one before. Not only did the summer pro-ams include guys who wanted to take down an NBA player, but there were pros who also wanted to let loose and kick butt. One of those was Charlie Scott. Charlie is a legend among a lot of players because he was the first Black scholarship player at the University of North Carolina. In his first five years as a pro, Charlie averaged about 27 points, five assists, and five rebounds per game between the ABA and NBA. An All-Star each season.

Later, Charlie played with Boston and the Lakers, and with Denver at the end of his career. That summer, between my rookie and second year, I played against him in one of the Denver pro-ams. We battled and, in one particular showdown, I started talking trash to Charlie. I told him, "When I see you in Madison Square Garden next year, I'm going to dunk on your ass!" Fast forward a few months later and, sure enough, on December 1, Denver visited MSG. Charlie was in their starting lineup. At one point in the game, it was just me and him. I caught him just like I said I would. I had the ball on a fast break, and I dunked right on him.

When I ran back up the court, all he could do was shake his head and smile. Later in the game, though, Charlie gave me some wisdom that only a veteran player like him could. When we were fighting for position at one point, he told me, "Listen, young fella. If you're in the game long enough, everybody is going to get dunked on." While I outplayed the veteran, who was in the last season of his career, I'd also gotten to know a little bit more about the league as a result. Thanks to Charlie.

* * *

Guarding various guys in the NBA provided their own unique challenges. One of them was Magic. When we played against one another, he and I always talked shit. Every time we matched up, we talked trash. He once said of me, "Sugar talks plenty of trach but he always was able to back it up." My whole thing when I played against Magic was that I wanted to try and post a triple-double against him. He was known around the league as the king of the triple-doubles. Someone who could score, dish assists, rebound, you name it.

Never one to back down, I wanted to outdo him at his own game. Sometimes I even managed to do just that—both in a game and in a single season. For instance, in 1979–80, Magic's rookie season, I led the league with seven triple-doubles. The following year, I was third. The year after that, I was second. In total, as a Knick, I notched eighteen triple-doubles. And as a Net, I added three more, for a total of twenty-one in my career. Today, that's good for 24th all-time in the regular season (tied with Kareem, Kobe, Kyle Lowry, and Chris Webber). And it wasn't even a stat we prioritized then. Not like today's stars like Nikola Jokić and Russell Westbrook do these days.

George Gervin was another elite player. He was the only man I ever feared on the court. George was big. Though only two inches taller than me, he felt *a lot* bigger. It seemed like he would lead the league in scoring every year. He was a machine, and one of the best players I've ever seen. When you'd play against him, he would tell you straight up, "If you serve me once, I'm going to serve you twice." Today, people talk about the GOAT and who was the best ever. In my opinion, Gervin doesn't get brought up enough. These ABA guys don't get the credit they deserve. Dr. J was who Jordan wanted to be. Those days, we all wanted to be Gervin. Today, George is in my all-time starting five, with MJ, Bob McAdoo, Kareem, and myself.

As for Jordan, I remember going up against him several times toward the end of my NBA career. We were both All-Stars in 1984–85 when he was a rookie. Later, my Nets teams usually took out his young Bulls teams. Back then Chicago wasn't nearly what they became in the following decade. Part of that was the league got old, and part of it was so many were lost due to tragic circumstances. Len Bias, Reggie Lewis, Magic, and me, to name a few. But Jordan, hats off to him. He kept his nose clean (and let his teammates like Charles Oakley, Horace Grant, or Dennis

Rodman do a lot of the dirty work) and stayed healthy and achieved it all.

But my Nets teams beat him four out of six times his rookie year. The second time they got the best of us was a game in Chicago on April 2. We were 37–38 going into the game and the Bulls were one game worse. While I played well that night, scoring 29 points with three steals, eight assists, and five rebounds, Jordan was *on*. He had 31 with three steals, nine assists, and eight boards. I played 46 minutes and he played 44. That was a good matchup. You could see his talent. But we got him the majority of the other times that season. Jordan was still young, though. And while it was obvious that he had the talent, whether I went up against a rookie or a vet, I feared no one. After all, they laced their shoes the same as me. If he cuts, he bleeds, just like me.

Mike and I would talk a lot of shit, though. That was just part of my game, as it would be his. Simple stuff like, "You can't guard me!" "Man, you can't guard *me*!" We'd get into each other's jerseys a little bit on the court. That's one thing about MJ, he's crazy competitive. I told him every time, though, similar to what Gervin told me, "Hey, young fella. You take one step, I'm going to take two." That was MJ. Of course, you can't talk Magic and MJ without talking Larry Bird. Larry was fun to play against. He always rose to the occasion. He *also* talked a mess of trash. Maybe the most. But he was a hell of a player. He could back up everything he said.

The one guy who didn't talk a lot was Dominique Wilkins, "The Human Highlight Film." He was a great player and boy, he could fly. You know a player has true hops when he doesn't jump off just one foot to dunk. When he jumps off both, he's got real skills. Whenever he was near the rim, he was going to put you in there, too, along with the basketball. He and David Thompson were the best at it. But I used to love to guard David. He would try to back you down on the foul line, then he'd turn around and jump over you to shoot. But I knew that as David started to bring the ball up, I could get him with my quick hands.

If he got the ball over you, it was over. That's why I would get him before he got it up. He was another who sadly had drug issues. That was the thing about drugs back then. They were everywhere. It wasn't a ghetto thing. It wasn't an NBA thing (though Spencer Haywood thinks 80 percent of the league was on drugs around then). It was an American thing. Actors and musicians like Whitney Houston used it. Baseball players, including those on the New York Mets did, too. Doctors were using it to get through long days. No one really knew the full danger until it was too late. The good news is I saw David Thompson in Las Vegas recently and he looked great.

* * *

After my second year finished, as we'd just missed the playoffs, I took stock of what I'd done. I wondered how many more All-Star games I could land. Eight, nine? That year, I shot 47 percent from the field and filled up all the major statistical categories. (I also led the NBA in turnovers—oops!) Making the All-Star team with guys like Magic, Bird, and Jordan was a high point in my life. I'd made history with my numbers, too. It was the total opposite of a "sophomore slump." But I knew that the mark of greatness wasn't climbing to the top of a mountain once. It's consistency. That was my challenge now. *Could I do it again?*

Memory Lane: Bob McAdoo

I went to Michael Ray's first press conference when he got drafted by the New York Knicks. I was one of the star players on the team in New York at the time, and he was our first-round pick. Willis Reed selected him, and I went to the press conference because I wanted to meet the new first-rounder on our team. And we've had a great relationship ever since then. From the NBA to Italy, we just have stayed in touch through the years.

He was a pistol! Him and Ray Williams were there in New York together and they got to the team in back-to-back years, near the end of Walt Frazier and Earl Monroe's time with the Knicks. And those guys were not patient! They were ready to play right away. But with Red Holzman there, Red wasn't going to bench his stars who he won championships with in the early seventies, so Michael and Ray had to wait their turn. But in practice, they would light it up every day.

Back then, Michael wasn't a big Studio 54 guy, but he used to like this club called Justine's. I think he got kind of fed up with the 54 scene. Because you'd go up there and there would be hundreds of people outside waiting. The bouncers would come out in the crowd and pick people out. They'd see me and it would be like the parting of the Red Sea. And I'd go right in. But they didn't know Michael as much at first.

But when I got traded—I'll never forget it. It was around four or five o'clock in the morning and my doorbell rang. I went to the door, wiping my eyes, and it was Michael Ray Richardson. I said, "What's up, man?" And he said, "Mac, I heard you got traded!" So my ears popped up and I said, "Go get my newspaper." I didn't have on any clothes! So, he went to my driveway and got my newspaper.

I opened it up and read that I'd been traded, and that's how I found out. The newspaper. And Michael Ray was the one who brought it to me. I was so dejected. I liked the team, I liked my teammates. But that's how it happened. Years later, we were both in Italy. He was in Bologna and I was in Milan. Then I left Milan after four years and went to Forli, which was closer to Bologna, so I was basically going there every week to see him, or he was coming to me in Forli.

We'd have our backgammon boards, and we'd go to the clubs. When he came to Forli, we would go out to restaurants. Michael was just a hell of a player, in the NBA and in Italy. He had the best hands, getting all these steals. Defensively, he was just awesome. In Italy, in Bologna, they just loved him. Sugarmania! That's what they called him. Sugarmania is in town! That ticket was hard to get, just like mine was in Milan. Everybody wanted to see Sugar.

7

TRYING COCAINE

IT was late in my third year with the Knicks when I first tried cocaine. For the majority of the season, the drug wasn't a part of my life at all. I stayed focused on my game, wanting to repeat my prior All-Star season performance. My extracurriculars were strictly girls and discos. It wasn't until the end of the year that cocaine and I would become acquainted. Even then, it was just dipping and dabbing, as I called it, trying it here and there. The first time I tried it, I didn't even like the stuff. It didn't work. But I'm getting ahead of myself here. Let me back up a bit.

* * *

In the summer between my second and third seasons, I went home as I usually did to work on my game. It was a new decade—the 1980s—and I wanted to improve both myself and the team. In Denver, I saw my mother and my family. I saw Renee and kissed my daughter Tosha. By now, Renee and I had split up. She hated New York and the women hanging around MSG, whom she called "vultures." But we were still friends, even if our lives had taken us different on different paths. She was a nurse in Denver, and I was a basketball player in New York. Still, despite the divorce, we vowed to always be good co-parents for Tosha. She deserved a happy family.

During the 1980–81 season, my third in the NBA, I was again an All-Star and first-team All-Defensive. I finished the year with an average of 16.4 points, 7.9 assists, 2.9 steals, and 6.9 rebounds. As for our team, we continued to improve. After finishing twenty games under .500 my first season, two years later we went 50–32 and made the playoffs. Knicks fans know today that, making the postseason in New York is nothing to sneeze at. No matter the team, it's a huge accomplishment. But making the playoffs in *New York*? Well, that's on a different stratosphere. Especially Red Holzman at the helm and the way we had played all season. That's perhaps why I let my guard down. Why I put myself in the wrong place at the wrong time. Something I'll never be able to get back.

* * *

Returning to New York from Denver a bit before the season began, I had some extra time on my hands. After rooming with Mike Glenn in Queens, I'd moved into my own place the previous year. I was now commuting to Manhattan from Jersey, a spot in a high-rise building in Hackensack. It was a nice little place in a nice little community. There was grass and trees outside finally. A lot of the apartments were rented out by New York Giants football players. During the week, I'd drive to Queens College for Knicks practice (we didn't have our own facility yet) and made sure to always leave an hour and a half early. With veteran status, it meant a lot to my teammates for me to be one of the first guys in the gym.

But during my free time? Rather than dedicating all my time to honing my craft, I preferred going out on the town with my teammates. While initially wishy-washy to the place, I began to enjoy the glitz of Studio 54 more and more. I was now getting into places for free—no more lines! I was becoming the toast of the town, enjoying the action and energy the city offered. Thinking about it now, I remember the stairs going up to the top floor at Studio 54. The place had dark stairwells with little yellow lights. There was an elevator, but I liked taking those stairs. They led you to the top where two bodyguards would be standing. If those guys didn't know you or if you didn't know anybody up there, they'd make sure to send you back and, even sometimes, kick you out of the place.

But if you got in? If you had the right connections and the reputation that you belonged? Then you were welcomed with open arms, rubbing elbows with the likes of movie stars, artists, musicians, and fellow athletes. New York was the best place to be a star . . . if you could hack it. In Studio 54, a DJ spun records on one side of the dancefloor while women danced everywhere else. In a way, it was like a normal nightclub, except not at all because of what you could get away with and who was there to be seen. There were certain private rooms on the third floor where you could go, places where I had some fun in my day. I mean, how could you not? Being young and famous in New York City at Studio 54? It would be a crime if you didn't take advantage of that once in a while, right?

New York in the seventies was *wide* open. Wide awake. And Studio 54 was leading the culture. All the stories you hear are true. But the NBA was a crazy place, too. No matter how comfortable you thought you were with a team, you could get traded in the blink of an eye. I remember when it happened to McAdoo during my rookie season. We were playing well at the time and Bob, an All-Star with the Knicks the previous season, was averaging nearly 27 points a game and close to 10 rebounds (I once saw him hit 18 shots in a row in a single game). Well, I was home one night when it flashed on the television. The Knicks had traded him to Boston. I jumped up and drove to his house. Bob was asleep. I rang his doorbell and said, "You've been traded!" He couldn't believe it. We were pissed, but there was nothing to do. It's just a part of the business.

* * *

As the season progressed, my judgment began to wane. It was hard for me to say no to anyone, or anything for that matter. When it comes to drugs and money, my whole thing was this: I never grew up with either. That's why I signed several shoe deals at once! As for drugs, I was never into them. I had friends who were, but that wasn't me. They'd go out drinking, partying. It just didn't turn me on. When I got to college, I had friends who got blackout drunk all the time. But not me. It was basketball first, women second. So when I first got into drugs, people in my life couldn't believe it. They were shocked.

My first few uses of cocaine were merely me being sociable. One of the crowd. It wasn't even that I was looking out for it. We just happened to be in the same place on the same evening. Now, every time I think of that night, I think, *Boy, was I in the wrong place*. Some might think that my diving into drugs was a rebellion. Or a complete dismissal of my upbringing; like a sheltered person who suddenly gets access to the world. But it really wasn't either of those. It wasn't that deep. Like I said, the very first time I tried cocaine, it didn't even get me high. But the problem came when I let myself try it again . . . and again . . . and again.

As most do, I began my use by snorting it. Later, as I spiraled, I would smoke it. You may ask, how could I let that happen? Well, I just let my guard down, accepting the drug from someone who I thought was my friend and wished me no ill will. After making it to the NBA, I'd achieved my dreams. I'd been an All-Star in back-to-back seasons. I began a nobody from little Lubbock, Texas, and those pig and cotton farms. After that was Denver, then the University of Montana. Now I was one of the best players the world, in the city that never sleeps. With all the hurdles I'd dealt with in life, and being in my twenties, I thought I could handle something that I could not. I thought I was invincible. After all, I was on top of the world. On cloud nine. There was no way some white powder would be able to change that.

Cocaine was a party drug. A fad. It was at Studio 54 and other places. And for years, it never crossed my mind. I'd see people hunched over mirrors and I'd walk on by. But cocaine is a sex drug, too. So whenever there's a lot of coke, there are lots of women around (my kryptonite). From a night or two being sociable with a drug that was everywhere in certain circles to getting hooked on it, my life changed quickly. Today, when I speak to recovering addicts, I always say that there isn't one person that was just sitting around, and drugs just hopped into their mouth. We all chose them. And that was my ultimate downfall.

* * *

Entering the first game of the season, I was twenty-five years old and ready to set the league on fire from the jump. In the second game of the year, I had 20 points, seven steals, 10 rebounds, and 13 assists and we won by 20. After leading the team in points and assists in our first game of the season, a victory over the Bucks, I dropped a triple-double in our second game against the powerhouse 76ers (with seven steals). We beat a team filled with greats like Dr. J, Darryl Dawkins, and Maurice Cheeks by 20 points (113–93) and started the season by winning 10 of our first 13 games. That was just how the year went.

To be the King of New York is a special thing. Our team had won 50 games for the first time in almost a decade. We had the third-highest attendance in the league. But the moment your head begins to inflate, you risk running into something that might pop it. Fall out of that cloud you've been on and right back to reality. And that's what happened to us entering the playoffs, where we'd face the Chicago Bulls, who had gone 45–37 on the season. While we'd split the season series with them at three games apiece, we expected to walk onto the court—our home court—and dominate, as we had done the entire season.

Stepping onto the court to start that game was myself at the point, along with Campy Russell, Ray Williams, Bill Cartwright, and Sly Williams. The Bulls countered with Artis Gilmore, David Greenwood, Reggie Theus, Dwight Jones, and Bob Wilkerson.

But in that first matchup, they were the better team. While we ended the first quarter up by 12, they took charge from there, outscoring us 78–56 the rest of the way. Gilmore had 13 points and 16 rebounds and four other players on the Bulls finished with double digits. I couldn't buy a basket, going 4-for-16 and just nine points (though I did pull down 13 rebounds, to go along with six assists). Campy had 17, Ray added 19, and Cartwright had 11 points, but we still lost, 90–80.

At that time, the first round of the NBA playoffs was not a seven-games series. It was a best of *three*. Now, we had to go to Chicago and win *just* to keep the season alive. A big part as to why we weren't our best was because we were without Toby Knight who, after a 1979–80 campaign, had missed the entire season with a knee injury. He was never the same after that, playing just 40 games the next season before calling it quits. His loss was massive. Still, we had to move forward. Every team deals with injuries and we couldn't use that as an excuse.

Going into a possible elimination game on the road, we knew we had to start fast—and we did. After scoring 36 points in the first quarter, we put up 26 in the second and went into the half up by 10, 62–52. But the game is played for four quarters and heading into the second half we let go of the rope. Though up by seven heading into the fourth, we led by 10 early in the quarter, but the Bulls tied the game with four minutes remaining in regulation. We got outscored in the quarter 26–19, and the Bulls—now with *all* the momentum— sent the game into overtime. Instead of seeing OT as a fresh start, we continued to fumble the game away and eventually lost, 115–114. Campy had 29, Ray had 24, Sly had 18, and I had 14 points with six steals, five assists, and six rebounds. But for Chicago, Artis Gilmore killed us, dropping 25 with 10 rebounds. If that wasn't enough, Greenwood had 19 and 12 rebounds and Dwight Jones had 11 and 14. But it was Reggie Theus who put the Bulls over the top with a whopping 37 points, 11 assists, and four boards.

After my stellar play all season, I couldn't get it going in my first postseason appearance. I went 8-for-33 from the field and missed all four of my 3-point shots.

The season was over, but not the memory of it.

* * *

At the All-Star Game that season, my second in a row, I scored 11 points, grabbed five rebounds, and four steals in 24 minutes. And we won (which we also did in my first ASG appearance). Back then the game was a lot more competitive than it is today, as us players really wanted to win. There was real money on the line for us, too. Winners got $1,500 and losers got $1,000. That was a big deal in the eighties—not to mention the pride that came with beating the best of the best. There were some real prideful guys on those teams. Gervin, Dr. J, Tiny Archibald, Robert Parish, Bird, Kareem, Otis Birdsong, Magic, and Moses Malone. We all wanted to beat the other badly.

Sure, when you walk into the locker room before an All-Star Game to get your uniform, you see all the guys congratulating each other, patting each other on the back. It's a good time. You can see that a lot of them like and respect each other. There's the occasional beef over a woman, a card game, or something like that, but all in all it was pretty chummy. On the court, though? It got serious. Everyone wanted to prove they were the best. The East wanted to beat the West. None of this layup line dunk contest shit the game has turned into today.

* * *

Founded in 1946 as an inaugural member of the BAA (before the league became the NBA), the New York Knickerbockers had a long, storied history (as does New York City with the game of basketball). And in 1980–81, we added to that history. For the second year in a row, we fielded an all-Black team. Years prior, the Boston Celtics were the first team to field an all-Black starting-five, which included the great Bill Russell. But now the Knicks continued the legacy of inclusion. The only problem, however, was that not everyone around the city or the country was on board.

The first year the team featured an all-Black roster came in 1979[en dash]80, and that led to a newspaper citing us as the "New York Niggerbockers." Yes, you read that correctly. What a disgrace. If that happened today, whatever paper that writer and his editors worked for would be shut down and sold for parts. But that's what passed for journalism in the *New York Post*, on October 23, 1979. The paper also chose to print each of our photos in squares like they were mug shots, like we were convicts. That's the kind of shit Black people have always had to deal with and shrug off. Even so, it eats at you. Gets under your skin.

We told ourselves we didn't need to worry about it. But the worst part was that no one in the organization and none of our fans made much of a deal about it. People knew it was taboo, I guess, but there was no protest, no outrage, nothing. It made the whole thing seem, somehow, more acceptable. That remains the worst part about it. I guess it was just normal to most people. But it was the *Twilight Zone* to me. There are a lot of things that went on back then that don't happen today, thankfully. Why? Because back then the players (mostly Blacks) didn't have the power. The coaches (mostly whites) did. But that's changed some today.

Now, a year removed from that awfulness, the Knicks fielded the best team it could, which again meant an all-Black roster. And we proved our mettle in 1980–81. We won 50 games, giving Red Holzman one more great year in New York. We also made the playoffs and I earned my second straight All-Star selection. If the best revenge is a life well lived, we were sure doing our best on the court. the power. The coaches (mostly whites) did. But that's changed some today.

* * *

After the playoff loss that season, I went back home to Denver to lick my wounds. Now, though, I was using cocaine about once a week. The thing about the drug—it wasn't just in New York. It was in Colorado, too. The "snow" was easy to find in the Mile High City. During the days, I worked on my game, played in pro-ams and stayed in shape. But at night I went out. And some of those evenings, I looked for the white powder. Dipping and dabbing. It wasn't a full-blown addiction. I wasn't reliant upon it. But it was snowballing, becoming too habitual.

During that summer in Denver, I hung out with guys I knew from high school, and they were doing it, too. I put myself in places I shouldn't—again. But I wasn't thinking much of it at the time, which was the problem. I let the stuff creep up on me from all sides.

I ceased my vigilance. While at one point it wasn't even on the list, it began to creep up as one of the most important things in my life.

As the summer progressed, I became more and more interested in finding and sniffing the stuff. Smoking it, too, unfortunately. And by the time the summer was over, I was beginning to look and feel worse physically. Unlike previous years, where I had worked all offseason to improve my game and go into the next season a better player, that would not be the case this time.

From there, so much went downhill, as any Knicks fan back then would tell you.

Memory Lane: Reggie Theus

Michael Ray Richardson and I crossed paths our whole careers. He was the fourth player drafted in 1978 and I was the ninth, and we battled on the court many times. We were friends in some ways, but we were also competitive. In those days, players weren't really *friends* with those we played against. You were respectful while also busy trying to walk over the next guy. But over time, especially after you retire, you reconnect with people. You realize that you are part of a different type of fraternity. That it means something more.

And that exact thing is something Michael Jordan once said to me when we reconnected after our careers had ended. Sugar and I played in Europe at the same time, too. God bless him, Sugar struggled with a stutter, but was also one of the funniest people I've ever been around in my life. He would talk shit—oh my gosh! He never stopped talking shit. Him and Ray Williams on the Knicks. With those two, it was just nonstop chatter to the point where I said, "I can't wait to kick y'all's asses!"

That's what made that playoff series we played against them in 1981 so much fun—for us at least! When we were playing the Knicks, Sugar and Ray Williams just talked so much trash. Because of Sugar's stutter, everything he said was funny. It was just in his delivery. No disrespect to folks who stutter, but Sugar, he was just hilarious. Even playing pickup ball, he would be saying so much to you. He couldn't turn it off! But more than anything, Sugar was genuine. Extremely genuine. And as it happened, I ran into him in 2020 at the NBA All-Star Game in Chicago.

When we saw each other, it felt like it was just yesterday that we'd seen each other last. It was pretty amazing. There's a difference between visiting Europe, which we've all done, and living there. It's hard to live overseas. So I would say this about Sugar, too. For all of the things that are good and bad about him, all the things that you've heard, and that people have told you, the life that he's lived—going over to Europe, a place that will get rid of you at the drop of a hat if they don't like you, if you don't fit. And he went over there and played for *fourteen years*.

He had a longer career in Europe than he did in the NBA! That tells you something about his personality. Something about the way people gravitate toward him. As crazy as he could seem at times, he wasn't that crazy. Crazy like a fox maybe! In the end, sometimes when you get a person out of a toxic environment and you put them in one that's different, a place where they can be more themselves, then they can morph into a different individual . . . and that's definitely what happened to Sugar.

8

SUGAR

EVER since college, people have called me Sugar. It started at the University of Montana and the nickname just stuck. When I first got to school, in one of our early games, I played really well. And since it was common for guys with the middle name Ray to be called "Sugar Ray," thanks to boxer Sugar Ray Robinson and later Sugar Ray Leonard, people started calling me Sugar, too. In Missoula, everybody thought I was a special athlete—sweet on and off the court—so the nickname became part of me. Today, friends call me Sugar without thinking twice. And I've lived up to it, even putting it on car license plates and gear shifts.

In later years, the name stuck because of my connection to drugs. The moniker was something of an ironic one, a commentary on my failures as much as my talent. It's strange how the two can intertwine at the top. The peak is so close to the fall. People think if you get to the top, it's easy to stay there. Hell, that's what I thought! But the hard part is not so much getting there as it is staying. I'd made the league. I was an All-Star. So when I started to do drugs, I thought I could stop it at any time. If I wanted to do something, I simply did it. It would be the same with my recreational habit, right? But I'd finally run up against something that was stronger than even me.

* * *

Human beings consume around 180 million metric tons of sugar a year. The US is the biggest consumer of sugar on the planet, as we take in 11 million metric tons per year. That's ten times what we should. America is a country of addicts and people looking to get high. As kids, we're taught candy is our friend. As young adults, we sneak into our parents' liquor cabinets. Caffeine is another one—the US consumes 146 billion cups of coffee per year! Later in life, we get high on other white powders or consume drugs that make us hungry and want, yes, more sugar. It's an epidemic. The stuff is everywhere.

Sugar comes from plants. Sugar cane needs warm climates to grow. So, a lot of it comes from places in South America. Historically, that's also where a lot of the United States' cocaine comes from, too. Even the world's most popular soda, Coca-Cola, used to have cocaine in it. Today, an average American consumes around 450 servings of Coca-Cola products per year.

* * *

Everything bad began when I decided to move from New Jersey to the Chelsea neighborhood of New York City during the middle of my third season. When I say things like, *Our stories are already written for us*, it's because of things like what happened next. The mover who took my stuff from Jersey into the city was cousins with one of the biggest dope dealers on the East Coast, a guy named Muhammad. And where exactly did Muhammad live? While he came from the West Indies, he now lived on the fourth floor of the building in Chelsea that I was about to move into. I would be a floor below him.

I'd decided to move into Manhattan because I'd gotten sick of the commuting and the city traffic. I wanted to be closer to where I worked, to MSG. Today, I shake my head. What the heck did I do that for? Muhammad's cousin introduced us. At the time, I didn't think much of it. I met new people everyday thanks to my profession, and Muhammad was a nice guy, someone who I thought was a friend. "Stop by anytime," he told me. Some nights, once I got settled in, I'd go up there and play cards or dominoes and shoot the breeze. Just passing the time. But the devil had a plan for me.

Then, instead of just playing games, Muhammad started passing cocaine around. That's when I sniffed it for the very first time. I'd just gotten back from a team road trip and decided to give coke a try just to be social with him and his friends. Like I said, when I first snorted the white powder, it didn't work on me. I didn't get high. So I tried it again, not thinking much of it. At Muhammad's place, he'd have other people over, even other NBA players sometimes. Coke was social, like alcohol. Shit, it was like coffee. But when I tried the stuff for a second and third time a few days later, I got hooked. My brain exploded. Then, a few weeks later, Muhammad brought out the pipe.

In a matter of about a month, I went from sniffing coke to smoking it, which is so much worse. When you smoke cocaine, it's called freebasing, and it's more potent. It's like cocaine on steroids, if you can believe that. But to do it was a process. You had to go out and buy this kit with the right pipe, a lighter, and other accoutrements. When he brought it out, Muhammad said, "I want you guys to try something." In Mike Carey's book *Bad News* about former pro basketball player Marvin "Bad News" Barnes, there are a lot of seedy characters mentioned. Well, Muhammad was one of those in my life. He loved to be around NBA players, and he got us hooked on him.

Muhammad was a big Knicks fan, too. So he knew who I was, and he liked me hanging around. But unlike Bad News, who was a hell of a player in his years in the ABA, I was never involved in any of the criminal activity, other than sniffing and smoking. I never hosted parties, sold drugs, or drove it anywhere. My problem was just using it—which is enough of a problem to have! While I wish Muhammad had never passed me the stuff and that his cousin had never introduced us, and while I wish I didn't move into that building in Chelsea or hire that specific moving company, at the end of the day I take full responsibility for my all of my actions. They were mine, and mine alone.

Since those days, I haven't seen Muhammad. I don't even know what I'd say to him if I did today. I'd probably let out a worn-down sigh—if he's even still alive. I still remember his voice, the look on his face, warm and generous, but flickering. "Just try it," he said. "It's not bad. Just try it." Me, being curious, I did. I liked it. I wanted more and I was naïve. But even in those days, in my third year and into my fourth season, I wasn't yet *dependent* on the stuff. It wasn't the most important thing in my life . . . yet. It was just something fun to do, dipping and dabbing, first on off-days then at home in Denver. Next thing I knew, though, I was in it. Bad.

Deep down, I know that I have a good heart. Even though I got into some rough spots, I'm not a bad guy. You get blinders when you're an addict. You're there, looking through your eyes . . . but at the same time, you're not all there. Because of that, when I would get high, I wouldn't want to go out in public. I didn't want to be in Studio 54, the Cotton Club on 125th, or anywhere in the city when I was using. I already knew I'd be paranoid, so I didn't need to be around people. On top of that, I didn't want anyone seeing me all fucked up. Addicts mostly want to be alone.

Later in my career, when I used drugs, I would either go to a hotel by myself, with a girlfriend, or with maybe one more person who was using with me. If it wasn't a hotel, I would just do it in my apartment. In New York, I wasn't yet a full-blown drug addict. But soon, I would go off a cliff. When you get like that, you lose all sense of yourself. You become a zombie. Your only thoughts are when you'll be getting high next and for how long. It's a parasite and you don't care about anything but pacifying it. That's what happens when the devil has you.

* * *

When I was in sixth grade, we lived around the corner from a convenience store. And after school, me and the other kids would all go there. One day, my mom gave me some money to get some candy for a treat. We were in a big group when we went to the store, but the owner would only let us in six at a time. When it was my turn, I went inside and looked around at the shelves, seeing what might catch my eye. Then I saw a Hershey's bar. I looked around the store and just put the bar in my pocket. When my friends and I left the shop, we walked out the door.

But that's when the owner came up behind me. He patted me on my back and said, "Come here, little guy. I think you have something that doesn't belong to you." He went in my pocket and snatched out the candy bar. Well, my mom had just gotten off work an hour prior and was already home, and the store owner made me call her. It was a fate worse than death. She came down there to the store and, in front of all the kids, beat my ass with an extension cord. When we got home, she beat me hard again. To this day, I can't eat even look at that brown wrapper.

Why I didn't just use the money that was in my pocket is beyond me. I suppose I wanted to keep it in my pocket. But doesn't mean I was going around stealing every day, either.

My point is that I wasn't a bad kid growing up, even if I tried to steal a Hershey's bar. The most I would try to get away with was taking candy from a store, something lots of kids do, and I couldn't even do that right! But even with that, ever since that day with the chocolate, I knew my mom would somehow find out. She made me think twice about ever doing anything bad.

But when it came to cocaine that fear did nothing to stop me.

* * *

Before new seasons, I would be in the gym every day. I was either working on individual drills or playing in pickup games with my teammates and former NBA players. In those games, let me tell you, there was a *lot* of trash talking. You might expect that among a group of high-profile hoopers. But what you might not expect is all the one-on-one games we played *full court*. Those really prepared you for the season because you had to guard your man the full length of the floor. If he got a rebound and you didn't check him right away, he'd dart up the hardwood and score on you. These games helped your footwork and stamina. If you didn't sprint, you were toast. Perhaps more than anything else, they got me ready for the new season.

And as the new year progressed, I was hot thanks to all my hard work. On November 27, 1981, I scored the most points I ever would in a Knick uniform, dropping 33 in a game in Cleveland. A young Bill Laimbeer was on that Cavs team, but neither he nor anyone else could stop me that night.

As for the season as a whole, I continued my strong play, making my third-consecutive All-Star team (though no All-Defensive team). I again played in all 82 games, and averaged 17.9 points, 2.6 steals, 7.0 assists, and 6.9 rebounds. I believed my best basketball was ahead of me. That a few more All-Star teams were, too.

While we had won 50 games and made the playoffs the season prior, we didn't do nearly as well in 1981–82, finishing 33–49. One of main the issues was that Ray Williams and Mike Glenn, two of my best friends, had both left. Ray signed with New Jersey and the Nets sent us back Maurice Lucas. Mike signed with Atlanta, and we got a draft pick. They were two big losses (for me and the team) in their prime, and I feel like the team didn't do enough to try and keep them. Why? Bad management, mostly. The rest of our issues, I chalk up to poor health. Toby Knight wasn't the same player, averaging just 5.5 points in just 40 games coming off the knee injury that forced him to miss the previous season. Things just didn't come together for us.

As a coach, Red wanted the Knicks to get the ball inside, which we did. But Bill Cartwright had a down year, only averaging 14.4 points due to nagging injuries (despite still playing in 72 games). Missing Williams and Glenn hurt, too. I didn't want to admit it, but I felt lonely without them. It was around this time that I gave my most famous (or infamous) interview. It happened on Christmas Day, 1981. We'd just lost our fourth straight game, this time to the Nets at home by one point. But just a few nights before, we'd lost by 28 to Detroit, then to Philly by 7 and New Jersey again by 16. So when reporter Harvey Araton asked, "What do you think is happening to this team?" I replied, "The ship be sinking."

He followed up quick, "How far can it sink?" And I replied, "The sky's the limit." While it was good copy and perhaps not the smartest thing to say, I don't regret it. We'd won 50 games the year before and were now plummeting. My only regret was not patenting the remark! It's now become a common refrain among fans when my name comes up.

We weren't playing well, and I was always honest with the press. If things were going great, I would tell them. And if they were going bad, I would tell them, too. One of the writers I was closest to at the time was Peter Vecsey. He had a fatherly quality to him. A lot of the players didn't like him and thought he was too harsh. But he and I became quick friends.

Peter and I still talk every now and then. Back then, if you played like shit, he would put it in the papers and roast your ass. That year, I got called for fouls a lot on defense and Vecsey would remind me of that in print. He'd always be in my ear about something. Today, few writers take players to task like that. But Peter was always fair. He spoke the truth. I called him

"Pistol Pete," because he was deadly with the pen. It wasn't our year and, as it turned out, Red wasn't long for the Knicks, either. The whole season, unbeknownst to us on the court, he'd secretly planned for it to be his last.

Red was around sixty-two years old now and had seen *a lot* of basketball. He was the type of guy to sit at the front of the bus with a big ol' stopwatch like a school master and he'd tell us that when the clock turned eight o'clock, no matter who was on or off the bus, it was leaving. "We're not waiting on anybody," he said. "If the bus leaves at eight then it leaves at eight." He was serious about it. Red and I never went out to dinner together, either. He wasn't sociable like that with any of his players. Occasionally, I'd go out with assistant Butch Beard or our announcer, Cal Ramsey. But never Red. He was old school.

* * *

In all my seasons with the Knicks, I played in almost every game. In four years, I missed a total of just 13 games, and 10 of those came during my first season when Red kept me on the bench. I was durable. During my career, thankfully, I never had the kind of injuries that kept me out long. In my later years, I played until I was forty-six. I was lucky that way. The one time I got hurt bad was in Italy in my forties; I was out for three weeks with just a bad bruise. But in the NBA, it was a jammed finger here, an ankle twist there, maybe a broken nose. But nothing serious. Nothing that kept me out.

The Knicks, however, wanted to change things up after the '81 season. They thought they had the answer that the roster didn't. It reminded me of my rookie season when the team traded away

Spencer Haywood and Bob McAdoo halfway through the year. They were two of the NBA's all-time greats, both former MVPs. Those two made playing point guard easy. They could fill up the fucking stat sheet—and I knew how to keep them happy. But the franchise wasn't concerned with the happiness of the players so much. They wanted to turn the roster over and bring new faces in and win. To prove management could get a title.

After games in the NBA, it can be hard to go to sleep. The matchups start after 7 p.m. and don't end until 9:30. Then there are showers, press responsibilities, and more. You get out of the arena by about 11 or midnight and then what? You're wired. Most people get off work around 5 p.m. and then they get to bed maybe five or six hours later, on an average day. Well, five or six hours after 11 p.m. is the wee hours of the morning. And if your game is on the west coast? It can be even worse if your internal time clock is set to Eastern Standard Time.

Players would hang out together after we'd just battled on the court. And drug-wise, everyone knew who had the hookup in every city. In the seventies, most players smoked weed. Some estimations had more than half the league taking tokes. But that changed to cocaine in the eighties. And the percentage of players on drugs went up, too. In fact, the *Los Angeles Times* once estimated that 75 percent of players were smoking or sniffing coke. Guys liked to use it after games to stay on edge and party. And in the bedroom, it made you go for hours.

* * *

The first time I ever freebased cocaine, it made me feel invincible. Like I was impervious to worry or concern. I was on top of the world. It's so cliché. Drug users always look for that first high again and again. It's like chasing a dragon, a ghost. You never find it. But when I got high, nothing else mattered. Not basketball, not my family, not even me, really. And after I came down, it hurt. I was depressed and I just wanted to be alone with my regrets. Then you get high again and run away from those feelings and toward that dragon.

A gram of coke cost about one hundred dollars back then and the high lasted for about an hour or two. New York was the place to be for it. There were parties and women and good times everywhere; the collective crash hadn't happened yet.

I remember one game on a Sunday, February 21, 1982. We had a home matchup at MSG against the Houston Rockets, and I'd gotten so high the night before that I'd forgotten about the game. I was still up and smoking around 8:30 a.m. when I realized that, in a handful hours, I would be on national television playing against Moses Malone and Calvin Murphy.

Once I remembered I had to play, I jumped in the shower and stayed under the hot cascading water until my fingers started to prune. Then I drank as much orange juice as I could fit in my stomach. I got to Madison Square Garden around 10:30 a.m. and took another shower and drank more OJ. I ate a breakfast sandwich and, before I knew it, we were warming up on the court before the game. I don't even remember when I put my unform on. But I kept talking to God, telling him to please just get me through this horrible mistake. If he helped me now, I would quit drugs cold turkey.

In that game, guess what happened? I scored 20 points, dished 11 assists, and grabbed eight rebounds (along with three steals). And we won! It was one of my best games of the year.

What did I do after that? I went out and got high for the next twenty-four hours straight. Our next game was two days later against Milwaukee. In that one, I had a triple-double, 15 points with 12 assists and 12 rebounds, to go along with a whopping seven steals. How is someone supposed to change when their production at work is better than most?

Well, I didn't change. Obviously. When players came into New York, they knew they could call me for the hookup and a good time. And when we went out on the road, I knew who to ask for the stuff. Sometimes, I'd even just go over to another player's house after a game, and we'd get high until dawn. "Yo, Sugar! Stop by, man!" And we'd get ripped until the next morning when I had to get on a plane for the next city. There was always a place to go, someone to ask for coke. All of a sudden, I cared more about scoring off the court than on. And it showed, slowly but surely, in missed layups and plenty of turnovers.

* * *

There is always something in this world that's more powerful than you. On the basketball court, I didn't think anyone was better than me. But in life, I was weak when it came to coke. I was so weak that I didn't care what situations I put myself in, in order to get high. I'd end up in run-down, seedy places where people in dark rooms and staircases were nodding off. I'd run up steps and meet people sitting with loaded Uzis. I couldn't stop freebasing. So I just kept going to places where I had no business going to find it. When you're sick like I was, you have no right frame of refence. The partying took on a life of its own.

One night I went to a place in Harlem. I drove my red two-seater Mercedes (with "Sugar" on the license plate). All these tough guys in the house there knew me. But the drugs were kept on the twentieth floor and the elevator didn't work. So I'd have to run up twenty flights, dodging junkies in the halls, and then run back down. I gave the guy watching my car fifty dollars and went sprinting. In a matter of two or three years, I must have hit that Harlem house thirty to forty times. That's a lot of stairs. After that, I managed to get my dealer, a guy who'd served time in prison, to meet me in a safe place on the street. I thought I had it made in the shade then.

The funny thing is that my dealer was a nice guy. In fact, he tried to get me to quit smoking the shit. We'd become friends. His name was Reni and he kept telling me I should put the shit down. "I hate giving this to you," he said to me. But he sold me the stuff anyway. Not because he was a hypocrite, but because he knew I'd go try to find it elsewhere and at least his coke wasn't laced with garbage. Later, when I went overseas to Europe for my career, Reni and I stayed in touch. I liked him; he was a good guy to me for years. But one day when I was playing in Israel, I heard he was murdered.

Reni was at a Harlem restaurant around two o'clock in the morning. His cousin had just beat up his own girlfriend, so that girl's brother was out looking for his cousin when he ran into Reni at the restaurant. He told Reni who he was looking for and Reni said he couldn't give his cousin up, even though he knew where he was hiding. So the guy turned around, pulled a gun out of his pocket, and shot him in the head four times. That's the life. Today, people ask me to name other NBA players who lived like that and who weren't caught. I was even offered one million dollars to rat on them in a book. I won't out anyone or take down the NBA. But I got stories.

* * *

Sometimes people ask me if me and Spencer Haywood ever got high together. Since he was famously shipped out of Los Angeles just before the Lakers won the title in 1980 during Magic Johnson's rookie season, he's been one of the players stigmatized as a drug addict. I know the feeling. They even portrayed him smoking on HBO's show *Winning Time!* I've been sober now for over thirty years, and people still think of me as the guy who got banned from the NBA. Well, I can say for sure that Spencer and I never did any drugs together, nor did I do drugs with the veterans on the Knicks. But I did sometimes get high with some of the younger players on the team.

Sly Williams was drafted by the Knicks in 1979, one year after I arrived. He was the twenty-first pick in the draft out of Rhode Island. Sly could score the ball, but he liked scoring coke more. He was a bad addict and it only got worse as he got older. In 2002, he was getting high one day when he ran out of drugs. So, he tied his girlfriend up and put her in a closet because she didn't want him getting more shit. Later, he'd come back to untie her. She left the house and went to work. She later told her friends what happened, and her friends called the cops. They came and got him, and he went to jail for about five years. That's an addict.

Me? I was never involved in anything like that before, during, or after my career. And I've never even been to prison. The only person I caused problems for was myself. I didn't take my shit and put it on anyone else. I know my actions hurt my family and embarrassed them, too. But I never intentionally harmed anyone. That's not in my nature. I just wasn't in the right frame of mind. Sly was out of the league in seven years after bouncing around between the Knicks, Hawks, and Celtics. Cocaine took a lot of good players down.

* * *

After the 1981–82 season, I stayed in New York, though I probably shouldn't have. While I had made it a routine of going back to Denver to visit my family and prepare my body for the next season, this was the first year I chose to stay in NYC. It hurt Renee, I know. I was beginning to make mistake after mistake for the sake of the drugs. I changed my whole routine. I got too comfortable. I thought I'd made it after three straight All-Star appearances. Even though the team did poorly that year and I didn't make the All-Defensive team, I didn't think anything was wrong. I was just dipping and dabbing, I told myself. No big deal. I could stop anytime and get my edge back. That summer, I didn't work out as often as I should have. Instead, I partied.

Shortly after the season, Red announced his retirement. If that had happened today, the team would consider asking its best player for input on the next hire. But I didn't get word ahead of time about Red or his replacement. And the man the Knicks hired to replace Red was Hubie Brown. Today, he is a beloved NBA broadcaster. But back then, Hubie was a fucking jerk. For me, the Knicks hiring Brown was probably the worst thing they could have done. In the end, the fallout wasn't anyone's fault but my own. But if I was already heading downhill, hiring Hubie was like sending me there with a wrecking ball.

Memory Lane: Corey Richardson

My dad has always been a hero of mine, a real-life hero. Having a famous dad was a good thing during my childhood, too. My first memory with him was probably taking my dad to my grade school for show-and-tell. All the kids couldn't believe it, like, "Wow, that's your father?" He came in and talked to the class and it was really special.

I have a lot of great memories with him—me and my dad just traveling the world. From a young age, it was normal for me to go to Europe for the summertime or for Christmas. My birthday is the day after Christmas, so I always spent it with him either in Europe or Colorado. I always loved that.

Me and him, we're actually a lot alike. We have the same type of personality. Our family members always say how we walk alike or sit and talk alike. We have the same mannerisms.

As kids, me and my brothers and sisters had the best of everything. Even though professional fathers can't be there on a regular basis, he was always around for us.

He was also a lot to live up to. I played basketball and football in high school. So, no matter what you do, you're trying to measure up to your dad when he's a famous athlete. But I'm so proud of just how strong he is as a man. No matter what he went through, he always put himself back on top again. He has the strength of a lion.

9

DECEPTION EVERYWHERE

HUBIE Brown was the only coach I truly never got along with. Sure, throughout my career, other coaches and I had our spats. That's normal. Professionals butt heads sometimes. But Hubie and I never got on the same page. I tried, but he was disrespectful to players and to me, especially. He talked to us like children. I remember reading about him saying he was naïve at his past stop as the coach in Atlanta (from 1976–81). Prior to that, he was with the Milwaukee Bucks in the NBA (as an assistant) and the Kentucky Colonels in the ABA (where he'd won a championship). His team had been full of drug users, and he just hadn't known what to look for. Now, as he came to New York, he was set to exert control.

Before the season started in 1982–83, the team held two-a-day training camp in South Jersey. Even with camp just beginning, Hubie and I already weren't getting along. I had respect for Red Holzman. He made me wait my turn as a rookie, and that was hard, but I respected him as a head coach and as a man. He may have been stuck in his ways at times, but he knew the game.

And he treated us like adults. Hubie treated his players like kids. With Atlanta, when he called a timeout, his players didn't go to the bench to sit down. Instead, Hubie brought them to the free-throw line on the court to degrade and cuss at them. That way the fans couldn't hear him scream obscenities.

I understand Hubie is a beloved figure today. He's a fine announcer, now in his nineties. But if Hubie did today what he tried back then, he would get a rude awakening. Guys wouldn't go for it. Back then, though, we had no choice. Players didn't have the power—the coaches did. We just didn't see eye to eye. He tried to use a heavy hand, and I wasn't for it. All of this culminated during a team meeting during training camp. That's when Hubie went around the room, talking shit to people. He called Bill Cartwright "Miss Bill," he told Campy Russell he was overrated, and then he came around to me. "Sugar," he said. "Every team has an asshole. And on this one, it's you."

He was about to lay into someone else when I raised my hand. I looked at our new coach in the eye and told him, "N-no, c-coach. On this team, there are t-two assholes. Y-you and m-me." If there was a DJ in the room, the record would have scratched. The gym got quiet. But Hubie wasn't a big man then, he just talked shit because he thought we couldn't talk back. But I did. I didn't give a fuck. Who was he? I was a three-time All-Star, the team's clear-cut best player. I played both ends and knew how and where to get my teammates the ball. But did Hubie care? Nope. He traded my ass the first fucking chance he got.

But while I was angry with Hubie, I don't hold it against him today. He did what he felt he had to do. Did he give me a chance? No. But at the time, I wasn't giving myself a chance, either. All I had time for was keeping up the lie of an NBA life and the reality of addiction. After training camp, I just left to get high. It was mostly what I thought about. Binging and then women. I'd hole up in a hotel and have ladies come in and out with food and more. I shake my head thinking about it now. It was a fantasy that quickly became a nightmare. I was no longer the next Walt Frazier. I was becoming the next famous burnout.

* * *

After that heated exchange, we had a preseason game in Landover, Maryland, against the Bullets. But even though he was trading me, did Hubie let me know? Nope. Instead, he let my ass get up at 6 a.m. that morning and get on the plane and fly down to DC with the team. From the plane, I got on the team bus. When we pulled into the hotel; I was the second-to-last person to get off the bus. That's when a Knicks official stopped me and pulled me aside. "You were just traded," he said. "You can go back to New York now." Huh? I was livid. But all I could do was get into a cab and go back to the airport.

Hubie, whose teams always played slow like snails, showed me who he really was with that one. Later, in an interview with some news crew not long after, Hubie bashed me. "Stop telling me about all this incredible talent," he said of me. He said that because of my "demons" I never lived up to my potential in a Knickerbocker uniform. That made me want to break a two-by-four over his head, but I had to swallow it. My mind moved on, as that of an addict quickly does. My next move was to call my agent. That's when a horrible idea got into my head. Probably the biggest mistake I ever made.

BANNED

The Knicks had dealt me to the Warriors on October 22, 1982—a week before the season started!—in a sign-and-trade, officially. The deal was me and a fifth-round pick for Bernard King, a prolific scorer who the Knicks badly wanted. But my agent, Patrick Healy, advised me not to go to Golden State. Instead, he recommended that I hold out and demand more money. It was the worst thought I could have considered. But really, I was just angry. I'd poured my heart into the Knicks. I loved the team and the city. And here comes Hubie, and then I'm gone? I was mad at the entire league. And all I wanted to do was chill and smoke in a dark room. So I listened to my agent and held out.

Considering these words today makes me shudder. Without anything to do for a few weeks, I turned to drugs more and more. I was living in Chelsea with my dealer one floor above me, so I didn't even have to leave the building to get high. I had no business doing what I was doing, but that didn't stop me. Truth be told, I was acting like a child. Hubie had tried to make me feel like one, and now I was playing the part voluntarily. I pretended my holdout was to squeeze more money from the Warriors. But really, I was just pouting. If Hubie hadn't been such a control freak, I told myself as I smoked bowl after bowl, I could be on the fast break right now setting up an alley-oop.

But it wasn't his fault that I was digging myself a deep grave. It was all mine. In the end, it was all born out of boredom. As Hubie even said, it was my "demons." As my agent worked to get more money, I relaxed. Looking back, I should have just reported to Golden State, played out the year, and kept it moving forward. But I couldn't accept that I had to leave the Knicks because of our coach. As the saying goes, idle time is the devil's mind. And for a few weeks, I had *a lot* of idle time. I was supposed to go to Golden State within seventy-two hours of the trade, but it took me weeks.

Thanks to my agent's advice, which he suggested because *he* wanted more money, I protested. I spent my idle time between the Big Apple and the aptly named Mile High City. While I was back home in Denver, Warriors coach Al Attles, who just recently passed away, came to visit me to try and convince me to come to Golden State. I wanted him to welcome me onto the team, but he wasn't a warm and fuzzy guy. I think I was lonely more than anything. Hurt by people I thought I could trust. From Jud to Willis to Red to Muhammad.

In early November, my agent and the Warriors were able to come to an agreement. It took a few weeks, which felt like months. By then, my dipping and dabbing had turned worse. And I'd already missed the team's first five games. But what made me feel a little better was that the Knicks had started the season 0–7. The ironic thing about me and Bernard getting traded for one another was that he also had a substance abuse problem. Playing for the Utah Jazz, King was arrested and suspended for using cocaine. (Later, he faced even worse legal issues.) That same year, in 1980, Jazz player Terry Furlow died in a car crash with coke in his system.

* * *

In my first game with Golden State, when I was finally back on the court doing what I loved. Coming off the bench on November 9, I played 16 minutes and scored eight points with two assists and four rebounds. But things took an unexpected turn, as I sprained my ankle in the game. It was probably the result of dehydration or whatever other side effects from smoking so much. I'd been so durable in my career, but taking the time away from the game, holding out and getting high, I wasn't in game shape. I tried to play on it, but I missed several games early on.

How did I get here? This was the first time I was unsure of my basketball future. Coach Attles had promised me a fresh start. But I came off the bench for the first four games with the team, missing several in between due to my ankle. In my fourth, I played 32 minutes and Attles, one of three NBA Black head coaches back then—along with Paul Silas and Lenny Wilkens—saw what I could do in extended playing time when I tallied 15 points, five assists, three steals, and seven rebounds. So he put me in the starting lineup after that in place of Lorenzo Romar. My ankle still wasn't healthy, but I gutted it out. I had to.

We had a solid starting five. It was me, Larry Smith, Joe Barry Carroll, World B. Free, and Purvis Short. We could all score. And World and Joe were All-Stars. But the team wasn't playing well. We started 5–12 and couldn't find any rhythm the entire season. Truth be told, I was out of it. This was the lowest point in my life, and I don't remember much of those first few months. Then, in January, I hurt my left ankle again. With that, I hit one of the worst stretches of my life. More and more, my existence became about smoking. I told myself I was just passing the time, but I was losing control. I missed the next 10 days with the team.

When I first got to Oakland, I was living in a Holiday Inn. Smoking, getting high almost every day—especially while I was injured. I dove into the famous Bay Area nightlife, too. So much so that the Warriors even hired private detectives to follow me. I think some part of me thought that if I got high enough then the bad dream of being in California would go away and I'd wake up back in Denver or in New York with a brighter future ahead of me. It was classic shoot-yourself-in-the-foot-escapism. Golden State hoped I would be the point guard they needed, but the whole thing was cursed. The team just couldn't win more than a game or two in a row. For the season, I couldn't bring my A-game because I was tiring myself with drugs.

After practices, I would leave the arena with screeching tires. I went into neighborhoods in the city that I definitely should not have been going to. And detectives followed me. I had a sense they were tracking me, but for some reason I wasn't worried. Game days, I would be hyper. I would yell at my teammates and coaches. Coach Attles called me a "nightmare." As former All-Star World B. Free said, a person would have to be sleeping under a rock not to see what I was up to. Even *Sports Illustrated* reported I'd flown back east to settle some drugs debts. But I wasn't the only one in the league like this. Some of the best and brightest were right there with me.

* * *

There was only one time when I was *sure* I was being followed. I was still playing for Golden State at the time, and I was driving around with a couple of my friends, Ron Brewer and Lewis Lloyd. But I wasn't getting high that particular day. Thank God. The three of us had just left practice and I'd stopped by my house on the way to taking Ron home. When I looked in the rearview mirror, I saw a car following us. The kind where when I switched lanes, he switched lanes, too. When I turned, he turned with me. It was something out of a movie. I kept watching him in my mirror as I drove.

After I dropped Ron off at his place, I turned around to drive back home. I got only a block and a half when I stopped at a light. I'll always remember this moment: I turned to Lewis and said, "I think there's someone following us, and I don't know who it is." When we came to a pharmacy parking lot, I turned into it. That's when the tail pulled in behind me. But by the time he'd gotten into the parking lot, I was able to do a quick U-turn and the guy got spooked. He must have realized I was onto him because he did a U-turn, too, but just sped off.

Other than that one instance, I can't recall ever being followed. I know Darryl Dawkins talked about a night in Boston when this cab driver was looking for me. "Where's Sugar?" the guy asked Darryl out of the blue. "We're going to get him." But I can't be sure if that's all true or not. Either way, when people told me that I might be being tracked, I didn't really give a shit. Because if they were already onto me then they were already onto me and there was nothing I could do. In that case, I thought, I was already caught.

By then, I already knew that I was doing something I had no fucking business doing (though I never did drugs before a game). So I didn't give a shit if I was being followed, because they probably already had pictures, witnesses, and all that on me. As for Darryl, we were friends, but we didn't hang out all that often. And we didn't party with cocaine together but a couple of times. The only time I remember doing cocaine with Darryl, who has talked openly about his use (including in his memoir), was in the summer when I got to New Jersey when I first got caught.

Then later some other night in Chicago. But I don't doubt he has his stories.

* * *

Back then, opposing players even got high with one another. For example, when David Thompson was in town with Seattle in 1982–83, we smoked together. One night, we were playing the SuperSonics and David wanted me to go out and get some stuff for that night. After the game, he came over and we got high all night. He had a plane to catch the next morning at 6 a.m., but at 4:30 he wanted me to get more shit. But there was no more. So I just took him to the airport around 5:00. That's how it went down on many a night in the NBA for those of us who were using. With the drugs, it was just something we started that got really out of hand. We weren't bad men. It's like many folks with alcohol.

No one starts out an alcoholic. And for us, it was coke. After about a month in Oakland, I got an apartment in Alameda, just outside the city. I would get high with other players there, especially while nursing my injury. On every roster, there were people who smoked cocaine and knew how to get it. One was Lewis Lloyd, who was later banned from the NBA in 1987, and died in 2019 from an accidental overdose (though had had a fixture at basketball clinics across the country, helping at-risk youth turn their lives around). But after his years in Golden State when he was playing with Houston, he could fill it up. Commissioner David Stern suspended him in 1987 and it lasted for two years. He played one more year after that, just 21 more games, before he was done.

In 1983, the NBA instituted a new drug policy in line with the United States' War on Drugs efforts. Players like Marvin Barnes in the seventies had been getting high (even sniffing coke *during* games) and, like myself, others were doing it in the eighties. So the NBA instituted drug testing and a three-strike system. After three failed drug tests, you were banned from the league *forever*. The only recourse was to beg for reinstatement after two years. But even then, the chances were slim. The league got Lloyd from "a tip," said *The New York Times*, adding that the NBA had security personnel in every league city and throughout the US.

In 1984, David Stern became the NBA commissioner, and he tightened things even further. Lloyd was suspended along with another player, Mitchell Wiggins. Before that, me and John Drew, the former Hawk and Jazz, had been the only ones banned from the league. But at Golden State, Lloyd and I would hangout late at night. Being injured is frustrating. The only benefit was that I had women coming in, bringing me food and spending "quality time." In Oakland, just to show you how far gone I was, I spent tens of thousands of dollars just on drugs. And I was only there a few months!

But on February 6, 1983, a day after notching a double-double in a win over the Spurs, I was traded. My prayers had come true. After 33 games with Golden State, between a holdout and a bum ankle, I averaged just 12.5 points and 4.4 boards. But I did manage 7.4 assists and 3.1 steals. I did okay, but I wasn't in any shape to play ball the way I knew I could play. And I wasn't living up to what Al Attles and Oakland's management expected. Al was a good coach and a good player in his day. I just wasn't listening. So they traded me to the New Jersey Nets for a young scorer named Sleepy Floyd and vet Mickey Johnson, who Nets coach Larry Brown had a big falling out with earlier that year.

The best part of the trade was that I already knew of Larry from Denver. When I was in college and coming home on weekends, he was coaching the ABA's Rockets. Now he wanted me—he may have been the only one—and I was happy as a pig in slop. I got word I was dealt from a Warriors assistant coach *during* a game against Phoenix. The guy said I didn't have to stay for the rest of the game after halftime. I went back into the locker room, showered, and bolted. I couldn't wait to leave.

The whole thing was a nightmare. I went home to pack, and knew I had seventy-two to report. You might be shocked, but I spent some of that time getting high. But once I got over that quick binge, I got on a plane and made my way across the United States to the east coast to meet my team in New Jersey. It was a fresh start, a new way for me to get back on track. But as all addicts know, there was still that voice in the back of my head, telling me that my old friends (like Muhammad) would be there waiting for me with the stuff they knew I wanted.

* * *

In the summer of 1986, several years after my time in Golden State, the *Washington Post* published a huge story about the NBA and drugs. The newspaper reported that the Warriors had spent as much as $20,000 hiring detectives to follow me and Los Angeles Lakers star point guard Norm Nixon. The Lakers were trying to trade Nixon, believing he was involved with drugs, too, and the Warriors were contemplating trading for him, which they never ended up doing. Nixon denied any drug use. Instead,

Norm, who was drafted a year before me in 1977, was traded to the Clippers in 1983, despite being an All-Star and champion for the Lakers.

The story in the *Post* also talked about Kareem Abdul-Jabbar trade rumors, whether teams hiring detectives was legal, and a lot more. It also mentioned David Thompson and his drug problems, as well as going in-depth on John Drew, who hid his use from his coaches on the Atlanta Hawks and Utah Jazz. "Whooooo, the rush," Drew had said about cocaine. "How it made me feel. I'd never felt that way before." With all of this swirling around, the NBA began to get more serious about drug testing and trying to rid the league of its problem players. The axe was falling . . . and I'd soon feel it in New Jersey.

* * *

After a night of smoking, I flew across the country to prepare for my Nets debut. My first game was a day later on the road against the Atlanta Hawks. With a new team now (and with the league's additional drug testing), I cut down on my cocaine use. I knew I had to get myself in shape, sweat out the stuff I'd been using and keep off it for a while. I'd been given a new start and though I was a drug addict, I hadn't fully admitted it to myself. For now, it was hard work and denial—two things addicts can be great at. In New Jersey, the Nets roster had some good guys, like Buck Williams, Otis Birdsong, and Darryl Dawkins. These guys were players. I knew that we could do something if we were all healthy and on the same page.

In my first game with the team, I came off the bench, only playing 16 minutes. We won the game, 115–109, and though

I didn't have much of an impact, the duo of Williams (28 points and 16 points) and Birdsong (18 points, six assists, eight rebounds) carried us to victory. In the following game, back in New Jersey, we beat Indiana by 15. Larry kept me coming off the bench, but this time I played 28 minutes, scoring 13 points with eight assists, two steals, and three boards. I got a block, too.

Then came the All-Star Game. I didn't make it (though, incredibly I led the NBA in steals per game that year), but I vowed to be back. What made it worse was that Larry talked to the press about me, saying that, physically, I wasn't the same player. Remember, this is before social media and the internet. Even though some games were on television, there wasn't the easy access of info that there is now. Playing on the West Coast, Larry hadn't seen much of me. Now, I was mediocre in his eyes. In a sense, I was making myself look bad. Still, like an addict, I couldn't see it.

The Nets even brought in former player Tim Bassett to baby-sit me. Bassett had played in the ABA and NBA for seven years, mostly with the Nets. But the thing about that was, Tim, may he rest in peace, was using, too! That's how rampant drugs were in those days—the guy they brought in to help me *not* use drugs was using himself! There was one time, I was over at a girl's house getting high as the peak of Mount Kilimanjaro when Basset came to get me. He knocked on her door. I answered and he convinced me to leave. . . but not before we finished off the rest of the drugs at the woman's place. Sheesh, that was quite the life. I wouldn't recommend it to anyone.

* * *

Larry Brown liked to call players "Kiddo." I wasn't sure if it was because he couldn't remember our names or what, but during practices it was "kiddo" this and "kiddo" that. But I didn't really care. I was just happy to be back on the East Coast. After coming off the bench my first few games, I started the rest of the season, finishing the year averaging 12.6 points, a league-best 2.8 steals per game, 6.8 assists, and 4.6 rebounds. I stayed clean for most of those final regular-season weeks, too, and things were going fine enough. I thought I might have actually been cured. I didn't have any withdrawal symptoms—those usually happen for those who drink or use drugs like heroin, which were never my go-tos. Maybe others have those symptoms, but I wasn't one of them. The drugs I used gave me mental highs, not physical ones. So if I wasn't around them, I didn't often think about them. It was just when I put my guard down that I got myself in trouble. Drug users know, though, that's just when you can fall off the wagon again. And so, thinking I was okay, I put myself in a bad spot (again).

* * *

After the All-Star break, we went 16–15 and finished the season 49–33. It was a good run, but the end of the year was as much about Larry Brown as it was me or the Nets. I'd fallen into my old habits toward the end of the year and Coach Brown had gotten wind of it. I'd started dibbing and dabbing again and was getting gassed by the end of games. I used to never get tired, and now I couldn't catch my breath So near the end of the season, with a week or two left in the year, Coach Brown called me into his office. He sat me down and said he'd heard what I was involved with. The night before, I had been up all night with a few teammates, like Darryl Dawkins and Albert King, trying to touch the moon.

But I didn't rat on them. Instead, Larry asked if I needed help and said he wanted to help me. There wasn't judgment in his voice, just care and concern. He then asked if I'd be willing to go to rehab. "If you want us to help you, we can help you," he said. I responded honestly, saying that yes, I wanted help, and I would go. Larry said the whole thing would be hush-hush; that the Nets would keep the whole thing a secret. I thought the idea was great. Why not? Larry gave me the name of the clinic in New Jersey and I went there in my Volkswagen the next day. Larry, to his credit, met me there, too. I met with a doctor and told him that, in my opinion, I didn't have a serious problem. After all, I was just freebasing a couple times per week.

Coach Brown and the doctor didn't quite know what to say about that. But do you know who *did* have something to say? The fucking newspapers. Because the next morning it was all over the papers that I'd been to a rehab center *during* the season. And there was more in the headlines. About how I was spending time in drug dens, running around in places that I never should have been, you name it. I'd thought the whole thing was supposed to be kept out of the press, but no. How could I get myself together now with everyone going mad? After that, things went downhill fast. I couldn't trust the Nets. The team, or some within it, didn't have my back. And what made matters worse was that, just days before the season ended and the playoffs began, Larry left us to coach in college.

* * *

We were 47–29 with just six games remaining in the regular season, which was third best in the Atlantic Division. With the playoffs guaranteed, Larry gave the team a couple of days off from practice. That was strange because Larry liked to run us to death all day during those practices. He'd told us to ignore any rumors we'd heard about him going elsewhere—rumors in the NBA were everywhere. But he said he was staying put with us. Well, a *Newark Star-Ledger* reporter named Mike Weber had heard a rumor that Larry was interviewing for another job, this time in college at the University of Kansas. Somehow, Weber got Larry's hotel and room number and he called him up. "May I speak to John Williams, please?" Weber said into the phone. The man on the other end said, "There's no John Williams here, but this is Larry Brown." To which Weber said, "Hi Larry, this is Mike Weber from the *Star-Ledger.*"

CLANG! Larry hung up the hotel phone. But, of course, word got out. And Nets owner Joe Taub was pissed off. He called Larry up for a meeting. Larry told him the truth. And Taub effectively fired him right there on April 6, with six games left in the regular season. Larry still made it to Detroit two days later and addressed us in the locker room before our game against the Pistons. "I screwed up," he told us. Buck Williams cried. I was upset, too. Larry was a major reason I was excited to play for New Jersey. My guy from Denver and the ABA. Now he was gone, too. Replaced by assistant Bill Blair.

* * *

Out west that year, Al Attles and Golden State finished 30–52, which put a smile on my tired face. But what was our reward for finishing 49–33? A playoff matchup against… the New York Knicks. The team that traded me the summer before. The team that chose coach Hubie Brown over me. The team that had let go of Spencer Haywood, Bob McAdoo, Mike Glenn, and Ray Williams. It was bad poetry. I was nervous to see my old team. I psyched myself out and just wasn't ready. Truthfully, I was lost. Hurt from the trade to Golden State. Depressed and lonesome in Oakland. Now I was lost and spiraling with New Jersey, especially with Larry gone.

But now I had a chance at redemption—even if I was nervous and broken. If I could somehow pull it together for a few games and play the Knicks like the All-Star I was, like I knew I was capable of, everything would come full circle and I would have hope and confidence at my back. My averages were the lowest since my rookie year, but that didn't mean I had to play poorly in this series, right? I could get it all together. Become the old Michael Ray Richardson. The guy the fans cheered for in New York. The multi-time All-Star. Okay, Hubie, bring it on!

* * *

The first playoff game was on April 20 in New Jersey. We were hopeful we could get a win, but the Knicks came out in the first quarter with a haymaker and stopped us in our tracks. They outscored us 35–27 and we weren't able to recover. Down by eight heading into the half, we were outscored by five in the third and were behind by 13 heading into the fourth. Even though we outscored them 31–29 in the last quarter, the game was long over. Bernard King, the man I was dealt for, who'd had his own issues, scored 40 points on us. I can just picture Hubie talking him up before the game, telling him to kill me out there. As for my part, I didn't play well, scoring just 11 points with four rebounds, three steals, and a single assist.

We had five other double-digit scorers on the team, but King was the difference maker. The next night, down the highway in New York at MSG, the Knicks jumped out to another great start and outscored us by nine, 32–23. Then, in the second, they outscored us again, 30–16. Losing by 23 at the half in an elimination game, we went into the locker room furious, and let it all out once the doors closed. Getting outplayed for six quarters, we knew the time was now to put up or shut up.

While we outscored them by 13 in the third, we didn't have the juice to finish the job, ultimately losing 105–99. I only scored eight points with two steals, four assists, and four rebounds. We were swept in the best-of-three series, and our season was over.

All in all, it was a disgrace. I was a disgrace. I put up just 19 points over the two games and let everyone down. First, it was the "ship" that was sinking. Now it was definitely me who was drowning. But I told myself that it had simply been a rough year. After all, who didn't have a bad year here and there? So I made a silent promise that I would return all the better the following season. But again, as users do so well, I was deceiving myself. While I knew I was making poor decisions, I had no idea how bad things were about to get. I'd only just got on the freefall ride. Now, it was time for the plummet.

* * *

Losing yet another coach didn't help my drug use. It's hard to pinpoint what, exactly, pushes an addict into blind abuse. But this sense of constant rejection and loss was, I believe, a part of it for me. I'd made the NBA. I'd bought my mother a house. I'd taken care of my family. Some part of me was exhausted. I just let go of the rope. I'd achieved all my dreams. They never tell you what to do after that. All the talk is about dreaming and chasing those goals. All of it was just getting to be too much. I needed a break. Drugs, of course, were the perfect portal out. Who cared about anything else, anyway? Not me. And it felt so good to use them in the moment.

One silver lining from my issues was the letter I received from Isiah Thomas. My foe on the court, the player I'd go into the visiting locker room to see and talk trash to, had now sent me a heartfelt three-page handwritten note saying that, if I needed anything, he had my back. I'll always be grateful for that gesture. In the letter, Isiah said he had family members going through the same things that I was and how drugs affected him and the people around him. He knew addiction didn't mean the addict was a bad person. He told me to call him if I ever needed anything. He said he'd pray for me and to be strong.

* * *

The sportswriter Peter Vecsey got tipped off one day that my car was in Harlem in front of a crack house. How did they know it was me? Well, my license plate said SUGAR. When police asked me about it, I told them I was waiting there for a girl. What was her name? I didn't know. What building was she in? Not sure. I was stuttering, jittery. I wasn't thinking about Renee, Tosha, my mother, my family, anything. Worse, the Nets started to drug test me. I'd gotten my first reprimand when news of my trip to rehab with Larry Brown became public near the end of the 1983 season, and I got my second shortly after when I was caught in Harlem in the offseason. Time for more rehab, newspaper attention and more apologies.

This time it was the Fair Oaks Hospital in Summit, New Jersey. I signed up for the program on May 13, 1983, which spanned seven weeks . . . but I stayed less than two. Most rehab places, if you ask me, are about making money. Why do I think this? Because when the patient's money runs out, so does their time at the facility. While not every facility is like that, enough are that I've seen. But that's not why I left Fair Oaks. I just didn't want to be there. I knew I used drugs, and I knew I used them too much. But the people there kept trying to convince me it had something to do with my childhood. And it didn't. Honest to God. My childhood had been just fine.

After I left Fair Oaks, I told everyone I was "cured." I knew I had problems, but I didn't think that place had the solution. Afterward, I got back on the court and in the gym and started working out again. At nights, though, I kept smoking. We had a new season ahead of us and a new coach in Stan Albeck. He was more laid back than Larry. While I loved Larry Brown, he and Stan were markedly different. Stan didn't fuss. Larry fussed. Stan was a former assistant coach with the San Diego Conquistadors under Wilt Chamberlain. He had most recently been the head coach of the San Antonio Spurs, with Artis Gilmore and the great George Gervin.

Players liked Stan. Even Dawkins spoke highly of him. But more than the season or the coach, what was on my mind was disappointment. The whole world knew about my drug use. Just because I was an NBA player, they got to find out. What was worse, my mom saw the news. That just killed me. She saw the private, bad parts of my life. I'd never wanted any of that to get out, let alone for my mother to see it. The rest of my family found out, too. Willie heard it on the news while driving his truck. Mom called him up one day to ask him what was wrong with me. That hurt. I was just happy Tosha wasn't old enough to understand.

* * *

On August 12, I checked into another rehab: the Hazelden Foundation Clinic in Minneapolis, Minnesota. I'd failed a league drug test and so I had to go to an NBA-sanctioned facility now in the Midwest. Less than a month later, I left "cured" again. How did I get out of this facility without any money? Well I signed up for a new credit card and bought a flight home . . . where I immediately got high. A few weeks later, I called a press conference and said I was "cured" once again. "I'll be more u-under c-control," I said. "And I'll be here start to finish." But I began to disappear again, a lot. Stan heard stories about me in all parts of New York and New Jersey doing God knows what.

At one point, I told the Nets that I'd been kidnapped. That I was being held hostage. I told the GM, "They're holding me, they're holding me." But I was in the Southgate Hotel across the street from Madison Square Garden. I'd checked in under Michael Ray Richards. Eventually someone from the team came up to my room and knocked on the door looking for me. "Hey, Michael!" they said. And I just responded, "How did you find me?" Not long after, the Nets simply waived me. I was cut. No longer in the NBA. Even though I was an All-Star and someone who my agent Don Cronson said, "Lit up a room." I guess I'd snuffed myself out.

* * *

Some today consider me the "poster child" for bad NBA decisions. It's a label I've had to live with for decades. But as I've said, everyone used drugs back then. From stars like David Thompson to others like Walter Davis, Fly Williams, John Lucas, "Fast" Eddie Johnson, George Gervin, John Drew, James "Buddha" Edwards, and later Richard Dumas. In his 2003 book, *Chocolate Thunder*, Dawkins talked about his own drug use. Early in his career, he wasn't getting enough playing time with the 76ers and it messed with his head, he said. So, while it wasn't a *good* decision, he turned to cocaine and pot as relief.

Wrote the big guy, "I think my overall frustration was the reason why I started doing more drugs than I'd ever done before. Which was very easy to do. At that time, I didn't know of more than a handful of players in the NBA who didn't snort cocaine or smoke weed or take the green uppers that we called Christmas trees." Even though Dawkins was known for big talk, I don't think he was exaggerating there. He also talked about how cocaine was a white person drug, at first too expensive for most Blacks. He asked, how did it even enter the league?

He's right. Coke wasn't looked down upon in the seventies and eighties. Richard Nixon had declared his war on drugs in 1971, and Reagan carried it on in the eighties, but early on, people weren't onboard with it. It's hard to believe today, but cocaine was seen as glorified in a lot of circles. A mark of wealth and fun. But the NBA and David Stern saw what it did to people up close and personal. And the league saw how it robbed people like Marvin Barnes and Fly Williams of their talent. They didn't want their already Black league seen as a drugged-up one, too— especially knowing how much money was there to be made.

* * *

It's funny, in a way. It seems obvious to punish a drug addict. If they can't act right, then get them away from the others who are trying. But drug addiction is a disease. The only one, as comedian Mitch Hedberg later said, that you can be yelled at for. But isolating an addict only makes their situation worse. So when the Nets waived me in the summer of 1983, many thought that, not only would my career be over, but my life as well. That I'd be homeless, lost, and perhaps even die young. It's happened to many others, including more famous people than me. But there was still hope.

Thanks to a new deal that the NBA and the NBA Players Association had agreed to in the summer of 1983—the three-strike policy—I was saved. "Our view," Stern later said, "is you can't waive somebody. The agreement is very specific. So the Nets, with a fair amount of behind-the-scenes urging by us [the NBA], reinstated me! I had another chance to play in the league. God had smiled down upon me. (At the time, the Lakers were even rumored to be interested in me.) It was like I was in the electric chair and a phone call came in from President Stern, who said, "He's pardoned." So, I went into a new rehab.

And, unlike all the previous instances, this time it worked.

Briefly.

On October 14, I entered a new drug treatment center, the third one in some five months. Less than two weeks before, I'd been caught by the team leaving training camp at Princeton University, which was located an hour outside New York. I'd gone into Manhattan to meet Muhammad, and I'd come back to Princeton and snuck into my room early in the morning, bed still made. But the Nets caught me, and they weren't happy. So now, it was back to square one and time for rehab again. And, well, the night before I went, I got as high as I possibly could.

Memory Lane: Michael Cooper

Michael Ray was actually Magic before Magic. He was the first big guard who could do those things like rebound, assist, and score. And he always included his teammates. Then Magic came along and just was a bigger version of him. But what Michael Ray had over Magic was that he was a better defensive player. He had quick hands and all the attributes that a good defensive player needs. Anticipation, tenacity, and all of that.

His career was very interesting because he didn't have the luxury of staying with one team—he went to many teams. But every team he went to, he was that force that led the franchise. He was the player that everybody feared. That's a rarity in the NBA, because people usually only fear you on one side of the court.

Stephen Curry, Dr. J, they were never feared on the defensive end. But Michael was that guy who you knew was going to bring game on both sides. If you didn't play good defense, he was going to get 30 and then stop you from getting yours. Those are rare attributes for an NBA player to have. The only one I can think of who could do that was the late great Dennis Johnson.

Michael was hard to guard. And he had another element that was rare at that time. He could talk a lot of shit! He was that type of guy—some players talk shit and can't back it up. They run their mouth, but when it's time to get down they don't. Michael Ray could talk shit, and his shit talking was more to de-soul you. It didn't scare me, but it scared a lot of other players.

Something I have to give Michael Ray credit for was that he brought a different element. If you were playing against him, whether it was with the Knicks or the Nets, you knew you were in for a battle. Not just physically, but verbally. Like, "Motherfucker, you can't guard me!" He brought that. For me, it was fun. It took you back to the street game.

One story I have to tell about him, who I love like my brother, was when I went to play in Italy and my team was playing his. And Michael Ray still had that competitive edge. The first time we met on the court in Italy, this fucking guy walks up to me and says, "I'm going to bust your fucking ass, Coop!" And the funny part is, it scared the shit out of my teammates!

They had never seen anybody do that. Michael Ray dominated that game. We'd lost before the ball went up in the air because of what he did in that moment. And that's just him. That's Sugar. He brought it every single night. It didn't matter who it was. Intimidation is part of being a successful basketball player, and Sugar was the best.

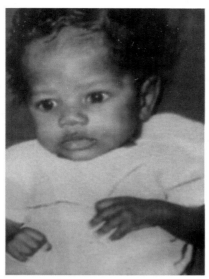

Baby boy Michael Ray Richardson. Born in Lubbock, Texas, who would have guessed what this cutie pie bundle of joy would become just a couple of decades later. Namely, a four-time NBA All-Star and European basketball legend. (Courtesy of the author)

Despite all the ups and downs of my career, I always have a smile on his face these days. (Courtesy of the author)

The cover of an old family-made scrap book that holds the clippings, media programs, and photos from my career. (Courtesy of the author)

MICHAEL RAY RICHARDSON #20
GUARD

Always for the fans, made sure to give the people what they wanted (both on the court and during meet-and-greets. (Courtesy of the author)

One in a long line of New York Knicks star point guards, from Walt "Clyde" Frazier to Jalen Brunson, I once had The Big Apple in the palm of his hand. (Courtesy of the author)

My hero growing up: the great Dr. J, Julius Erving (No. 6). As a kid, I had dreams of playing against him, telling my family that I'd dunked on "The Doctor." Now my dreams had become a reality, as I had the honor of sharing a basketball court with my idol. (Getty Images)

(Left) Before joining the Nets, I made sure to scorch them every time we stepped onto the court, whether shooting, dishing, or stealing. (Getty Images)

(Right) Defense was a key to my game, and I took it just as seriously as I did my offense. Wearing my signature Converse leather All-Stars in a game against the Bucks in 1978, I block a shot by one of the all-time greats, Norm Van Lier. (Getty Images)

(Left) You gotta earn 'em! In a game against the Hawks in '78, I'm making sure to help my team from the charity stripe. (Getty Images)

(Right) Though we had a rocky start, Knicks Hall of Fame coach Red Holzman helped me take my game to the next level (as the great Earl "The Pearl" Monroe leans in to offer some wisdom). (Getty Images)

(Left) Showing off that sweet athleticism, I nail a George "Iceman" Gervin–esque finger roll layup over Kevin Porter and the Washington Bullets. (Getty Images)

(Right) Nobody can guard me! Driving to the hoop against Wes Matthews, they didn't know if I was looking to score or hit the open man for the assist. I was a puma about to pounce, and there was nothing they could do about it. (Getty Images)

(Left) You need to put in the work to lead the league in steals three times. No one was safe from my craftiness. With cat-like reflexes, one second they had the ball, and the next second it was mine. (Getty Images)

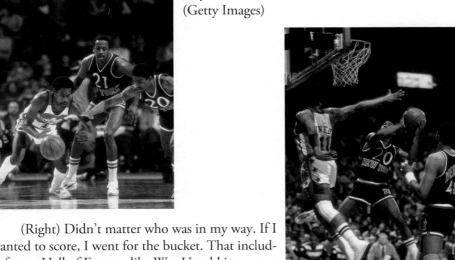

(Right) Didn't matter who was in my way. If I wanted to score, I went for the bucket. That included future Hall of Famers, like Wes Unseld in a game against Washington in 1982. (Getty Images)

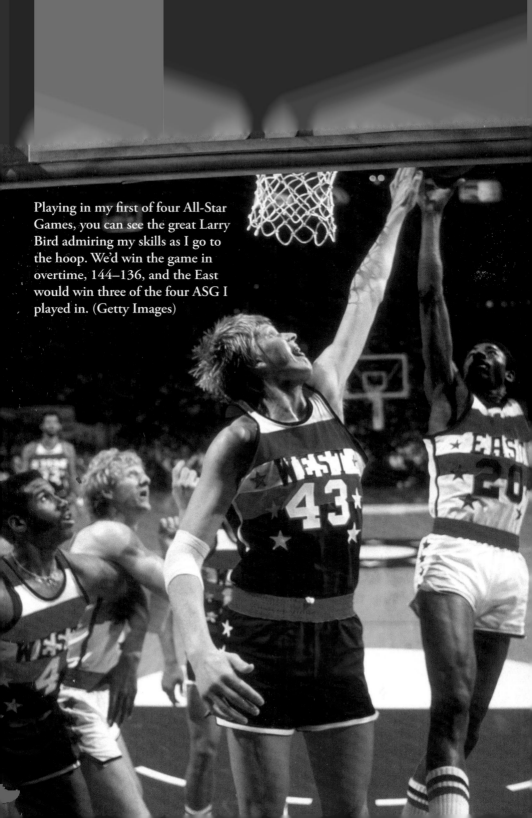

Playing in my first of four All-Star Games, you can see the great Larry Bird admiring my skills as I go to the hoop. We'd win the game in overtime, 144–136, and the East would win three of the four ASG I played in. (Getty Images)

Some guys just look the part—I was the part. Now playing for the New Jersey Nets, I always kept my eye on the prize, no matter the opponent. (Getty Images)

(Left) You have to keep growing as a baller. While I initially went to the hoop, as I continued my career I knew that I needed to extend my game. That meant hitting sweet jumpers, like this one against Andrew Toney and the Philadelphia 76ers in 1984. (Getty Images)

(Above, right) Didn't matter who was guarding me. If I wanted to score, I'd score. If I wanted to hit a teammate for an assist, I'd get that dime. Even the great Maurice Cheeks knew that, which is why he knew he couldn't press. (Getty Images)

After upsetting the 76ers in the first round, we battled the Milwaukee Bucks for six games, though ultimately losing the series. Here I am driving on future coach and NBA father, Mike Dunleavy Sr. (who obviously stood no chance when I turned the corner). (Getty Images)

Watch out, Italy! The Sugar Man is in town—and Sugarmania is on its way! This cover of the sports magazine Triste Sport portends a great career overseas for Richardson. (Courtesy of the author)

Though we had our ups and downs, NBA Commissioner David Stern always had my back. We never let our professional relationship get in the way of their personal ones, and were friends until his passing in 2020. (Courtesy of the author)

Looking dapper at the National Collegiate Basketball Hall of Fame with my good friend John Zelbst. (Courtesy of the author)

The Doctor is in! Though we battled on the court, I have nothing but love for the great Julius Erving. (Courtesy of the author)

"Sugar Ray" Enters Grizzly Basketball Hall of Fame

by Dave Guffey
Grizzly Sports Information Director

His nickname is "Sugar" and for the many thousands of fans who saw him play at the University of Montana and in the Big Sky Conference, there's no doubt that Micheal Ray Richardson was one of the "sweetest" players to ever play in the Northwest.

Montana's all-time scorer with 1,827 points, Richardson joins an elite group of 51 other former Grizzly greats as he is officially inducted Saturday into the Grizzly Basketball Hall of Fame. Because of his hectic schedule playing for the New Jersey Nets of the National Basketball Association, he was unable to attend

Sugar Ray is Montana's all-time scorer.

the induction, but hopes to come to Missoula in the fall for a formal presentation.

Richardson will be this year's only inductee, and it is only fitting, since he is in a class by himself when it comes to basketball ability. Last year's inductee was Missoula's Ben DeMers.

An All-American while playing for the Grizzlies, Richardson was not only a great scorer for the Grizzlies, but a great all-around player. He is the Montana all-time assists leader with 372 and sixth in career rebounding with 670.

The 6-5, 190-pounder from Denver, who played at UM from 1974-78, is the No. 4 career scorer in the Big Sky, 20th in rebounding and sixth in assists.

He was an All-Big Sky first team selection three times and Grizzly MVP three times as well.

"Micheal Ray was certainly one of the finest basketball talents I have ever been associated with," said Grizzly coach Mike Montgomery, who was an assistant with Jim Brandenberg MR's last two seasons. "He had an explosive ability that is rarely seen."

"He made other players better because of his abilities and could rise to the occasion for the big ball games," Montgomery said.

After his illustrious career at Montana he was picked in the first round of the NBA draft by the New York Knicks, then coached by Willis Reed. He was the fourth pick overall in the draft.

At the time coach Reed said, "He can play with anybody. He has great quickness like Walt Frazier used to have. He also has size, passing ability and is a strong defensive player. He's the first big guard we've had since Frazier. . . ."

Richardson is a four-time NBA all-star and named to the league's all-defensive team twice.

He was recently featured in a 14-page spread in the February 4th issue of *Sports Illustrated* (ironically the same issue in which Larry Krystkowiak was featured). The article traced his college career to the NBA and his much-publicized problem with drug dependency.

He has become "one of the most dramatic comeback stories in sports," wrote SI's Bill Brubaker.

The plain facts are that he's having an excellent season, averaging 19.2 points a game, along with 8 assists and 2.9 steals. He is the ninth leading assists man in the NBA and first in steals.

His outstanding season was rewarded recently as he was named to the NBA All-Star team.

Over a four-day period in late December he averaged 28.7 points, 6.7 assists, 4.5 rebounds and 3.5 steals a game. Four days after being named NBA Player of the Week for his previous heroics he scored 26 points, had 12 assists and grabbed 11 rebounds in a game against Phoenix. It is believed to be the only "triple double" in Nets history.

He fouled out of his first collegiate game in 1974-75 and by the third game of the season was a starter. He was already a strong defensive player and averaged 7.5 points a game for a team that went 21-8 and lost by three points in the NCAA tournament to eventual champion UCLA.

A look at more of his accomplishments at UM:
—Highest single game average in UM history at 24.4.
—Most points in a single game, 40 (tie) vs. Montana State, 1976.
—2nd highest single season point total, 683, 1978.
—1st team All-District 7, 1977, 1978.
—Named to 3 all-tournament teams.
—Participated in several postseason all-star games, 1978.

"It's a great honor," said Richardson by phone Wednesday. "The fans were super. If I had it to do all over again I'd do the same thing." He said his most memorable moment was his 40-point effort against MSU. Welcome to an elite group, Sugar . . . How sweet you were . . .

Richardson was a first round draft pick by the New York Knicks in 1978.

19

I was honored to be inducted into the University of Montana Grizzly Basketball Hall of Fame, and appreciate everything the school has done for me! (Courtesy of Bill "Grizzly Bill" Schwanke and the University of Montana)

Leah Lichausser

Marc Taylor

11/29/82

Dear Michael Ray,
You are my favorite basketball player. I think you are the best player in the league. I was really sorry to see you go. The Garden won't be the same without you. Everyone always got on your case about trying to take situations into your own hands but I understand that you was just trying to get the team rolling. You showed me in the All-Star game that you can be very effective under control when you have some talent to work with. You and World should be explosive. I hope that you can help the Warriors go far in the playoffs.
Enclosed is a scrap book that I've kept of all the Sugaresque moments that you've had as a Knick. If you get the chance, I'd appreciate it if you could send me an autographed picture of you. Thanks
Sincerely
Marc Taylor

Getting the appreciation from the fans is a gift every player treasures. Here's a letter from one such fan, Marc Taylor, showing love and support for his "favorite basketball player." (Courtesy of the author)

Posing with my son, Michael Amir Richardson, who has grown up to not only be an incredible soccer star (and Olympic bronze medalist!), but a great man. (Courtesy of the author)

A father is always proud of his kids, no matter what they do. Here at Tamara's graduation, along with her sister Tosha. (Courtesy of the author)

It's a family affair! Spending time with my boys Amir, and Corey (and his son, Chase), along with my girls Kimberly and Tamara. (Courtesy of the author)

Basketball is an international game. While working for the NBA, I got to visit some incredible places, including New Deli! (Courtesy of the author)

So proud of my kids! Enjoying a day out with Corey, Tosha, and Tamara. (Courtesy of the author)

My brother for life! From our playing days to the work we do in the community, Otis Birdsong has been by my side through it all. Lucky to call this man my friend. (Courtesy of the author)

Orange you glad to see us! Spending time with my beautiful wife, Kim. (Courtesy of the author)

No words for the love I have for my adopted country of Italy. They embraced me (and Sugarmania), and I have so many incredible memories of my time there. Even all these years later they give me such love, including before a game between Virtus Segafredo Bologna and Happy Casa Brindisi in 2019. Two thumbs way up! (Getty Images)

10

DEFEATING DOC AND MOSES

GROWING up, family was everything to me. We lived in a lower-class neighborhood in Denver, and my siblings and I were raised by a single mother. But we always had each other. My sister Sherry once said that I was the one who took care of all the girls in our family, like a surrogate father. I made sure no one messed with them and made sure they were home safe before dark every night. One time, I caught my sister Ienda high after smoking weed beneath the school's football bleachers. I saw her eyes were so red. I threatened that I would tell our mother and that scared her straight. She never smoked again.

It's not bragging to say that I was my mother's favorite, either. Everyone knew it. She would come back home from work dog tired. She would sigh, "My feet are killing me." So I'd say, "Mama, sit down." And I'd get lotion and just rub her feet. I'd coo, "Mama, you alright. Mama, you alright." That's when I made the promise to buy her a house so she didn't have to work on her tired feet anymore. But no one believed me then. No one thought I'd ever make the NBA. My sister Dorothy was taller, and she would always beat me when we played one-on-one. But I knew that one day I would be better than her. And get better than everyone else, too.

So I kept pushing. I would wake up my sisters and tell them about my dreams. How I dunked on Dr. J in some of them. I wouldn't back down from anything (or anyone), even when I was asleep. Little did I know that my biggest professional achievement would come against Dr. J, and little did I know the difficult road I would have to walk just to get there. And the journey I would take after that. Life is hard. Life is strange. Curious. But the key is to just keep going. Push forward. You don't know what's ahead. And what's even further ahead from that. One day at a time leads to a life well lived.

* * *

In rehab, there are a lot of group sessions. A lot.

There are always a lot of doctors, preachers, and even judges walking around the facility. The thing was, I didn't enjoy rehab (though I doubt many do). And it was not just because I wanted to get high. It wasn't about that. My problem with the facilities is that they try to *tell* you why you have issues. The centers tried to break me down to my core, looking for "trauma" from my childhood. They tried to tell me that I use drugs because I had problems. And my whole thing was, I didn't have problems. Not ones that made me smoke. I got high simply because I liked the way it made me feel.

"But no, you have problems with your father," they told me. But I really didn't. If I had such deep issues, I would have gotten stuck on drugs or alcohol much earlier in my life. But I didn't even start drinking until my second year in the pros. For me, my problem was the rehab guys telling me I *had* problems. Telling me it was my childhood when it wasn't. I was like, come on, man. I just liked the effect drugs have on me. Looking back on it now, I can see that the feeling drugs gave me was more powerful than I am. I had no control over it. It was stronger than me.

But it had nothing to do with my childhood. Until cocaine, I was always the person who could stop something if I put my mind to it. I'm the same guy who, as a freshman in college, drove eighteen hours each way, from Missoula to Denver, to see Mom on the weekends. I always thought I was mentally strong. But those drugs were the toughest shit I ever met. Today, I don't put myself in those places anymore. I don't go around drugs and alcohol. I feel confident that I could control myself if I did, but why take the chance? Why tempt myself? I don't, and that's why I'm clean to this day.

* * *

Thanks to the newest round of rehab, I missed the first two months of the 1983–84 season. My life and emotional state had by now gotten so bad that I even considered retirement. While I never wanted to quit—I loved the game so much—my head just wasn't in the right place. I was exhausted.

Making it in the NBA takes all you got, and to stay there takes reserves you didn't even know you had. In my case, add to that years of narcotics and a person gets fatigued. By this point in my career I'd gone through several agents, more cars than I could remember, and a wife. I'd never felt so low. But even though I thought about crawling into a hole, I never really wanted to run away. I was fucked up, that was for sure. But I wasn't *that* fucked up.

Still, my friend Charles Grantham, the former union executive with the NBPA, pushed me to meet with people from a place called the Life Extension Institute, which the league has partnered with ever since the early eighties when the *Los Angeles Times* reported that three quarters of the NBA snorted coke. But instead of going to Life Extension, on October 14, 1983, I checked into Manhattan's Regent Hospital. At the time, even the great Kareem Abdul-Jabbar used drugs. In his memoir, *Giant Steps*, he admitted to using heroin, weed, coke, and LSD. And Earl Monroe, in *his* memoir, talked about once trying angel dust.

People get curious. And, as they say, addiction is a family disease because it affects the whole family. Now I was living that, but as a twenty-eight year old.

Beyond all that, my drug use made me a target. So much so that my teammate Darryl Dawkins thought the league was following me. Not just one person, like that time in Golden State, but that the whole NBA was on my trail. Waiting for me to slip up. "We believed the NBA was targeting Michael Ray," he said in his memoir, adding that he thought the NBA was tracking him at times, too, along with other players in different cities.

But it didn't bother me when Darryl told me his stories. Like I said, if they had people stalking me, I was done for anyway. While other players were getting popped here and there for smoking pot, it seemed the NBA had a hard-on for me. I was the guy they wanted. An All-Star, but not Magic, Bird, or Kareem. I wasn't a media sensation. My stuttering didn't help me get any commercials, and I played in New Jersey—not New York, Los

Angeles, Boston, or Chicago. Perhaps I was the perfect sacrifice. I'd soon find out, no matter who was chasing me or driving cabs in Boston. That was just the way it would be.

* * *

Because of the NBA's new three-strike system, I was reinstated with the Nets. If drugs hadn't been around, many of us would be remembered more fondly than we are today. It's like a generation got wiped out. I could have been thought of as one of the greatest of all time, but that's life. We have different paths to walk. As the old saying goes: *Man plans, God laughs*. And that season, because of all my problems, I was only able to play in 48 games.

Despite my off-the-court issues, I was always well liked by my teammates and the people around me. That included New Jersey Nets owner Joe Taub, who stuck with me even through all my mistakes and indiscretions. I'll always love him for that. Taub, a successful businessman, was so pro-player that he even cancelled a practice once on our behalf. I thought Stan would explode. I rejoined Taub's team in December 1983 after months of rehab in Manhattan. Then I had another non-drug-related setback in mid-January and missed about 10 more games. It wasn't until February 4, 1984, that I became Sugar on the court once again.

As many people around the league already knew and as I soon found out in person, Stan Albeck could coach. The new hire for the Nets was the glue that kept the team together all season. Stan was an offensive genius and someone who knew how to talk to people. He never got too angry at any time, and generally kept an even hand. George "Iceman" Gervin's former coach with the Spurs, Stan knew what he was doing. He was what they call a player's coach. And I needed all the positivity I could get. Stan was sensitive to my situation. He acknowledged that some people were treating me like a "leper," but said he knew I felt bad about my actions, which was true. I apologized to everyone in the organization for every slip-up I made, not wanting them to think that I was OK with hurting the team.

My teammate, the always well-coiffed Mike Gminski—the guy looked like an actor playing a professional wrestler—said that I had a chance to succeed marvelously now or fall flat on my face. That was accurate. But again, I wasn't the only one. For almost my entire time in New Jersey, we had this assistant coach John Killilea, who would actually leave games to go to the locker room and take shots of whiskey. His excuse was that he had to piss. John died in 1996 of cardiac arrest. Life ain't easy, that's for sure. And there were numerous players in the league who also abused alcohol over the years, with too many to name.

* * *

By now, I'd found a new woman and we'd gotten married. Her name was Leah, and we had a daughter together, Tamara Nicole Richardson, who everyone called Nikki. Leah also had a daughter from a previous marriage, Naomi, whom I adopted. Naomi's father had gotten involved in some trouble and one day had been found dead at the end of a subway train line tunnel all shot up. Today, Tamara is a doctor in Long Island, with a little girl, Harper, and she just gave birth to a new baby. While Tosha and her mother lived in Denver, I settled in with Leah and our daughters in New Jersey.

When I first got traded to the Nets, I lived in the Hilton hotel in Hackensack, New Jersey, for the season. But now that I was still on the team and trying to get my life together, Leah and I all moved up to Mahwah in North Jersey to live in a house in the suburbs. I kept clean for chunks of the season and began to get my old form back. I played in 48 games, starting 25 of them. Though my numbers were down based on previous seasons, I did have a few bright spots, including scoring a season-high 25 points in a loss to Cleveland and tallying 14 assists with eight steals in a win against Philly. For where I *could* have been in my life then, I'd take that output. I dove on the floor for loose balls and fought for my teammates when they got fouled hard, doing all the things I'd done throughout my career.

On February 4, I hit a buzzer-beater 3-pointer to beat the Bulls, 108–105. In the huddle with just 10 seconds left, Stan drew up a play. He told me to take the ball to one side of the court and dump it down to Darryl in the post. I was chewing my gum frantically like I often did, and said, "Got it, c-coach." But when I got the ball in my hands, I took it, faked my guy, and hit the three. Before it hit twine, I said, "We win," and ran into the locker room as the team stayed on the court. I was out of the showers before they got back. "I told you motherfuckers," I said. Larry Brown would have gone mad. But Stan told me, "Hell of a shot, Sugar."

Later that month, after going 2–6 the games after my buzzer beater, we picked ourselves up and went on a streak, winning 11 of 12 games. And while we dropped our last two games of the regular season, we had won five in a row before that, finishing the season with a 45–37 record.

For the season I averaged 12 points, 2.1 steals, 4.5 assists, and 3.6 rebounds—far from my best numbers. While it was a down year statistically, I was just happy to still be playing, even if I'd been erratic on and off the court. Even though we'd finished the campaign eight games over .500, we finished 17 games behind the Boston Celtics and seven behind the second-place and defending champion 76ers. Magic Johnson had led the league in assists, dishing 13.1 per game. By now, Magic had two rings, and both Bird and Dr. J had one. I didn't have any. But for a single playoff series, at least, I was about to redeem myself.

* * *

Overall, we had a solid roster. We were up and down during the season, largely thanks to me and some untimely injuries, but we had talent between Otis, Darryl, Mike Gminski, Albert King, Buck Williams, and me. Even though we showed that we could hang with the best of the teams in the league, no one gave us a shot when we matched up against the defending champion Sixers in the opening round of the 1984 playoffs. It was a microcosm of my career: long odds against a beloved opponent.

The three-seed Sixers had home-court advantage, but I'd made my bones in underdog situations like this, whether in high school, the University of Montana, the Knicks, and now with New Jersey. But this wasn't high school, or college, or those previous playoff series. These were the Sixers . . . and the Sixers were stacked. With Moses Malone, Julius Erving, Maurice Cheeks, Andrew Toney, and Bobby Jones, the team was coached by Billy Cunningham, who'd won a ring as a player with Wilt Chamberlain and as Philly's coach the season before. As a kid, I used to dream at night about playing Dr. J, and when he was in

Denver during the ABA days, I'd watch his every move. Now, here we were. In the playoffs. On the same court.

The twinkle was back in my eye. The fans were loving me in New Jersey. I was finally getting good attention, even hearing comparisons to Magic again. Down the stretch, I'd played some of my best basketball since I'd been in the league, even if my averages didn't show it. And Stan had a lot of confidence in me by now. He told me, "Sugar, just go out there and play." I stepped up as a team leader, and our guys had great chemistry. Now it was time to prove that we belonged. That we were here, and ready to dethrone the defending champs.

* * *

We were ready from the jump. In the first game of the series, with a raucous Philly crowd, we stepped onto the court ready to put those asses back in their seats . . . and that's just what we did. Finishing the first quarter up by 10 and never taking our foot off the gas, we not only quieted the fans in The Spectrum, but all the doubters out there, beating the Sixers by 15. Writers called the victory for us on the road a "shocker." We were jumping in passing lanes and dunking all over the older Philly team.

Before we get on to the next game, I need to point out that I had not played up to my standard in my previous two play-off series. Both two-game losses (to the Bulls and Knicks), I'd shot less than 30 percent from the field and averaged just 10.5 points a game. Those games were not me at my best, and I was determined to show that I was not only someone that my team could lean on during the season, but when it mattered most in the playoffs as well. So, in our 15-point blowout in Game One,

I scored 18 points with nine assists—both playoff career highs—to go along with six rebounds and five blocks. But that was only the beginning of my rebirth.

In Game Two, the Sixers continued their poor play. We were up by 17 at the half and won handily, 116–102. I felt like I could not be stopped that night, as I put up 32 points with nine rebounds and seven assists. Our big Florida-born center Darryl Dawkins dominated as well with 22 points and we felt as though we had the whole thing sewn up. As we headed back home for Game Three, I remember Darryl chugging Heineken cans in the back of the team bus. He polished off his own "sixer" in less than five minutes. For a Nets team that had never won a *single* playoff game in its eight NBA seasons, we'd already gotten two.

In the next two games were at home and, instead of staying aggressive, we let go of the rope. Our goofy mascot even came out at center court with a broom. Stupid. Everyone had sweep on their minds, but it wasn't meant to be. Philadelphia won games Three and Four (thanks, in part, to a few questionable calls).

The series was now tied, and the 76ers had gotten their confidence back. Big Moses killed us on the glass and Dr. J wasn't going out so easy. But that's when "The Doctor" gave us our ace in the hole. After their game four victory, he was interviewed and said that we "weren't going to win in Philadelphia." Then he added, "Mail in the stat sheets." That wasn't confidence, that was arrogance.

Stan Albeck showed us what he'd said on the bus the next morning. We were snarling. We drove to Philly for the fifth and final game, knowing we had to win on the road or go home knowing we'd let our series lead slip through our fingers. Both of Philly's stars—Doc and Moses—were playing a ton of minutes and we could see that they were wearing down. We weren't scared.

Even from the outset, Stan had said of our playoff matchup, "If it's Philadelphia, then let's get it on."

After a back-and-forth game, we entered the fourth quarter tied at 76 apiece. The Sixers went up seven points with just seven minutes to play. The score was 90–83. But we weren't ready to go home yet. I knew we could win. I sliced into the lane for a finger-roll layup as we scratched and clawed our way back. The whole team fought. And in the deciding play, Albert King tipped in an Otis Birdsong missed layup and that was the difference. Bye, bye, Philly! And after we won, reporters called me the "driving force" behind the victory—the biggest in Nets team history since joining the NBA and my personal history. Coach Billy Cunningham could only look on in disbelief. Had this ragtag team from Jersey outdone the champs? Yes!

In Game Five, I'd scored 24, dished six assists, grabbed six boards, and stole the ball six times. Adding a big three-point play near the end. Great players dominate when the lights get the hottest. We celebrated the win like we'd just won the championship. I always knew we'd had a chance. For the season, we'd played Philly well, splitting the season series 3–3. Their guards just couldn't handle me and Otis. And Doc, bless him, was just too old to hang with athletic Albert King. We had a theme song that postseason, "Ain't No Stoppin' Us Now" by McFadden & Whitehead. And after the game, we played that over and over again. Music never felt so good.

* * *

Now, in the second round of the playoffs, we faced the East's second-seeded Milwaukee Bucks, who had just defeated Atlanta and young Dominique Wilkins. While the series against Philly went five games, the one with Milwaukee went longer. Coached by the innovative Don Nelson, the Bucks roster boasted Marques Johnson, Sidney Moncrief, and Bob Lanier. We'd beaten Philly in Game Five on April 26 and had to fly to Milwaukee for game One in the Eastern Conference Semifinals just three days later. Most newspapers predicted that we'd be too tired in that opening game . . . but they were wrong again.

While we got off to a slow start, being down six at the half, we outscored the Bucks by ten in the third and came away with the win, 106–100. We were riding high, and Darryl Dawkins was the main reason for our win, exploding for 32 points and eight rebounds. Our Buck—Buck Williams—grabbed 17 rebounds and scored 15. Otis had 18 points and I got 14 with eight assists, four steals, and six rebounds. We'd just won our fourth playoff game, with all of them coming on the road. This led to me saying in an interview with Peter Vecsey, "Pete, there's no place like *away*."

But Game Two was a different story. While we kept the thing close through four quarters, we lost it at the very end. On a bad call. Down 94–92 with just 13 seconds left on the clock, I was coming down the court with the ball, about to tie the game. Slicing through the lane, I saw the 6-foot-11, 250-pound Bob Lanier standing in my way. I made a move to pass, but the ball didn't get to Mike Gminski. Instead, it just bounced unattended near the free-throw line. I knew I couldn't touch the ball again (or else be called for a self-pass travel) so I tried to box out a few Bucks players until one of my teammates could grab the ball.

That's when referee Earl Strom whistled me for touching the ball first, which I did *not* do. After the game, replays showed I didn't touch it. In fact, it was Buck Williams who had touched it, legally. But because of that call, the Bucks got the ball back and won the game, 98–94. We should have won that one, but when you play in someone else's gym, they're going to get some home cooking from the referees, no doubt. That's just the way it is. In the end, it was a big letdown that would follow us home to New Jersey for Game Three.

In our third matchup of the series, we lost by seven at home in the Meadowlands, 100–93. Dawkins had another big game, scoring 31 points while Otis added 20, but I played poorly, as did the rest of the team. After the game, Buck told reporters, "We're world-beaters on the road. But we come in here and put on a different game face."

Down in the series and looking for our first home playoff win, we responded . . . though it took us three quarters before doing so. Down 10 at the half and nine going into the fourth, we outscored the Bucks by 16 in the final quarter to take the 106–99 win. Buck backed up his talk with 18 points and 10 rebounds. I scored 24 and Mike Gminski, our big spark in the game, added 20 off the bench. With the series tied and heading back to Milwaukee, Game Five would be another seesaw.

While we'd been able to come back in Game Four, that spark didn't light in game five, and the Bucks beat us handily, 94–82. Dawkins was our lone bright spot with 20 and eight, and Milwaukee's balanced attack simply outdid us. But even though we were one game from elimination, we still felt good and ready for Game Six. Trouble was that another bad call would screw us.

With 1:32 left in the fourth quarter, I sunk two free throws to tie the game at 95 apiece. Then shortly after, the Bucks' Paul Pressey made one of two free throws to put his team up, 96–95, with just 1:20 left. Then Paul hit a jumper with 41 ticks to go to give them a three-point lead. I scored again after Buck Williams got a big a offense rebound for us to make it 98–97. Downcourt, the Bucks' final shot was blocked, resulting in an airball just as the shot clock expired, but the refs wrongly kept their whistles quiet. It should have been our possession.

Instead, there was a fight for the ball as it rolled on the court and that's when Moncrief got the "rebound" and sat on it. Time just ran out but it should have been our ball, down by a single point with four or five seconds or so to get a shot off with an out-of-bounds play. We could have easily won the game. But no. After the game, we were pissed off. Nets executive vice president Lewis Schaffel filed an official protest with the league. And like the call in Game Two, the replay showed the Bucks' shot never hit the rim. In the end, it didn't matter. We lost, despite Dawkins scoring 29 and Otis adding 22.

And just like that, after everything the team and I had been through, the playoffs—and our season—were over.

Despite the two bad calls, it was a better end to the year than they way it started. And it was better than the year prior and our playoff loss to the Knicks. In the two playoff series against Philly and Milwaukee, I managed to average 16.8 points, 4.9 rebounds, 7.2 assists, and led the playoffs in steals with 3.1 per game. Once we were beat by the Bucks, I watched the Boston Celtics beat the Lakers in the Finals, which gave Larry Bird two rings to go against Magic's two. But now I had to figure out my future. Would I sign a new deal in New Jersey? Would I stay clean?

The answer to both of those questions were a resounding "Yes."

Memory Lane: Tamara "Nikki" Richardson

My dad is the best! He's reliable, helpful, and always there for his family no matter what. He's the type of person who will drop anything—whenever I need him, he's there. My dad is also a very funny guy; we're always laughing together. Some people say we even have the same laugh.

My first memory of my dad was probably living overseas in Bologna, Italy. I would travel back and forth, going to school overseas one year and in the United States for others. Colorado, Bologna, Antibes (France), New York, back and forth splitting time.

Today, my dad and I are very close. I like to say I'm his favorite child. I live in New York and see him often now that he travels here to do stuff with the Knicks and Nets. So I get to see him a lot during the basketball season and in the summer while he's doing his camps.

We talk every day on FaceTime. He's an amazing grandfather. He spoils my kids like crazy! Even though I'm thirty-eight, I say he spoils me, too. If I ask him for something, he might argue, but he'll always get it for me. My dad never says no to us!

My favorite story with him would be the time we spent overseas, traveling around the globe. He gave me and my siblings exposure to a world of different cultures. That's the biggest impact he had. At some point, all of us were in Italy together when we were young. It was great.

For as good an NBA player he was, I would say he's an even better dad. It's funny, with my siblings, it feels like we all had him at different stages in his life. While I didn't see a lot of his struggles growing up, I did have a lot of very positive memories with him, which I'm thankful for.

11

BACK TO THE ALL-STAR GAME

PRIOR to the playoffs against the 76ers, I think everyone—including their mothers and their dogs—counted me out. I was a lost cause. A has-been.

I had played in just 48 games due to several stints in rehab, and there was no expectation that my career would last much longer.

But during the 1984–85 season, I refound my game. My passion. Even Larry Bird said after my Nets had beaten the 76ers that I was "the best basketball player on the planet." That was quite a compliment from one of the best *ever*. He and I always talked a lot of trash, too.

After several years in which I'd spend the offseason either using or in rehab, I was able to keep myself clean during the summer and into the year. I felt great and saw this as my redemption season. The one in which I reminded everyone, including myself, who I was. On the court, I was a beast. Off of it, I kept my composure. Only the strong survive.

After our great series win against Philadelphia, the Nets and owner Joe Taub rewarded me with a new four-year, $3 million deal. Considering I'd been in and out of rehab and nearly waived by the team just the year before, this was a huge moment. I also participated in an anti-drug video produced by Charles Grantham, *Cocaine Drain*, which told young people and other NBA players why they shouldn't use drugs (also in the video were John Lucas and Kareem). I passed every one of my weekly drug tests administered by the team. And when the new year began, I was as ready as I ever was. Yes, the 1984–85 season was my comeback.

Around this time, though, Taub was negotiating to sell the team. He wanted out of sports (though he later bought back in around 1991). He and I were friends, so before he sold the team, he wanted to take care of me, to make sure I had the contract I deserved. Thankfully, he did what he said he would. Even today, I'm close with his family, though he has since passed away. Taub also used to be close friends with the baseball player Larry Doby, who was only the second Black player in Major League Baseball, after Jackie Robinson. But when the two of them went to the movies, Larry had to sit in the balcony while Joe sat downstairs.

Joe always hated that. When Larry died, Joe built a baseball stadium in Paterson, New Jersey, in Larry's honor. And today, me and Otis Birdsong conduct basketball camps for underprivileged kids in Paterson as part of the Taub Foundation. Me and Joe stayed friends until the day he died in 2017. When one of Joe's daughters passed away, I was the only former player at her funeral. I flew in from France, where I was playing then, to attend, sitting right next to Joe. After that, I spent time with him at his home and he said to me, "Look, I was there when Sugar Man was going through his shit and now he's here for me."

I was also able to build a great relationship with Larry Doby. He was an incredibly nice person. He would even come on the road with me sometimes when I was with the Nets. We'd hang out together, go eat and see movies. Thankfully, by then we could sit wherever we wanted in the theaters. It wasn't like that old racist Black and white shit was still going. Thanks, in fact, to people like Larry Doby, who sacrificed their life to push the limits of what Blacks were allowed to do. Today, we stand on the shoulders of giants like him.

* * *

In training camp, I roomed with Darryl Dawkins. What could happen, right? In all seriousness, Darryl was one of the nicest guys you'd ever meet. He also loved chicken. He'd eat *everything* on a chicken bone, down to the little pieces that stuck to the joints. After practice, we would go to this little chicken joint and the fucker would order, I kid you not, seventy-five wings and a gallon of water. Back at the hotel, Darryl would take his bottle of tabasco sauce and would get butt naked and sit his big ass on the side of the bed and eat the wings one-by-one. And when he got done with that chicken bone, it would be clean.

He was also one of the funniest guys I've ever met. He said he was from Planet Lovetron. But as a player, Darryl was one of the most skilled big men that ever played the game. He was fast, could handle the ball, and had a nice little 10-to-15-foot jumper. He could pass, too. He was known for breaking backboards on thunderous dunks he named (if he wanted out of practice, he'd try to break one). Darryl just had one problem: he didn't want to be *great*. He wanted to be good and have fun. If he got a few fantastic dunks in a game, he would give you all he had. Other than that, it was all laughs.

* * *

To open the 1984–85 season, over the first dozen games, I scored double digits in each game, including two games with more than 10 assists. Though I started out strong, we sat at just 6–6. In the summer, the Nets had drafted European star Oscar Schmidt, but he'd decided not to come over. He could have helped, but oh well!

Stan Albeck was back for the year, and it was the first time I had the same coach in back-to-back seasons since Red Holzman and the Knicks. I scored 28 points and then 31 points in back-to-back games against the Celtics in early December and had 32 in a win against Washington a few days later—one of the best stretches of my career. And on Christmas day in 1984, I was able to get my revenge against Hubie Brown and the Knicks.

We traveled to Manhattan to play New York on December 25. To start that one, they came out and went up 34–27 in the first quarter, increasing their lead to 64–54 at the half. But that's when I took over. We outscored them 66–50 in the second half, and even though Bernard King, the guy who I was traded for, scored 60 points, we won thanks to my 36 points, four steals, four assists, and five rebounds. The headline the next day read, "King's 60 Soured by Sugar." That game then began a streak of eight for me during which I dominated.

For the entire year, I had 24 games with 25 points or more, 14 games with five steals or more, 28 double-digit assist games, four double-digit rebound games, and notched two triple-doubles. Getting clean looked good on me. As Magic Johnson was getting love for winning rings and notching his trouble-doubles, I was doing my thing, too. With the ball, I wasn't no Curly Neal. As a shooter, I wasn't Steph Curry. But I had enough of both and a quickness that no one could match. I wouldn't play with the ball, I'd just put my head down and use my first step to go by a guy. I was always taught not to dribble unless you're going to do something with it.

With one move I'd be *gone*. And when I was matched up against smaller point guards, I licked my lips. If people like Magic couldn't stop me, little guys like John Stockton sure wouldn't either. I'd have to tell Utah's coach Jerry Sloan to get John off me because I was taking his lunch. I was one of the only guys Zeke *and* Magic feared. And I prided myself on that fact. You had to make them work! During the 1984–85 season, I was back to my celebrity status in the NBA. Everyone from all walks in the New York area wanted to hang with me. But my best friend on the team was Mr. Otis Birdsong.

A four-time All-Star, Otis was a strait-laced, no-nonsense guy who only drank beer. But Otis could score with the best. There was one game, January 29, 1985, when he and I were battling George Gervin and the Spurs. We were in San Antonio on a road trip out west. Here we were, three of the best guards in the league. In that one, Otis scored 22 and dished six assists, while I had 26 with six assists and three steals. Albert King added 24 off the bench as well, but Gervin got the best of both of us that night on his home floor, scoring 47. That's how good the

"Iceman" was. And he needed every point, as we lost the game by just three points, 130–127.

* * *

Finally clean and back on my game, I made the All-Star team for the fourth time in my career. I didn't have any slip-ups that year, and I didn't even miss a game. I in all 82 while averaging 20.1 points (the highest of my career), 8.2 assists, 5.6 rebounds, and a league-leading three steals (my second highest total ever). I was clean and on track. Back on a mission. I'd proved my mettle and did what I'd needed to do. I was so good that Buck Williams even said the last two minutes of every game were *mine*. Yes, I showed I could be an All-Star. And at the annual game, there was even a new first-time participant: rookie Michael Jordan.

When it comes to Jordan's career, there about a million what-ifs. What if Len Bias and Reggie Lewis hadn't died? What if Magic hadn't left in the early nineties? And what if I was never banned from the league? See, MJ didn't scare me. No player and no situation did, to be honest. During Jordan's first year, my Nets beat his Bulls four out of six times, including the final game of the year when I had 20 points, 12 assists, and six rebounds to Michael's 29 and nine assists. In all fairness, Mike wasn't yet the gamechanger he'd grow up to be. Still, we got him. For me, every time I got on the floor with someone hyped like MJ, I took it personally.

Jordan, Isiah, Magic, Bird—I wanted to play my best against all those guys, and I wanted to bust their asses, too. I always thought, no matter who I was facing, *these guys cut and bleed the same way I do. Lace up their shoes the same way I do.* So I feared no one, even if they were great. It was just how I approached the game. I was also rewarded for my attitude and drive, being given the NBA Comeback Player of the Year Award. I was ecstatic.

The award was only given out seven times ever. And during the course of its seven-year lifespan, the Comeback Player of the Year award was given out three times to guys who had come back from substance abuse, which was the reason the league stopped handing it out. The first winner was Nate Archibald, and I was the award's second-to-last recipient. Others included Bernard King, Gus Williams, Paul Westphal, Adrian Dantley, and Marques Johnson. Later, the league adopted the Most Improved Player Award in place of the Comeback Player of the Year. But I'm proud to have been one of the seven original recipients.

* * *

While I showed my resolve, we finished the season 42–40. Sadly, we were bit by the injury bug. Albert King only played 42 games with a hurt back. Darryl Dawkins only played 39. And Otis Birdsong only suited up for 56. It was a rough season, even if Buck Williams and I were both able to play all 82. While the season had plenty of bright spots for me, it didn't end well. While we earned the five seed and still made the playoffs, our opponent would be the Detroit Pistons. With Detroit had the higher seed, we started off at their place.

I wish I could say we played well in the series, but that would not be the case. We lost the first game by 20 points, 125–105. Buck played well, grabbing nine rebounds and scoring 23. I had 12 points and 10 assists, but we just couldn't hang with Detroit. We had six guys in double-figures, but some of that came in "garbage time" when the game was out of hand. And for all my trash talking, Isiah had a great game against us with 21 points and 11 assists. He was really building something in the city. Bill Laimbeer added 23 and 13 rebounds. Detroit also had six guys in double-figures. Three of them had 20-plus.

The next game, also in Detroit, was a bit closer, but not by much. While we were down by just five at the half, we lost by ten, 121–111. We played better as a team, but they just outdid us. I had 22 points, 14 rebounds, and eight assists, while Buck added 23 and 11 boards. Albert King, feeling healthy again, added 27. For Detroit, Isiah had 29 points and 14 assists, with Laimbeer adding 18 and 12. Beyond their play, what killed us, though, was not having Otis for the series. Injured, Otis wasn't even able to suit up. He couldn't even be a decoy, and that spelled defeat. Nevertheless, we did our best in Game Three back in New Jersey without him. Sadly, it wasn't enough.

Back in New Jersey we came out strong, hitting them with everything we had. We finished the first up 33–22 but, in every quarter after that, they crawled back and crawled back. We ran out of gas in the fourth, and they outscored us 32–24 to win by a single point, 116–115. Their secret weapon? Longtime role player Terry Tyler, who scored 23 off the bench with 11 rebounds. Earl Cureton (who sadly passed away earlier this year) added nine points and a couple of rebounds as a reserve, too. Just like that, we'd been swept. In a few years, the Pistons would become the "Bad Boys" and win back-to-back champions in 1989 and 1990. Sadly for the Nets, it was in the series against us where Detroit set that very foundation.

* * *

With the season over, New Jersey fired Stan Albeck. Management had high expectations for us, and we just didn't come through. But it wasn't Stan's fault we didn't win enough, even if he took the blame. It was just injuries and bad luck. We couldn't get on the same page. Stan would be fine, though. The next year he'd coach Michael Jordan and the Bulls. As for me, I wouldn't be so lucky. My disease came back strong, and I'd let it. I'd been good all season. I didn't go out, I'd promised myself I'd be a homebody for the year. Then I slipped up. I let my guard down and, again, started putting myself in places I shouldn't have been. It was the same story, and I'd soon pay major consequences.

My drug habit had already cost me nearly $75,000. I'd heard of some players losing millions, so I suppose there was a silver lining. But my life was set to be mostly rain clouds for a while now. Not only was I soon to go down the same dark, rocky roads that I had in seasons prior, but Joe Taub was now gone from the team. He'd been like a father to me, something of a guardian angel. I didn't want him to walk away from me or the team. But it wasn't my decision. Thank goodness I had my $3 million contract in hand, along with Leah and the girls.

That all provided some security . . . until my actions put all that in jeopardy. But as I soon realized, I'd put myself in a bad position and no contract, wife, baby, or helping hand could get me out of it. I would have to be the one to help myself. If I could slip up, get too comfortable and get on the pipe yet again, then I had to pull myself out from those issues, too. It was on me. Shit, I was the same guy that Larry Bird had once called the best on Earth. If I could achieve that honor coming from where I did, then I could kick a nagging drug habit.

Right?

Memory Lane: Buck Williams

If you want to talk about the point guard position—people were always calling me the "poor man's Moses Malone"—well, with Sugar, I would call him the step-brother of Magic Johnson, because of his size and his skill set. He was probably one of the greatest point guards to ever play the game. It's unfortunate that he got banned and that it derailed his legacy, but he's truly one of the groundbreakers for that position.

I don't think there's too many players in the history of the game like Michael Ray. He came with the full package. Back in the day, you had point guards who were floor generals. And Michael was a floor general, but could also score the ball, pass, steal, and defend. He had a well-rounded game, similar in many ways to Magic. And he was fearless. I saw him intimidate many point guards while we played together. He played mind games with so many of them in the league.

And what he did for me, if I had an exceptional matchup that night, before the game, we'd be stretching and warming up, and he would tell Lonnie Shelton or Maurice Lucas, "Buck is going to kick your ass tonight!" And he'd come back to the other side of the court, and he'd start laughing and telling me what he told Lucas. Sugar got me in a lot of situations in a lot of games against the greatest power forwards because he was instigating. Telling my opponents I was going to kick their behinds that night!

He got off on that and he'd do it almost every game. But with those Nets teams, Sugar was the main ingredient. He set the tempo on both ends of the floor. He got us into the fast break and set the offense. Michael made sure players got the ball where they wanted it, too. He was a great floor general.

Exceptionally fast. He could lock down the best point guards in the league.

The dude was the best point guard I ever played with. The other thing I can say is that I think Michael has a big heart. He was really unselfish. His big heart extended off the basketball court, too. I think that's why he got into so much trouble and got banned. He never wanted to disappoint anyone, always trying to appease everyone. And that's why he was an exceptional point guard. I love Michael. He's one of the bests teammates I ever played with.

12

"WHERE'S SUGAR?"

THE 1985–86 season would be my last in the NBA. Going into the season, the Nets replaced Stan Albeck with Dave Wohl, a former point guard in the league with a handful of teams, including the Nets. He'd also been an assistant with the Nets, Milwaukee Bucks, and Los Angeles Lakers. Wohl had won a ring the season prior with Magic and Pat Riley in LA, so the Nets thought he could come in and spin his spells and get us to the promised land. But it wasn't meant to be, largely in thanks to me and my drug problems and the curveball I threw the team. Dave was a good coach. He understood the game. He was also my sixth in seven years.

When the season started, I was thirty years old and entering my eighth pro campaign. I was in the second year of a four-year deal, and I felt like I had the world by the balls. Wohl had given me the ball and said, "Run the club." So, on October 30, I nearly did the impossible—in a good way! I was one steal shy of recording a quadruple-double against the Pacers, notching 38 points, 11 rebounds, 11 assists, and nine steals. We won that game 147–138, too. Beginning on December 7, when I scored 33 points and notched 12 assists and nine rebounds in a win against the Trail Blazers while holding Clyde Drexler to just 17 points, we began another long win streak, taking nine out of the next ten games. The only loss was to the Hawks, and that was by a single point. We were rolling, and so was my game. By the end of December, we were 20–13, and I was once again playing All-Star–quality ball. But I'd soon shoot myself in the foot. Majorly fucking up everything. I'm not proud to say it here. I can only look back now and sigh. It all started with a nice little team Christmas party. A break for us when we were playing well, heading into the holidays.

* * *

The festivities began the night after we beat the Pistons at home on December 26. When you play Detroit, there was always drama. I remember there was about 30 seconds left in the game and we were up when the Pistons' big forward Rick Mahorn set an illegal screen. Rick was one of the dirtiest players ever, him and teammate Bill Laimbeer. So he sets this screen on me, and I said, "If y-you do that again, I'm g-going to hit you upside the head with the b-ball!" Rick replied, "Yeah, yeah, okay. Fuck you." The next time down, he did it again, so I picked up the ball and popped him in the head with it. Rick ran after me, but everyone broke it up. He told me he'd see me after the game at the team hotel. I said, "Okay, I'm in room 2204!" But Rick's ass never showed. But in the game, I'd scored 23 points to go along with 10 assists, five rebounds, and two steals that night.

I was at the top of my game . . . but I got way too comfortable. I relaxed again. The next night, the Nets threw a Christmas party for the players and staff at George's Restaurant in Moonachie. A month before, I'd missed a team flight to San Antonio and the following game on November 11, which the team announced wasn't due to drugs. But in that game, I had one of my lowest scoring outputs of the year, notching just 12 points.

I was quickly slipping back into old bad habits. It was another car crash in the making—I just couldn't see it, even though everyone else could. I never thought drugs would take over again . . . but I was wrong. I was having fun during the party, and even had a few drinks, which was unlike me. I was dancing with my wife, dancing with PR people in the organization, just having a great old time. At some point, some of the guys, including Darryl, said they were going to a hotel bar for a little after-party. They asked if I wanted to come. To this day, I wish I would have just gone home. But instead, I sent my wife home to be with the baby and my sister, who was visiting for the week.

I told Leah I would be home soon, and went to hang with the guys. The after party was at the Sheraton Hotel in Hasbrouck Heights, a place where pro athletes often went to get drinks (and a place where certain women knew we'd be). There, one thing led to another and I made one of the biggest mistakes of my life. I'd already let my guard down with the drinks at the team function. Now I was on the precipice of being right back in the shit. Ironically, outside, it was snowing like the North Pole. I thought that I had to pass the Sheraton on my way home, so why not stop in? Besides, I was feeling good from the drinks, and it was the holidays. Let's party!

At the Sheraton, my teammates, Dawkins and Bobby Cattage, were trying to look out for me. But when they turned around for a minute, this hot-looking blonde walked up to me and began whispering in my ear. Next thing I knew we were driving away in a convertible with the top down in the middle of winter, heading to her place. There, we freebased and fucked all night. And into the next day. Then, when she was gone, I just stayed in the hotel and smoked the rest of the shit she'd left behind. I barely remember what the woman looked like, and I cannot remember her name. I just recall the paranoia that set in when I finally realized what I'd done.

* * *

The paranoia burned into me. News flashed that I was missing on the screen's scroll. By the time my brain turned on again, I'd missed two practices and a game. Fuck. I'd done it again. My mistakes, of course, coincided with the height of the NBA's drug issues. Former NBA player Johnny High died in June 1987 in a mysterious car accident after testifying in court about his drug issues. As Dawkins has said, the NBA was employing detectives. He even thought the blonde woman was planted by the league and that she set me up. I don't know what's true, and, in a way, it didn't matter. Blonde or no blonde, I'd fucked up.

I'd taken the wrong road again and put myself, my family, and my team in jeopardy. Articles were written about me being missing. No one knew where I was, not even Leah. I was so ashamed. I felt regret every time I woke up from a drug haze in my life, but never more than this time. I'd finally gotten my life together, and now I'd let it fall apart again in just one night. I was all out of excuses. After a few days in the hotel, I called my friend and de facto agent Charlie Grantham and told him I needed help. As recently as a few weeks before I was telling my teammates like Buck Williams that I would never use drugs again. Now, in a moment of weakness, I'd blown it.

During the team party, Coach Wohl had told me how proud he was of me, that I was the reason we were playing so well. That I was playing as well as any guard in the NBA. We'd hugged when we parted that night. But in the aftermath, it was "Where's Sugar?" So, after my three-day binge, after wallowing in self-pity, saying, *What did I do?* I returned to the team and the Nets put me right into rehab. I was down to my last chance, my final strike. I'd tried to stay clean for over a year. I wasn't a bad guy. I just couldn't control myself when it came to cocaine. I had bad judgment. That was my crime.

* * *

The rehab center the Nets sent me to this time was in Van Nuys, California. By this point, I'd visited facilities in New York, New Jersey, Minnesota, and Southern California. I was in the facility for seventeen days. And when I came back shortly after, I apologized to everyone. They asked me what happened, and I could only shake my head. You think about what you're doing until you take that first hit and, once you start getting high, you don't think about anything else . . . until it's over. By then it's way too late. In my absence, the Nets had gone 6–5. And my first game back was on January 22. Where was the game? Denver, of course.

What should have been a triumphant return home in front of my family was instead a game marked by disgrace. Not only that, but we lost by 13 points. From that point on, I only won four more games in my entire NBA career. Between those, we lost 11 more games, including eight of my final nine in the league. From my first game missed until my last in the NBA, the team was 11–17.

What a mess.

* * *

In January 1986, about a month before my banishment, me and the Nets still had a sliver of hope that I could stay on the straight and narrow. The problem was, though, I hadn't yet hit my rock bottom. Plenty of people would have seen my situation and thought I had, but not me. I was still pushing the envelope, even though I was one strike away from permanent banishment from the NBA. After I left the Van Nuys rehab center and got back with the team in Jersey, I continued to go out. I went into seedy drug houses, hanging around the New York city streets. I even went to upscale places like Studio 54, where people were passing around coke like soda.

Nowhere was safe. Even the doctor the Nets connected me with was freebasing crack. No joke. After the California rehab, the Nets' general manager went out and found a counselor for me who was supposed to "cure" me. He was located in Maywood, New Jersey, and I visited him the day I got home from California. We were set to talk because he was going to be my new full-time counselor but, during that first interaction, he handed me one hundred dollars and said, "I want you to go into the city and buy me the same stuff you were using. Because I want to see what it is, I want to test it." That was strange, but I did what he asked. And, of course, I got some for myself, too.

The next day, I brought the doctor six vials of coke and he thanked me and told me to come back the next morning at 9 a.m. But when I got to his office the next day, he was sitting in the exact same place as when I left him, wearing the exact same clothes. He looked like a zombie on zero sleep, still buzzing. Even *this* motherfucker was on the shit. So how was he supposed to help me if he couldn't even help himself? Shit. This sports therapist was nothing but a liar. Two weeks later, I heard he was pulled over buying drugs down in Washington Heights and his doctor's license was taken by the authorities. But now, stupidly, I was hooked again.

* * *

As I said, in 1985, Joe Taub sold his 40 percent share of the Nets to Ray Chambers and Lewis Katz for $150 million. In a flash, my friend and protector was gone, though he did maintain a small stake in the team. My biggest regret is not getting clean while Taub was the main man in Jersey. Truly, I didn't realize what I had in him as a team owner. He actually cared about his players. That was both rare and special. Now, though, I thought I still had one more protector in the organization. After my All-Star season the year prior, I thought I could manage myself; using drugs and maintaining my status in the league. But I couldn't.

One way I tried was by bribing one of the Nets team doctors. It was the wrong thing to do, but I didn't care. That's the power of narcotics. I don't want to say the doctor's name, but after I'd started dipping and dabbing again I was paying him $200 each time to hide my positive drug tests. To get rid of the dirty urine and to put clean urine in its place. But without telling me, he stopped protecting me after that Christmas party. Of course, I got popped again. While I can't blame him, I was sure angry at the guy in the moment. I know he was just doing his job and by not covering for me he was, in a way, protecting me by no longer enabling me.

After another failed drug test, the Nets and the NBA were on to me, and I'd lost my last chance. Two strikes now. It didn't help that I'd missed a practice and couldn't be found in early February again, either. While the NBA said I hadn't failed a drug test, the whole thing foreshadowed what was about to happen to me in a matter of days. I was suspended by the Nets for one game in February. It was as if I had one finger left holding onto the edge of a cliff and, if I let go, my entire life would plummet to some fatal end. I held on as tightly as I could, but no amount of hope would lift me up. Not for a while, anyway.

* * *

My third and final strike came after yet another failed drug test. Somehow, after the Christmas party, I'd gotten one more chance. Yet even after rehab, I still wasn't clean. I kept using, knowing I shouldn't.

Before we were set to leave Jersey to play Atlanta on February 22, the Nets team doctor stopped me and said I had to take a urine test on the spot. My piss was dirty, but I thought he might keep covering me. After I peed in a cup, I flew with the team to Atlanta, where we lost to the Hawks by 29 points. Two nights later, we played the Washington Bullets and lost by 10. Then, after the flight home from DC, some men stopped me when we arrived back at Newark Airport.

League officials had been waiting for me by baggage claim in the airport when I got off the plane. I knew what it meant. I'd been getting away with my switched urine tests for about three months now, but my luck had officially run out. I never found out why the doctor stopped switching the tests, but he had. The Nets probably caught him. Even still, it was all my fault. And now I'd officially run myself out of the league. I'd gotten high about five days before we'd left to play the Hawks. Now, league officials were telling me they'd seen my dirty test, and that I was going to be banned from the NBA. It was the lowest I'd ever felt in my life.

The encounter in the airport happened on February 25, 1986. The night before, I'd played what would be my last game in the NBA. And on February 26, David Stern announced my lifetime banishment. My failed drug test came just a day after I'd been taken in by police on February 20. I'd gotten so high that I broke into my own house in Mahwah. Leah and I had been having our problems. When I was away, she got the locks changed and a court order to keep me out. But she never told me. So what did I do? Locked out, I kicked in one of the glass windows beside the door, shattering it. That pushed the NBA to test me for the final time. And, of course, I failed.

The *Newsday* headline in the paper after my banishment read, "Sugar Fouls Out!" Others called me "naïve" and "semiliterate." Worse, I'd broken my mother's heart. A four-time All-Star, I was the first player to be banned from the NBA for drugs.

When most decorated careers end, it's with fanfare and applause. For me, it was with a whimper. When I saw NBA security in the airport, I walked right up to Mr. Horace Balmer, the NBA's head of security. "Anything wrong?" I asked. "You know what's wrong," he said. "Strike three." That's when my life flashed before my eyes. When everything hit home. Like an addict, I never wanted to feel the reality of my actions. But I did then. Like a wrecking ball.

Drugs hurt my entire family. I never wanted to face that. I once told a *Sports Illustrated* reporter, "I'll be playing basketball until, you know, until the day they kick me out." Well, I wasn't wrong. In the Nets' first game after my banishment, the team lost to Golden State to bring their record to 30–30. After that, the team signed my old teammate Ray Williams from San Antonio. They went just 9–13 the rest of the way, finishing the season 39–43 and sneaking into the playoffs (only to get swept by the Milwaukee Bucks, 3–0). The team's nightmare season was over . . . but I wasn't paying attention. I was getting high and having as much sex as I could until I couldn't take it anymore.

And then, reality finally set in.

* * *

David Stern is one of the most important people in the history of the NBA. Bill Walton said he's *the* most important. Stern helped negotiate the NBA and ABA merger, and parlayed the Magic Johnson-Larry Bird rivalry into league success, paving the way for Michael Jordan and his tongue wagging.

He also saved my life.

Stern became the commissioner of the NBA on February 1, 1984. Two years later, I was out of the league. Yes, one of his major concerns at the time was drug use by the players—especially Black players. There were rumors of white players' nosebleeds on the bench and covering their heads with towels, but there were no headlines about them. Still, I love Stern to this day.

While I denied my drug use at first, my agent Charlie Grantham didn't appeal my ban. In total, I played in just 47 games in my final year, averaging 15.7 points, 8.2 assists, 5.3 rebounds, and 2.7 steals. I'd tallied 556 NBA games over nine years with averages of 14.8 points, 7 assists, 5.5 rebounds, and 2.6 steals. And in 18 career playoff matchups, I averaged 15.7 points, 7.2 assists, 5.5 rebounds, and 2.8 steals. But the thing about Stern was that he wasn't happy about banning me. He said that having a three-strike program looked good "on paper," but at what expense?

Stern cared. He said I was now facing potential ruin, the end of my career, maybe homelessness. He said kicking me out was one of the worst things he ever had to do as commissioner. He called it a "tragic day" that I was now "permanently disqualified from playing basketball in the National Basketball Association." My friend Larry Doby spoke on my behalf, too, saying that I wasn't a "problem child," but a "child with a problem." Bulls GM Jerry Krause, who everyone called "Crumbs" for all the donut crumbs on his shirt, said that I'd made my own "bed." I bet Krause was happy. Now Jordan didn't have to deal with me on the court.

Not only was my basketball life going down, so was my marriage with Leah. She'd gotten a restraining order and we'd gotten into a huge fight the night I kicked the window in. That night, eight or nine cops showed up. Luckily, I was friends with Allendale's police chief. I knew he wasn't going to throw the book at me, but the cops still had to make sure I didn't do anything stupid. In the end, I was booked for assault. My friend Brenda bailed me out, paying $2,500. After all of that, after my banishment and after using drugs for weeks upon my dismissal from the NBA, I'd finally hit rock bottom.

Addicts will tell you that, for someone to recover fully, they have to hit their lowest point. Around the league, a lot of guys were hitting theirs, too. I wondered why the league wasn't able to do more for its workforce besides hiring undercover agents, suspending guys, and kicking them out. But recovery, in the end, is about your own personal choice. It was up to us, as individuals. No one can do it for you. But when I got banned, you best believe a lot of players put their pipes down. Today, there are few if any highlights from my games on NBA television or in promos.

* * *

Today, when I think about what happened, the only problem I have is my inability to really pinpoint how it all got started. Growing up, I was a kid good. My mother, the warrior, taught me right from wrong. So, I still wonder, *How did I ever get involved with drugs?* I can't even think of a time when there was a massive change in me. All of a sudden, I was just hooked, binging on cocaine. Stupidly. That's why I've come around to the idea that our stories are already written before we arrive. I'm not a particularly religious person, though I do believe in a higher power. My mistakes were part of my scripture. God doesn't give you anything you can't handle.

13

BANNED

MY whole life, I thought I was a winner. But by February 27, 1986, newspaper men like Tony Kornheiser were writing my obituaries. They were saying I knew the rule and that even if I couldn't read it, the rule was read *to me*. Lewis Schaffel, executive vice president of the Nets, said the team did all it could for me, sent me to the "best rehabilitation center in the nation." But, as Schaffel told Kornheiser in the *Washington Post*, "Ultimately, we all failed." My addiction had won. Maybe it was always going to. But there was a silver lining. I had lost my career, but not my life. There was hope. Room to improve. I knew that I had gotten myself into this, and the only way to get myself out was to do step up and do what was necessary to turn things around.

* * *

In the offseason, the Nets drafted my replacement, "Pearl" Washington. The team was trying to forget me as soon as it could, from cleaning out my locker to drafting the next hot young guard. Drafted from Syracuse, Washington—who took the same nickname as my former Knicks mentor—grew up in New York City and was rated as the top high school player in the country. He was the thirteenth pick in the draft, but only lasted three seasons in the league. Despite being a dream job, the NBA is not an easy lifestyle. And here I was, too. Unemployed, dealing with my now-estranged wife, wondering what would happen next. The one thing I knew, though, was that I had to stay clean.

I couldn't let this be my final chapter. Some lives went down the drain as a result of drugs. But others, like John Lucas, were able to pick themselves up. People said he was walking around alleys with no socks and shoes, controlled by his addiction, looking for the pipe. But he turned his life around. He now runs a treatment center in Houston. If he could do it, so could I.

The first thing I had to do, though, was face what I'd done. Next I needed help. And to look in the mirror.

* * *

As a kid, I loved candy. One of my fondest memories is going into the corner store near my house with my friends and getting a chocolate bar and some gummies. Today, I keep a drawer full of candy next to my bed. Inside, I've got Snickers bars, sour cherries, cinnamon candies. In my heart, I don't know if I'm an addictive person, but my behavior would certainly indicate as much. So once I'd come to grips with what my drug use had done, after I finally put the pipe down and stopped looking to forget my problems through coke and sex, I told myself I was done for good with drugs forever. I'd messed up my career and family life, and now I had to fix it.

The first step was to stay clean. The next was to go to the gym and start working out. I told Leah not to worry about money; that I was going to figure it out and be sure to still take care of her and the baby. Even though our marriage was on the rocks, I knew I had a responsibility to both of them. I told her, "I got us into this. So, I'm going to g-get us out of it." She said she believed me and let me get to work. I wanted to get in tip-top shape. While the NBA was the best league in the world, it wasn't the only game in town. At the time, there was the CBA (Continental Basketball Association), USBL (United States Basketball League), and other minor leagues, as well as leagues overseas. But first, I had to get my wind back.

At the time, the Nets still owed me one more paycheck. With that, some $250,000, I bought myself a little bit of time. I could have stayed in a dark room and killed myself with the pipe, but I wasn't going to go out like that. I could have sat back and blamed David Stern, blamed the Nets, blamed my father, the rehab centers, Leah, Renee, my teammates, drug pushers, anyone and everyone. But what was the point? Was that going to change the past? Was that going to get me my career back? No. All that would help now was hard work. Though given a "lifetime" ban, I was essentially suspended from the NBA for at least two years (barring a review). I vowed to get back.

* * *

At the time, I was also in debt to creditors, despite having made over $1 million. I needed to get that straight, too. Charlie

Grantham told reporters on my behalf that I had an "illness." Now, he said, it was time to put my health over basketball. I had to get my shit in order. After I was banned, I laid low. Charlie set me up with some doctors, therapists, and outpatient programs. But when a writer from the *New York Daily News* rang my doorbell, I said, "All I need is some peace." Back in the Meadowlands, a reporter quoted Dave Wohl as saying he and the team were going to have a "primal-scream meeting" to vent all their frustrations. That made sense.

Mike Gminski equated my situation to a family member with a "fatal disease." He said, "You keep hoping for him to pull through, but somewhere in the back of your mind, you're prepared for the inevitable." It all made sense; I couldn't argue. Shit, I was the same guy who just did an anti-drug film. Now look at me. As much as I hated to say it, I couldn't be trusted. Even my old coach Willis Reed, who was an assistant with the Atlanta Hawks at the time, said I was "very impressionable" and a "person who could be led around" and "a victim of the times." It seemed like the whole world had an opinion on me.

Buck Williams, one of my closest friends on the Nets, defended me. "He is one of the nicest guys I've ever met," Buck said. "If you needed anything from him, he'd give it to you. The last dollar out of his pocket." Buck also said, "I don't care what he's done. I know him and I still love him." That meant a lot. But more than the world having my name on their lips, what I needed to worry about now was staying clean and finding a way both back into basketball and making money. Those were my new goals. Said Charlie Grantham, "If Michael Ray doesn't play any basketball at all for two years, it will be terminal to his career."

* * *

On June 19, 1986, Len Bias passed away. The standout college player from the University of Maryland, Bias was picked by the Celtics with the second overall selection in the 1986 draft. Two days later, he died from heart issues related to a cocaine overdose. He'd reportedly had a five-year, $1.6 million deal set up with Reebok, too, along with his NBA contract. A few of his teammates were charged with coke possession and, in 1986 and later, President Reagan signed the "Len Bias Law," which punished dealers whose drugs led to others' deaths. The whole thing was horrible for everyone, Len especially. He'd just been excited to make the NBA and had his entire life (and career) ahead of him.

In the wake of my banishment, other NBA players got the axe, too. John Drew was banned for drugs in 1986, as was "Fast" Eddie Johnson in 1987. Chris Washburn was banned in 1989. Roy Tarpley was banned in 1991. Richard Dumas got the boot in 1993. More recently, Chris Andersen was banned in 2006, O. J. Mayo in 2016, Tyreke Evans in 2019, and Jalen Harris in 2021 (though all were later reinstated).

If I had talked about everything I knew at the time—either to the league, to the newspapers or to some sort of government agency—there would have been a lot more guys with punishments in their histories. But I just couldn't do that. I had no interest in taking the NBA down. The league hadn't done anything but give me a chance to excel, and I'd blown it. Now I had to think about what really mattered. Revenge? No, not one bit. What I realized, though, is that I still loved the game of basketball. That I knew for certain. So I'd decided to build myself back up from there. One of my specialties on the court was rebounding. Now it was time for a big one in real life.

My next move was to play in Israel. To some, it may have seemed odd. But when I was with the Nets, we'd traveled there to play some preseason games against the Suns. I loved my time there, and knew what to expect if I decided to play overseas. In order to go abroad, Leah had to rescind her legal complaint against me, which she did, knowing that I had to earn a living to help her and our child. The Allendale judge also dropped the criminal charge for the Mahwah windows. So, October 28, 1986, I signed a $60,000 contract with the Hapoel Ramat Gan, a mediocre team that wanted to compete with the big guys in Israel, including Maccabi Tel-Aviv.

And with me, now they could.

* * *

Israel is seemingly always on the brink of war in some part of the country. And when I went over there in 1986, there were consistent bombings and conflict. But it wasn't all bad. The food was tremendous and the women were beautiful. Though the first time I'd been to Israel, I kissed the ground upon returning home to the United States, now I was overjoyed to be heading back.

But there were problems. People and politicians objected to me coming to play. They'd claimed that they didn't want a drug addicted American in their league. Really, Maccabi Tel Aviv didn't want an NBA All-Star ruining its championship chances. It was always something.

What I'd heard was that Tel Aviv and FIBA, which was based in Munich, conspired to keep me from playing. Who knew exactly what reason they gave? I didn't care. I was coming there for a new chance as much as anything else. So I decided to stay in Israel for a year and try coaching. Everyone seemed okay with me doing that. Though wishing I could be on the court instead of on the sidelines, I stuck around and coached Hapoel Ramat Gan for a season, about eight months. Then, all of a sudden, just after getting comfortable and doing well on the sidelines as an assistant, I had to figure out my next move. Stay in Europe, or go back to America? In the end, I missed my kids and my country. So I went home.

Memory Lane: Scott Tesser

My father-in-law Joe Taub passed away about six years ago, and he and Michael had a very close relationship. When he passed away, I don't know how it happened, but I became very close friends with Michael. I love him. For me, though, it's a bit surreal. I grew up a Knicks fan, and my own father was a crazy Knicks fan. Michael was actually my father's favorite player. As a kid growing up, I remember watching him play for the Knicks and my father talking about him all the time. Life's funny that way.

Now, I find that my father's favorite basketball idol is a close friend of *mine*. In fact, Michael and I were playing golf one day and it was around the time my own father was very sick. We knew there wasn't a lot of time life, so I said to Michael, "Do me a favor and call my dad. We won't tell him who's on the phone. But please just get on the phone and start talking to him, okay?" My dad really wasn't well at the time, but he gets on the phone with Michael and they start talking. He didn't know who it was. Then my mother leaned in and told him.

My mom said it was like my dad just came to life for a while after that! Look, we all know that Michael went through a tough time in life. But today, he's one of the nicest guys I know. There's nothing in the world that he wouldn't do for anybody. My father-in-law Joe was a guy who grew up in Patterson, New Jersey. He never had much when he was younger, and I think he always had a fondness for guys that just kind of had a little trouble in their lives. He stuck with them. And Sugar and him just laughed and had a great time together.

Today, my family sponsors the camp in Paterson that Michael and Otis Birdsong do together. And I also sponsor the camp they do at the JCC in Tenafly. That one is for younger kids. I went there one day asked him why he did camps like this one, with such young children running around. He said he just loves it. He wants them to have fun and hopes he can do a little good for them. It's a great thing. How many ex-NBA All-Stars would spend a week with six- and seven-year-old kids, teaching them how to play basketball? But that's just Michael.

14

THE MINOR LEAGUES

THEY say "time heals all wounds," and that's largely true. But hard work goes a long way, too. With the NBA's three-strike system, a player could apply for reinstatement two years after his banishment. And now, after my time in Israel, one year had already passed. I was now thirty-one years old, but still had to figure out what to do next.

So it was time for a stint in the minor leagues. At the time that meant either the USBL or the CBA. The latter was one of the more successful minor leagues in the US, with big names like Cazzie Russell, John Drew, and "Fast" Eddie Johnson, among others. My buddy Earl Cureton, too. There is a long list of former NBA players that played in the USBL and CBA.

Now it was my turn to be a part of the USBL. I signed a contract with the Long Island Knights for the 1987 season. Our coach was former Knick Dean Meminger, and the roster included past pros like Steve Burtt, Geoff Huston, and Dexter Shouse. It also included legendary women's basketball player Nancy Lieberman, who is in the Hall of Fame today. A 5-foot-10 point guard from Brooklyn, Nancy played in the USBL for a few years and even competed against the Harlem Globetrotters with the Washington Generals. She's done everything in basketball, from coaching in the WNBA, NBA, and Big3 league to playing with the guys. People called her "Lady Magic."

To this day, me and Nancy are the best of friends. And we were roommates on the road with the Knights. All the guys tried to hit on her and I was like her big brother, swatting them away. Back then, Nancy was near the end of her playing days, but it was a triumph nevertheless for her to be on the roster. The sad thing was, though, I didn't stay with the Knights for very long. The team, which finished 13–15 that season, let me go in early June, saying I was shooting too much or something. In addition, Dean Meminger and I didn't really get along. But the club said my release had nothing to do with drugs, and that I'd passed all my tests. With one door closing I opened another and signed that same year with the USBL's Jersey Jammers, coached by Henry Bibby.

The Jammers had Tony Campbell, big Martin Nessley, and Bob McCann on the team. But the competition in the USBL wasn't like the NBA, let me just say that. The league was the last stop for many players at the end of their careers, or a place for younger guys trying to get noticed. For me, a player in the middle of his prime, it was unusual. Even so, I told myself to just put my head down and dominate. I knew that I was back at the bottom, and the only place I could go was up. In my first game with the Jammers, I remember that I scored 14 points in 35 minutes.

In the end, my time in the USBL only lasted a few months. The Knights and the Jammers, which finished 13–17 under

Coach Bibby, both made the playoffs, and both got bounced ahead of the finals. But I'd done my job well enough. I'd played, stayed clean, and showed that I could still ball. Unfortunately, the USBL was a bush league compared to the NBA. I knew I had to keep working both on myself and my game if I wanted a chance at playing at a higher level. I also knew that if I failed another drug test of any kind, my NBA ban would last forever. With that in mind, I went back to the discipline that helped me get to the top of the league and stayed away from places where I shouldn't be. I even started to go to AA meetings. Then my next basketball break came. The CBA called, and it was Bill Musselman and the Albany Patroons. It was time to make some history.

My plan all along was to come back to the NBA after my two-year ban was up. As soon as I was able to apply for reinstatement, I intended to do so. I'd had the dream of making the NBA from a young age (which I did), but now I had it all over again in my thirties.

I played well in the USBL, scoring and dishing assists while pulling down rebounds as usual, but I didn't love playing for Meminger. And all the cheap hotels and bus rides killed me. So after my stints in the USBL season, I went home and tried to repair things with Leah. It was important to me that she and I were at least on good terms, especially now as I was getting sober and was ready to be a better co-parent.

Bill Musselman had heard I was making a comeback. One thing to knew about Bill was that *all* he cared about was winning . . . and, having a roster with the best players possible helps get you wins. Naturally, he called me up. Musselman wanted to know if I was still hungry and if I still had game. I told him yes and yes, and so he invited me to come in and try out. When he saw I still had my skills intact, he gave me a contract on the spot.

In November 1987, after my brief successful tryout, I signed a new deal to play in the CBA with Albany.

I was headed to upstate New York to play with the Patroons, perhaps the most famous minor-league basketball team in history. While I wasn't in *perfect* playing shape, I could handle the CBA and knew I'd work myself into better condition as the season progressed. On the roster we had Scott Brooks, Tony Campbell, Rick Carlisle, Sidney Lowe, and Derrick Rowland. That was a great start. I was set to make about $500 a week (a large drop from my last NBA contract), and would also be subjected to weekly drug tests. All of that sounded fine to me. I just wanted to play and win . . . and that's exactly what happened.

If you want to know about Bill, he's the guy who said, "Defeat is worse than death, because you have to live with defeat." He was an intense guy with a singular eye on grinding out victories. Bill coached in the ABA with the Virginia Squires and then in the NBA with the Cleveland Cavaliers. To start the year, we went 11–0. Tony Campbell was killing it for us at shooting guard and was later called up to the Lakers, where he appeared in 13 regular-season games and 15 playoff games, winning a ring with Magic that very season. Working my way back into top-level shape, I came off the bench at first and played well, scoring and grabbing steals. Soon, Bill saw that, to get the team going, I'd have to be a starter.

Later in the season, when some of our players were called up to the NBA, I finally got my chance to start, and my play improved immediately. The biggest source of drama that year didn't come from anything on the court or anything in my personal life, it was my coach. Bill Musselman was the fire that burned brightest and hottest that season for the Patroons. When I say he was a sick man, basketball-wise, it would be an understatement. He was one of the craziest motherfuckers I ever played for! But Bill also knew basketball. And at the end of the day, he didn't care about anything but winning and I respected that. Any tension he caused was a means to an end.

Prior to the season, Bill had won three CBA championships *in a row*. He'd won the 1984–85 ring with Tampa Bay and then did it again with them the next year. Musselman earned his third CBA ring in a row in 1986–87 with the franchise, which had then relocated to Rapid City, South Dakota. Now he wanted his fourth ring in a row with us and the Patroons. And I was his key to doing so as the season progressed. We finished the season with a record of 48–6, and Bill won the CBA Coach of the Year for the second time in a row. We were first in the CBA's East Division and set for a long playoff run. We had an unbelievable team and a wild man as a coach.

During the year, we had won something like 25 games in a row when we found ourselves in Biloxi, Mississippi, playing the Jets, a squad that once boasted the likes of Craig Ehlo. But even without Ehlo, the Jets took us to triple overtime and we lost the game. Bill came into the locker room afterward and shouted, "I'm trading all you motherfuckers! You let me down!" Coach Musselman wanted to set records. He was on a mission in the CBA. Then after every game, he'd go to a bar and get drunk. His face would turn red as a tomato. The man, I'm sorry to say, suffered a stroke after coaching a Portland Trail Blazers game in 1999.

The next day in practice, after his tirade, he took the whole team aside and said, "Do you remember that shit I said yesterday at the end of the game? Well, fucking forget about it." Bill was a hilarious guy, all things considered. Sometimes he would call me piss drunk at three in the morning, complaining about something I did or didn't do on the court. And at halftime in one game, he threw a chair at the players, so I threw one his way. He told me, "Sugar, you've never won anything in your life!" And I yelled back, "Just four NBA All-Star rings!" That shut him up for a little while.

Amazingly, despite all of that, we ran through the CBA playoffs, going 12–4 and winning the championship. Even though we had dominated all season, the championship did go down the wire, with us having to pull out Games Six and Seven against the Wyoming Wildcatters. Bill got his fourth ring in a row, and we hugged after the final buzzer. We finished a with CBA record of 65–10, which still stands to this day. It was the first for the Patroons since Phil Jackson won it all with the team in 1984. Of course, not all of it was wholesome and good for us, though. Fans in the minor leagues often took shots at me from the stands. Drunk loser guys who wanted me to turn around and say something back to them. "Hey, Sugar! Just say *yes!*"

* * *

Musselman was hired the following season to coach the Minnesota Timberwolves, the newest expansion team in the NBA, for the 1988–89 season. The league is the hardest of the major sports to break into. Hockey, baseball, and football all employ rosters and coaching staffs larger than the NBA. When I played, there were less than three hundred players in the entire league. It's super selective. So when Bill got the chance to coach in the NBA again, he had to take it. Now, I had to keep going. Keep rising through the ranks and making sure my nose stayed clean, literally and figuratively. I had to stay sober. That was my top priority, along with killing guys on the court.

* * *

I recently read that the NBA took marijuana off its banned substances list, and it probably stopped testing for the drug a long time before. Why? Because a lot of the players use pot for various ailments and for recreation, too. Cannabis is legal in many states when you're at home, but it's (obviously) not legal to smoke and drive. Nor should it be legal to get high and play in an NBA game. But the reason it's off the list is because no one would be able to field an NBA team if the league made it illegal, so it's funny how time changes people's minds.

Of course, cocaine and crack are different than pot. But given all this, people ask me today if I'm angry at the NBA. The answer is that I'm not at all. I'm a little disappointed in their marijuana policy but, that aside, I'm happy with our relationship. I want the league and its workforce to thrive. I want them to learn from my example—the good and the bad of it all. We're in different times today. Socially, politically, and economically. There is so much money in the league and so much celebrity, too. These NBA guys are media talking points, athletes, and celebrities all at once. It's not an easy task for anyone.

Yet, look at LeBron James. The guy has never been in trouble. Not once. In the age of phone cameras, that's incredible. He's one of only a few billionaires in the world who can say they earned their money in the public eye. The few others are also athletes and entertainers, like Michael Jordan and Jay-Z. LeBron should win an MVP just for that. Just for keeping the league in good standing around the globe. And I hope he was able to learn at least a little bit from my story. I know LeBron is a student of the game, a historian. He knows his stuff. And that's what makes me proud about the NBA today. People like him.

* * *

After all the success with the Albany Patroons, I was now looking for a new job. The team, which was formerly coached by Phil Jackson before all his success with the Chicago Bulls, has a long history of former players and coaches who have gotten new gigs after playing for the club. Now I was hoping to be the next on the list after Musselman and his job in Minnesota.

The ace in the hole? My now-dear friend Bob Hill. The former Knicks coach had been coaching in the CBA when I was playing with Albany, and I'd roast them every time we played. So when the year was over and I'd gone back home to New Jersey to recuperate, Bob called me up.

I'd now been sober for two years and was going to AA meetings several times a week, along with being tested at least once a week. I personally wanted records of everything, so that when I applied to the NBA for reinstatement the league could see all the good I'd done. When I finally got things in order and my two-year ban was up, I sent it all to the NBA and waited. In the meantime, FIBA lifted whatever ban it had on me and Coach Hill offered me a job to play overseas. Later, he would guide the

San Antonio Spurs to big-time winning seasons. But now, he was making his way and doing so with a first-division team in Bologna, Italy.

His first call? Me, of course.

15

SUGARMANIA!

GOING to Italy to play basketball was the best decision I ever made in my professional life. Maybe my personal one, too. I'll forever be grateful to Coach Bob Hill for asking me to join his team in Bologna. Some may hear my story and wonder why I would ever go overseas to play and risk being forgotten by the NBA. But folks have to remember that the NBA wasn't what it is now. Today the league is *booming*. But when I was making All-Star teams, the league only showed one game a week on national television. While the players loved the NBA, it wasn't yet competing to be the country's national pastime.

There were good crowds in Boston and LA, but while I was a pro I remember playing games against the Nets in Piscataway at Rutgers University. Today, the Nets' home in Brooklyn is a basketball palace. But to make the league and the game what it is, a lot of us had to put in a lot of work. The same, in fact, went for leagues abroad. Before I headed to Bologna to meet Bob Hill, I went to Houston to play in a pro-am with some other big names, including Moses Malone and John Lucas. Once I got my

wind up to speed running with those guys, I hopped on a flight
to my new home.

* * *

But, before I'd left, on February 25, 1988, I'd applied for reinstatement to the NBA. After receiving my application, the league
interviewed everyone in my life, from Leah to people with the
Patroons, Jammers, and Knights. All of my records and drug
tests got reviewed. Then, on July 21, David Stern said, "On the
basis of our extensive investigation, it appears that Micheal Ray
Richardson is drug free and constructively dealing with his addiction. When a person attempts to conquer his drug addiction, no
one can be absolutely certain that he will not suffer a relapse.
However, there is no evidence of any drug use by Micheal since
his last inpatient treatment."

The commissioner added, "On the basis of all circumstances of
this case, I think it appropriate that Micheal Ray Richardson's..."
I'll pause here for the drumroll. "... be granted." *Wahoo!* With
that, I was officially part of the NBA family again. The question
was, did I want to come back? And if I did, would another team
have me? What would the Nets want as compensation? For now,
those questions were on the backburner. But my statement upon
hearing of my reinstatement was, "I'm grateful for the NBA for
giving me another opportunity to play basketball. I'm thirty-
three years old and I think I have paid my dues." With that all
now behind me, it was time for Italy.

* * *

By now, Leah and I had patched things up. I was sober and working hard—both in my personal and professional life. And so, we got back together. But leaving for another country isn't great on a marriage, especially when one person doesn't want to be there. Leah didn't want to live in Europe, instead preferring to stay home and work in the US. And that was fine with me. It was her choice. She left about a month in (and a year later, we broke up). But I was lucky in that our little daughter, Nikki, decided to live with me in Bologna and enroll in an international school. Nikki was about five years old when I played for Virtus Bologna. And to help me with taking care of her, I got a full-time nanny, who stayed with her when I went away a few times a month for road games.

It was such a benefit to my spirit to have Nikki with me during that time. I was in the process of starting my life over again—in many ways, starting with my playing career. By having my daughter with me helped the transition to a new country, language, and team. Nikki would stay with me overseas for a handful years, actually. She was about twelve when she moved back to the States but, in between, we had a grand old time. Some people might think it was hard to be a pro athlete in a foreign country as a single parent, but I'm of the mind that I'd do anything for my kids. I used to take Nikki to school in the morning and pick her up in the afternoon on my moped every day. She had her own little Barbie helmet. Her classmates treated her like a queen since she was my daughter. On weekends, we'd go shopping at the fancy Italian stores. I really think her growing up and becoming bilingual really helped her in her adult years. The international schools offered a lot of one-on-one teaching and Nikki, who would grow up to be a doctor, loved the experience. I was glad I could provide it.

BANNED

Many fans in Italy remembered me from when I visited the country in 1981 as part of a convoy of NBA stars, including Dr. J and Moses Malone, who played in a first-of-its-kind exhibition game against an Italian All-Star game in front of 12,000 fans. Now I was back to play *for* some those same fans.

What also helped was how much the city of Bologna loved its basketball. Back then, the game in Europe was really growing. A big part of that was because of the former NBA players who went overseas and to Europe, especially guys like Bob McAdoo, Spencer Haywood, and Mike D'Antoni, who played the game there at a high level and who showed the young players in the country what to do.

In 1988, I signed a contract to play in Bologna for $400,000, tax free. I also had a car and a house supplied by the team. While in some ways it felt sad to have to retreat abroad, in another way it felt like a gift. I would soon learn about the passion the fans had there. I would hear them chant, *Shooo-gaaah! Shooo-gaaahh!* It would be called "Sugarmania!" But first, I had to meet the people of Bologna. I was looking forward to seeing Bob Hill, too. The last time we'd seen each other in person, I was destroying his team in the CBA. I was also looking forward to seeing my old teammate Bob McAdoo, who I used to crush in backgammon all the time.

Coach Hill knew I could play. He knew that once the ball went up at tip, I could only do it one way. He liked that about me. I was a great competitor. That's why I was his first call when it came to setting up the roster for his new team, Virtus Bologna, also known as Knorr Bologna (for its food and beverage company sponsor). This would be both of our first year overseas in the city. But while Bob was only going to stay for a year (he would go

200

onto be an assistant in Indiana with the Pacers and then a head coach for them, San Antonio, and Seattle), I would stay for nearly fifteen more. And here, now, all we both wanted to do was win.

Each Italian team at that time was allowed two American players. The other one on my Bologna team was Clemon Johnson, a 6-foot-10 center who'd played for Portland, Indiana, Philadelphia, and Seattle over his decade-long career. He held NBA averages of about five points and five rebounds, and won a ring with Philly in 1983 with Dr. J, Moses, and Earl Cureton. But now we were teammates on Knorr. Prior to my arrival, the team hadn't won an Italian League championship since 1984. So, what did we do? We finished the first season 21–15 and won the freaking 1989 Italian League Championship Cup! How's that for a first season?

* * *

When David Stern reinstated me in 1988, I had the chance to go back to the league or remain in Europe. And at one point, the Philadelphia 76ers asked me to come play for them. The team offered me a contract after their point guard Johnny Dawkins torn his knee in the beginning of the 1990–91 season. I was thirty-four years old at the time, and it was probably my last shot to make the league again. I asked Philadelphia to give me a two-year guaranteed deal, but they wouldn't guarantee the second year. So I said thanks, but no thanks. Besides, Knorr was already paying me well for my services. Why not stay?

The guy who owned Knorr Bologna was named Gigi Porelli. The team has a long list of guys from the US over the years who've played for it, from Travis Best to Earl Boykins, Mario

Chalmers, and Orlando Woolridge. But I was one of the first. That, combined with my reputation coming to Italy, had Gigi scared when Bob Hill told him I was going to be on the '88 team. Gigi wanted me to come to Bologna early to meet him. That was fine. When Bob and I arrived in the city for the first time, we met Gigi in a hotel and I signed my contract. Gigi shook my hand and said he was looking forward to the season starting that September.

By the time I got back home, the first $50,000 had already been transferred to my account. That got me excited for the chance to play for Gigi's team. And when Bob and I went back less than a month later, we arrived two weeks before the season and hung out together and got to know one another. Gigi actually set it up, almost like a vacation before all the hard work. Then when I saw our arena for the first time, I saw the big ol' sign welcoming me to Bologna. *Welcome Home Sugar.* That was a nice touch. It felt like I *was* home. Even today, the fans treat me well. I went back to Italy for a jersey retirement ceremony in 2023, and the fans cheered me like I was a rock star.

* * *

When I arrived, the culture, fresh food (milk and veggies), women all blew me away. (I just had to make sure I had a bottle of Tabasco wherever I ate.) I wanted to learn Italian and fit in as soon as I could. So I enrolled in a school to learn the language, but only spent three days there. I couldn't absorb it how they were trying to teach it. You don't learn words off a chalkboard as a kid. You just hear them. Instead, I started to go to restaurants as often as I could just to listen to people speak. That way, you can hear people say the same thing over and over. What I really wanted was to learn the language to understand what people in the country were saying about me—if they were giving me compliments or talking trash!

* * *

At the time, the Italian professional basketball league was the best one in Europe. What was immediately clear to me was that the players could really shoot, and their fundamentals were on point. Even the big men could bomb from distance. But the Italian players weren't quick like those in the NBA. That was their biggest flaw. They were slower. Noticing that, I took advantage of their heavy feet because I was still as fast as a fox—even then! Fundamentally, I was sound, too. I could shoot, handle, pass, and everything. But mostly, I was a lot quicker than the other players, and used that to my advantage.

My first preseason game with Bologna, I scored 65 points against the Cantù team. I was staying clean and on a mission. Plus I wanted to play well for Bob Hill, who had taken a chance on me. I wasn't at all concerned with the NBA; I wasn't scoreboard watching or wondering who might need me to come in and play a role in the league. My focus was on my team in Bologna. Something I noticed early on was that all my teammates were hard workers, skilled, and in great shape (European players would soon make a big impact on the NBA). The problem was that Bologna hadn't won anything in some six years. It was time to change that.

It's not ego to say that I didn't have many—if any—bad games with Bologna. I could score 30 points easily and even managed more in some games. And after we won the Italian Cup in 1989, earning the victory in Forli (our rabid fans traveling with us to see the final game), I felt like a cult hero. Our squad was the talk of the country, which is what everyone had hoped when they raised that banner for me: *Welcome Home Sugar!* There wasn't anything else I wanted other than to stay in Italy. Winning felt great. Winning fixed a lot of problems. Sugarmania was in full effect!

* * *

Thinking about my first year in Bologna with Bob Hill, a lot of stories flood back. I enjoyed a long, rich basketball career, but it may be my time with Virtus that tops everything. I recall one time playing against the other Bologna professional team, Fortitudo, on their home court and, let me say, I had a largely (though playfully) contentious relationship with their fans because I was both so good and so outspoken. Well, in this particular game, one of their players made a nice move and dunked the ball. His team's fans went nuts, though I didn't see anything particularly special about it.

Well, our next time down, I inbounded the ball and threw it to our point guard, Roberto Brunamonti. I ran down the right side of the floor, circled underneath the basket, and came out the left side. I got the ball and hit a three—*swish*—on Fortitudo's weak zone defense. As I ran back, I turned at half court and grabbed my crotch and flipped off the fans in the stands. I can't describe how freaking crazed their fans got in that moment. It was like a confetti cannon of people burst from a lightning bolt. Bologna fans are famous for throwing things on the court, like batteries and whatever else is available, so I had to duck out of the way!

Oh, and we won the game.

In Italy, they will suspend you quick for fighting, but all I wanted to do was rile up the opposing team's fans. Give them a story to tell their neighbors the next day at work. Coach Hill could only shake his head and smirk at my antics. But it wasn't just the other team I got on top of. I remember a game when me and my teammate Mike Sylvester, who had dual American and Italian citizenship, got into a fight and were suspended. Coach liked Mike because he had experience with the American game. Though he never played in the NBA, he was drafted by the Detroit Pistons in 1974.

In our absence, some of the Italian players who came off the bench but who thought they should have been starters, began to talk some smack to us. I told them, "Y'all sure do run your mouths a lot!" Funny, coming from me, of course. "Well, now is your chance to prove you got what it takes to win without us." But we lost that game, which fell on a Sunday. Well, we had the next day off, but in practice on Tuesday we were running competitive four-on-four-on-four drills. On their own, they can lead to fights, but with all the talking around our recent loss, it definitely did. One guy on my team said something slick to me, and so I hit him in his face. He got knocked out.

Then I heard another guy running his mouth at the other end of the court, and I chased after him but he ran out through the back door! All the while Coach Hill was shouting at me to cool down, but I'd just heard enough. Besides, sometimes a team needs to get a fire under its ass. It can rally troops, not quell them. Coach Hill jumped on my back and rode me like a pony out the door as I chased after my cowardly teammate. When I calmed down, coach said he understood what I did but sent me home anyway. The next day, everything was fine and we went back on our winning ways.

* * *

There's another story that comes to mind from this era of my life. We'd gone through the regular season my first year and, ahead of the playoffs, had a bye and a week off. To keep us fresh, Coach Hill set up some exhibition games for us during that spell. But I didn't want any part of that. Instead of traveling to another Italian city to practice, I wanted to rest and stay in Bologna to boo the other hometown team while they played in their playoff game and also spend some time with Nikki. Call me petty, but it was just so much fun to get into it with fans! But Bob made me get on the bus the next morning.

However, that didn't mean I had to like it. That's why, in our away exhibition game, I dogged it in the first half, jogging up the court and hardly shooting. We were down 25 at halftime. In the locker room, coach threw an entire chalkboard in my direction and shouted my head off. His face was redder than I'd seen anyone's face get. He told me I'd lost a step and that I couldn't be the man anymore. Along with him, my teammates weren't exactly thrilled with my effort either. I nearly undressed to go home right then. But, putting my sneakers back on, I got back on the court. Guess what? I played out of my mind in the second half and brought us back.

We won that game, too! With about two minutes left, the game now in hand, coach took me out and I went to the end of the bench to take my shoes off and untape my ankles. With the sticky white tape now in my hands, I threw it at coach and it got him in the side. We laugh about that today, but it wasn't funny then. On the bus after the game, Sylvester and I got into a big fight. In the showers after the game, he'd threatened to fight me because I'd stolen his towel. Then, on the bus, as he was setting up a card game for the ride home, I took his money off the table and he lost his mind! Mike called me names and even threatened to kill me.

In response, I got a glass Gatorade bottle, smashed it on a railing, and threated him with the jagged thing. Coach Hill jumped on my back again and thankfully cooler heads prevailed. We made it home, though I didn't eat with the team that night. And while these events aren't my proudest, I know that they can also galvanize. If you can survive them, you can survive anything. In a way, I was testing our metal, looking to jumpstart the single-mindedness it takes to win. And, well, we won it all that year. I was also pretty lucky that Coach Hill really liked me. But after the year, Bob went back to the NBA while I stayed in Italy.

* * *

After our year together, I wished Bob well. He and his family went back to the United States, and he built quite the coaching resume for himself, winning 121 games in two full years with the Spurs, and also coaching stars like Reggie Miller, David Robinson, Ray Allen, and numerous others. But I was more than happy to stay where I was; to see what year two would have for me. And beyond. The Bologna coach for my second year was the thirty-year-old Italian Ettore Messina. For an encore, our team went 22–13 for the 1989–90 season. Well, we won yet *another* Italian Cup. We also won the FIBA European Cup, beating Real Madrid 79–74, coached by the up-and-coming George Karl.

If I remember correctly, I had about 30 points and 10 rebounds in that contest, which was held in Florence. But it wasn't all that easy. Our point guard had twisted his ankle pretty bad early in the game, and so I knew I would have to pick up the slack. Keeping our momentum, I went off from the jump, right as the team needed me to. I wanted to win badly and prove that my presence in the country was worth the hoopla—which is exactly what I did. When we won, the fans rushed the court and picked me up over their heads, tossing me around from outstretched hand to outstretched hand. The love Bologna had for me was unbelievable, incredible.

Our team was now on the map in a major way. In Italy, if you win, they'll celebrate you until their voices go hoarse. You can play forever if you keep on winning. For me, it was easier in the Italian leagues—not because the competition was so poor, because it wasn't. I felt the league was better than the NCAA even, to be sure. But the thing is, the teams only play one or two games a week. That's the secret. In the NBA, it can be three or four or even five games per week. That allowed me much more time to recover. I also had more time to travel and see the sights with my daughter. And when I did, people would stop me in the streets, "Shoo-gah! Hello! Basketball!"

Sometimes, though, during the games, the crowds would get rowdy. As I previously mentioned, they would even throw bottles. They'd yell and get red in the face like they had too much wine. It was intense. But it wasn't anything I couldn't handle. I was just happy to be there. That's the thing; when you get so low in life and begin to finally bounce back, you're grateful for what you have. It's humbling for the world to know your failures, but it brings a sense of calm and appreciation later. After all, everything is a balancing act. And after my success in Italy, I knew I wanted to stay. I knew I would never play another game in the NBA again, and I was totally comfortable with that.

The one thing I want people to know, though, is that I wasn't banned from the NBA *for life*. At least, not in the long run. I was reinstated. And the 76ers did reach out to me (even if they denied it in the press). I could have come back. Philly's owner, Harold Katz, and general manager, Gene Shue, offered me $800,000 to come and play for the season when Johnny Dawkins went down. It was my choice to decline. Not David Stern's. Yes, I'd broken the rules. Yes, I'd gotten my three strikes. And yes, I'd been punished. But while I was the first player ever to be banned from the NBA for drugs, I was now its first to be reinstated. It's important to me that people know that.

When you're on drugs, you can't feel or know what you've lost, what you've given up for the sake of the narcotic. And when I woke up from years of mistakes, I realized I'd lost the thing that I loved the most: playing the game of basketball. Life had given me chance after chance to stop, and I just never did. Over and over. It took hitting rock bottom, getting my life as an NBA player taken away (and rightfully so). I'd taken my life to the limit. You can't really play out your future at any given point. That's what I've learned. You just have to take each step as it comes, and hope you do the right thing along the way. Hope you make the right choices. Now, I finally had.

* * *

In my third year with Bologna, we finished 22–14 on the season. We lost in the quarterfinals of the Italian Cup playoffs and the quarterfinals later of the FIBA Cup, too. But it was still a good year. Sadly, me and Coach Ettore didn't see eye to eye, so I left the team. I'd loved my three years in Bologna— the year before, I'd set the Italian All-Star Game scoring mark with 50—and I hoped I'd be back. The people treated me like a king, and I couldn't have been more grateful. And the food! Yes, I was a little older now, but I was still fast on the court. I could get to the rim, dish, and score. I still had my quick hands, too.

However, it was time for a new challenge. After three great years with Virtus Bologna, I decided to sign with KK Split in Croatia.

People could especially see how quick my hands moved as I gesticulated on the court. And during the occasional in-game scuffle, too. When I play, my lips and hands get going and I can't stop them until the buzzer sounds. The fans loved me for it. My opponents, not so much. I remember Lakers great Michael Cooper told me that he got so sick of my trash talking every game. Plus, Cooper said the referees in Italy protected me. "We couldn't touch you!" he said. I just told him, "Hey, that's just what I earned in Bologna, Coop!" Now I was leaving. But I'd done well. I didn't have any drug mishaps. Really, it was a complete success.

Memory Lane: Bob Hill

Michael Ray Richardson got caught up with some wrong people and got kicked out of the NBA. But he was a four-time All-Star and was heading for a great career. David Stern just felt it necessary to kick him out and keep him out. So when I decided to take a head coaching job over in Bologna, Italy, I went after him. I knew Michael then, but not very well. Even so, I knew him well enough as a person to bring him over and to know he had just made a mistake.

When I got the job to coach the team in Bologna, I wanted to bring over an American who was dynamic, athletic, and had a heavy background and reputation. But when I brought up Michael's name, the Italians over there got nervous right away. They weren't sure it was a good idea because of his past. But I told them I didn't care what they thought and that I was going to sign him. And that he was coming.

He jumped all over the chance to play in Italy. At the end of the day, we became very close. I'm like his white dad and he's like my Black son. We're as close as we can be. In Bologna, he played great for me. He was awesome in the Italian league. We always played on Sundays, and he'd come over to our house every Sunday morning and my wife would make him an American breakfast. There are just a lot of little stories and tidbits like that, which brought us close together.

Because of his past, the guys in Italy didn't think that he was going to show up after he signed. That's why they insisted we come over two weeks early and go to the Italian Riviera. Well, they took care of us on the vacation, and Michael and I got ever closer after that. To be honest, I never knew the side of Michael that got involved with drugs. The Michael that

I know was a committed player who wanted to win. And that's what he did over there in Italy.

If he didn't think one of his teammates was practicing or playing hard enough, he would tell them. He wouldn't hesitate. The things he wanted to do on the basketball court, I wanted them to do, too, so I always had his back. Michael won a lot of games overseas. In Bologna, where we played, there were two professional teams. So, you can imagine the rivalry was pretty big. And Michael would get after the other team's fans. Ha! They didn't like him!

It wasn't an honest hatred, of course. It was more, "I'm going to show you! We're going to beat you!" He loved to go to the other team's games. If they were playing and we were off, Michael would go and sit in their stands and piss their fans off. To be honest, there wasn't much I didn't like about Michael Ray. And, by the end of the season, once we'd finished, there wasn't anything I didn't like about him.

Soon, the people in Italy learned to appreciate him. Not just because of his talent. It was his willingness and desire to win. Whatever it took. Whether that meant getting a rebound, a steal, a blocked shot, a bucket, a free throw. He was willing to do it. Willing to accept all the responsibility of that the team. The authentic basketball fans grew a deep appreciation for what Michael stood for at the end of that year in Italy.

Early in my NBA head coaching career, there was only one European player, Šarūnas Marčiulionis. And he could really play. But you take a look at the rosters today and see that there are many European players impacting the game now. Today, Nikola Jokić is the best player in basketball. We've come a *long* way, and a lot of people had a lot to do with it, including Michael Ray Richardson. He showed Italy what the NBA was all about.

16

TOURING EUROPE

THERE was a rumor that I'd failed a drug test in Italy, leading the NBA's Gary Bettman (now commissioner of the NHL) to say that if it was true, I would not be allowed back in the league. Of course it wasn't. It was just nasty rumors likely made up by Coach Ettore Messina, whom I didn't get along with, so he wouldn't have to keep me on the team. In truth, I'd passed every drug test I'd been given. People just love to talk bad about others, but so often they get it wrong. Something that didn't change, though, was the fans' support. They all wore Sugarmania T-shirts, hats, and held up signs for me wherever I went in the country. Even if my old coach was an ass, I knew the fans would always support me.

With the positive test rumors, and after three years in Bologna, I signed with KK Split in Croatia. The problem was, at the time, the country was in turmoil. Even getting there was difficult. If Israel had seemingly always been on the brink of war when I was there, then Croatia was even worse. The team had been successful of late, but now the country was *at war* when I got there in 1991–92. The country had declared independence from Yugoslavia, and the troops were called. Bombs, guns, artillery. It was so bad that by the time I got there, KK Split didn't even play in its normal Croatian League. It was too dangerous. Instead, we played in the European league.

The team lived in a hotel in La Llacuna, Spain, just outside Barcelona, some one thousand miles from Croatia. We played around one game a week. During the Christmas holiday, though, some of the Croatian players wanted to go back home to see their families, and took that opportunity to go back to Italy. Not long after, KK Split's coach, a Yugoslavian guy whose name I no longer remember, wanted me to fly into Croatia and practice with the team. I had no concept of what war was like, so I agreed. I took a car from Bologna to Trieste, Italy. Then I took a speed boat from there to Croatia to meet the squad.

When I got there, I saw the country was a mess. Refugees were sleeping on the floor of my hotel lobby. At midnight, the whole city was pitch black. I stayed for three days and then got my ass out of there. Before I left, though, I practiced with the team a few times. During one, an alarm went off. One of those sirens saying a bomb might be dropped at any moment. We were in the gym shooting and all the players took off running. I kept shooting, not knowing what was happening. The guys yelled to me, "Come on, man! Come on, man!" So I followed them and we huddled in a little room for nearly an hour, waiting to see what would happen. This was on my third day.

On another occasion, during my three days in the country, I remember being at a restaurant when soldiers came in and casually put AKs at rest on the floor, on their tables. They put smaller explosives on their laps. I was paranoid as all hell. I didn't have a clue what was going on. Or if I'd be a target somehow.

I quickly realized that I had no business being there. It just wasn't safe. I told the coach I would meet him back in Spain, that I wasn't staying in Croatia another night. Luckily, I caught another speed boat back to Trieste, and from there got my butt back to Bologna. Then I caught a flight to Spain. It was an unbelievable few days.

The country itself was beautiful—blue sky, clear waters. It was sad to see the people destroy it with their weapons. I wish I could have had a different experience there. The country is known for having some great basketball players, including Toni Kukoč, Dražen Petrović, and Dino Radja, all of whom had played for KK Split and won big. But I was never able to play with them. Later, I heard KK Split won a Croatian Cup, but I wasn't there for that. Instead, I was there when we played teams from Germany, Spain, Italy, and Russia. We had a fine year, dealing with all that was going on. But when the season was over, I went back to Italy.

The biggest highlight of my year in Croatia, though, was when KK Split got to play Bologna. Boy, did I want to stick it to my old coach, along with the team's head man, Alessandro Mancaruso. We played the game at a neutral site in Spain, and I ended up winning the game for us with two free throws. Afterward, I went back into the locker room and came back out with a big fake nose on, making fun of Mancaruso, who had a big ol' schnoz. He'd liked the news about me failing a drug test and I wanted to embarrass him, as if to say he was Pinocchio with that big honker. In the end, I wasn't long for Croatia, but I *loved* beating Bologna.

* * *

With Croatia in my rear-view mirror, it was time to return to Italy—this time with Livorno. Located in Tuscany, which was about two hours south of Bologna, I played there for the 1992–93 and 1993–94 seasons. I couldn't go back to Bologna because of the rumored failed drug test, which was never true in the first place. No one, not even Mancaruso, has presented evidence—to this day—of any failed tests of mine in Europe, despite the rumors. So, fuck them. But Livorno was on Italy's northwestern coastline. The ocean comes right up on the beaches. It was a beautiful place. While the team was never especially good during my time there, I did enjoy another highlight game against Bologna.

This time it was *in* Bologna, shortly after Christmastime. And what did I do for an encore? We beat the favored Bologna team on the back of my 30 points, part of a nice winning streak for us during which we beat a handful of the top teams in a row. While management had tried to forget me, the fans hadn't. They chanted "Shoooo-ggaaa!" the entire game. It was Sugarmania all over again. I still smile at that one. Playing in Livorno was fun, and life was easy. Though I was getting a bit older, I still knew how to play the game and was adapting my style to my body. Maybe I was slower than I had been, but I was still quick compared to most of my opponents. I knew how to box out, keep my dribble, and in turn my shot also improved.

The Livorno team didn't do anything particularly special in my two years there. So it was time for something new. I was looking for another job in Italy, and I'd just gotten off the phone with a team in Trieste when I got another call from my former college teammate, Lee Johnson, who was now the general manager of the French team in Antibes, the Olympique Sharks. Lee had played in the NBA for about a dozen games for Houston and Detroit. Now, like me, he was in Europe. Lee asked if I wanted to come to France to play for him. I told him about my phone call with Trieste, and he said into the phone, "Don't move. We need you. I'm coming to get you."

He told me not to sign with anyone. Instead, he got in his car and drove six hours from France to Italy and picked me up. He knew that if he didn't come down and intervene, I would have signed with Trieste and he would have lost me. We arrived back in Antibes around 2 a.m. I got an offer from Trieste at 9 a.m. but, because of Lee's efforts, I decided to sign in France. I liked the idea of a new challenge in a new country. Lee was offering a little bit more money, too. (Euro teams sometimes even offered more money than the NBA!) So I put my name on the dotted line. I was happy to see, too, that the Antibes team was solid. Lee was a good general manager and had set the team up for success.

He'd brought me into the fold in 1994 to replace David Rivers, who wasn't getting the job done. A former point guard at Notre Dame, David had also played in the league for a few years. With him out the door and me incoming, Lee was excited about the upcoming season—and he was right to be enthusiastic. Just like my first year in Bologna, for my first season in France we won the LNB Pro A, the top-tier French league championship. We had the best record for the year, finishing 21–5, and defeated Pau-Orthez in the finals, three games to one. I stayed with Lee and Antibes for two more seasons and, while we didn't win another championship, the time was a blast.

I enjoyed learning French and about the culture there, too. Again, the food and women were amazing. Everywhere I went! Around this time, I also became an investor in a restaurant in Juan-Les-Pins, a small town in the French Riviera not far from Antibes and a few hours from Cannes. The whole region was right on the water, just beautiful. And the restaurant, Le Mardrian, was a hot spot on the weekends. The owner, a guy named Richard, wanted to bring some star power to the place, so he got me to invest. Athletes also hung out there after games, which definitely helped bring people in to eat. They sold lobster, fish, lamb chops, and even pizza. But while I'd enjoyed my time in Antibes, it was once again time to move again.

* * *

For the 1997–98 season, I decided to stay in France, signing with Cholet Basket. The team was on the other side of the country, about a ten-hour drive northwest from Antibes. But just ahead of the season, the NBA came to France. Today they are maybe the second-best basketball country outside of the US (even playing the US in the gold medal game of the Olympics). It's an historical powerhouse thanks to players like Victor Wembanyama, Nicolas Batum, and Tony Parker. In 1997, the league helped put on the McDonald's Open in Paris, which featured the Chicago Bulls. At the peak of their fame. Michael, Scottie, Dennis, Phil, and the whole circus.

Anyone who has seen the documentary about Jordan, *The Last Dance*, knows about the Bulls' visit to the city. MJ in a black beret. It was the preseason before the team was set to make its final championship run. Now they were spreading basketball goodwill in Paris. I was on hand for the spectacle, as was David Stern. Fate is funny. This turned out to be one of the most important moments of my life. I was now forty-two years old, and I'd spent the past decade or so getting my life back together in Europe. And here was the NBA coming overseas to where I was. It was a giant to-do.

The guys who played against Jordan were asking him for his armbands and autographs after the game. At this time, MJ was the most famous person on Earth. But at halftime of the game, I went up to Stern and we hugged. I sat next to him there in the stands and I told him that he'd saved my life. With that, David's face lit up. I think he was scared I'd be angry, hateful, or cause a ruckus. But I told him how I honestly felt. That I could have been dead in a gutter somewhere if he hadn't given me my ultimate wake-up call. I didn't know it at the moment, but me telling Stern that would be the start of a beautiful friendship.

* * *

The season in Cholet couldn't live up to my moment with Stern. It was a fine time playing for the team, but after the year, I was on to new surroundings. As time went on, despite regular trips home during the offseason for a few weeks, most often to see mother back in Denver, I began to feel less American and, in a way, more European. There wasn't any of the racial prejudice I knew in the US here overseas—at least, I never felt it. Everywhere I went I had fans screaming for me. They all loved basketball and they all loved me! By now my personal life was up and changing, too. Leah and I were officially divorced, and I'd met someone new, a French woman, Ilham Ngadi, with whom I child with. A little boy we named Michael.

We didn't know it then, but Michael would grow up to be a big-time pro soccer player. Today he's playing on the world stage. Yes, life was going well, but it was time for another move. With the 1998–99 season coming up, my next team would be Montana Forli. The pay was good, especially for a forty-three-year-old. I was twice as old as my youngest teammate on the squad, too. I have to laugh at that; playing with guys who could be my kids. One of my teammates in Forli was a guy named Rodney Monroe. He was thirteen years younger than me, but he could hoop. He played a year in the NBA for the Atlanta Hawks in 1991–92, appearing in 38 games.

Even though I was one of the older players in the league, I was still doing well, notching 33 points in one game, 30 in another, and 27 in a third. Around this time, the famed basketball writer Scoop Jackson interviewed me for *Slam* magazine. And I told Scoop, "The show is still goin' on, it's just a little slower." After Forli, I played another season for my old team in Livorno. It was around this time that comedian Chris Rock made a documentary about me with the TV channel TNT. Rock, with his raspy recognizable voice, talked about watching me play with the Knicks and Nets.

In the doc, Rock said I was one of the most exciting players he'd ever seen. The whole thing followed me and my career, in all of its ups and downs to that point, up to showing me overseas. It made me happy that I could tell the world about my new life and my continuing professional career.

And continue it I did.

For the 2001 season, I made it back to Antibes for another year. Then next up in 2002, I thought about playing a final season as a professional with AC Golfe-Juan-Vallauris, but financially it didn't quite work out. With that, I officially retired at forty-six years of age. Take *that*, Tom Brady! I even earned dual-Italian-American citizenship for my time in Europe.

For someone who was banned from the NBA because of drugs, you know what? Today I wake up and throw kisses to the sky, counting my blessings. Here I was, sixteen years later, still playing until forty-six. How could I be mad? I was no saint, but I was no devil, either. And aside for a few extra losses on the Nets, I didn't hurt anyone but myself. My only regret was not becoming the oldest professional basketball player ever in Europe. That honor went to Ron Anderson Sr., who played in the NBA until 1994 and later went overseas, playing in France and retiring at the age of fifty-two. Even his son later played the game in France.

* * *

Everyone always points to the "Dream Team" in 1992 for the expansion of basketball abroad. But that team—with Michael Jordan, Larry Bird, Magic, Charles Barkley, and the rest of the stars—they had to play somebody in those games. How did those players—born in Croatia, Italy, France, and everywhere else—learn the game? Well, part of that education came thanks to guys like me, Bob McAdoo, Spencer Haywood, Earl Cureton, and others. We went overseas in the eighties and taught the young up-and-comers how to navigate pick-and-rolls, how to shoot off the dribble, how to play with faster, more experienced guys. We showed them what the NBA was all about. The sport grew.

I'm proud of that. But I got a lot back in return from Europe, too. It was an unbelievable experience living over there. It gave me an understanding of how other people in the world lived and that life doesn't have to be the "American Way" all the time. Things can be freer, more relaxed. We can take a siesta or two and the world won't come crashing down. We can play two games a week instead of four or five. It's okay. In the summers in Europe, whether you're rich or poor, everyone takes a vacation. In America, people get a week or two at most. In Europe, I'd see people in their seventies and eighties riding bicycles, eating fresh foods. I loved it.

While I wish I didn't have to leave the NBA under the circumstances that I created, I also know that I never would have seen the world in the way that I did if it wasn't for how things turned out. It's strange to say, but there were major silver linings. That's why I always come back to the idea that God has a plan for us all. He doesn't give us things we can't handle. And our stories are written before we take our first step. I believe that, feel that deeply. All of what happened to me was part of a plan—for better and for worse. It just somehow makes sense to me that way. I can't explain it any other way. You go through things to become a better person. A different person.

* * *

When I retired, I was making about $10,000 a month. I could have played another year or two, but I started getting wind that my salary was going to be cut to about half. That's when I decided to take myself and my career in a new direction yet again. I declined the idea of playing another year. Hell, I wasn't no spring chicken. I could still hoop, but it was getting harder and, toward the end of my career, I was playing small forward more frequently now. So I called it quits. That's when my friendship with David Stern provided me with a new opportunity. The commissioner got me a job working for the NBA's regional office in Paris, France.

Living in the City of Lights, I would fly around to different countries and be an ambassador of the game. Part of my job was to hold basketball clinics for kids in places like Germany, France, Italy, and elsewhere. My reputation was still so big abroad that Stern knew I could help get the next generation of young athletes excited about basketball and the game, so he put me to work. I kept that job for two years and it was great. At that time, I also worked in partnership with one of the biggest sports agents in Italy, Luciano Capicchioni. He was a tough guy with a weathered face, but he was well known.

But soon my time overseas would come to an end. Yes, I was lucky. In my career, I never had any major injuries, no surgeries. I'd made a name for myself in the NBA and all over Europe. I'd played the game I loved well into my forties and proved I could beat the demons that hindered my game in the US. I did it all on the court as a player, knocking off champions, becoming an All-Star and a Comeback Player of the Year. It was time for something new. And while I didn't quite yet know what that was, I knew it would be something in the game of basketball. Thanks to David Stern, I got another assignment.

Memory Lane: Earl Cureton

My first encounter with Sugar was in New York. He and Ray Williams were the backcourt for the Knicks, and I thought they were one of the best I'd seen my rookie year in Philadelphia. They had so much size and strength and bulk. Every game we played against them, we would be down at halftime because of their explosiveness (though we would try to overpower them in the end). And Sugar was just incredible. Add Ray to that and we had a lot of good duels on the court. That always stood out to me.

I didn't get a chance to really know Michael Ray until we were both out of the league. But when I was with Detroit, we played a playoff series against him and the Nets. I was really close to one of his teammates in New Jersey, Darryl Dawkins, back from my Philly days. And I knew they were close friends. So, I *heard* a lot more about Sugar than I experienced firsthand early on. But to me, he's one of the best big point guards. A lot of people referred to him as "East Coast Magic." He could handle, distribute, and he and Magic even had the same college coach.

When the news about the drugs came out, well, there were a lot of stories going around. A lot of people were pulling for Sugar to get through because he was such a good guy. It seemed like he would be clean for a while and then, all of a sudden, he'd binge and fall off track. A lot of people were rooting for him to get himself straightened out. We all knew what kind of talent he could be. I always thought he'd get over those problems. I was one of those people pulling for him back then.

Later in his career, when he went overseas, Sugar pretty much took the NBA with him to Italy. He was that good, playing there until he was about forty-seven years old. I played in Italy in 1989–90, and when I went over to visit him, I remember he was talking about Oscar Schmidt, the so-called best player to never play in the NBA. Sugar told me all night before the game that he was going to destroy Oscar. Sure enough, Sugar locked him up at both ends of the floor. In Bologna, I'd see Michael's name written all over the walls. He told me, "There's Sugarmania here, t-too!"

Sugar always speaks his mind. Even through his stutter— Darryl used to call him "Stutter" Ray! But Michael is the kind of guy who gets his point across, one way or another. Over the years, I got to know him well, and I've only grown fonder of him. He's one of the best people I've ever met. Michael is truthful and straightforward. He knows he made mistakes and is not ashamed to talk about them. Today, people mention his issues, but they forget to say how good he was on the court. Sugar had a sickness. But if wasn't for that, his story would be very different.

17

I'M STILL HERE

I HAVE made many homes in cities and towns throughout my career, and one of them has been in Denver, Colorado. Knowing that, my friend David Stern helped me get a job with the hometown Denver Nuggets after I'd retired from playing ball in Europe. Prior to every season while I was overseas, Stern and I would talk, just catching up. I would update him on where I was in my life, and he'd tell me how he was doing. We built a relationship where many might not have predicted or, if they were in our shoes, been able to. I was grateful for and proud of my friendship with Stern, who always asked if I needed anything.

So when I got back to the US, the commissioner helped me get a new job. When a player hangs up his sneakers, there is always a wonder of what's next. Basketball is often all we know, so it helps to try and stick around the game and use your expertise. That's what I wanted to do. More than anything, I wanted to coach. I thought I knew a lot about the game and how to win and wanted to impart that knowledge onto younger players. But it can be hard to break into the coaching ranks. There are few jobs and lots of politics. But Stern helped me get in the door with a team in 2003.

What he was able to do was get me into an organization. While Denver's coaching staff was stocked with names like Doug Moe, Scotty Brooks, Michael Cooper, Adrian Dantley, and others, Stern helped me get a job with the team as a community ambassador. Knowing I was from Denver, and that I knew the area, it was a win-win. Stern called Denver's GM, Kiki Vandeweghe, and Kiki hired me for the team's community relations team. I knew Kiki from our playing days (he had been a two-time All-Star with the Nuggets), and we'd also talked when he was visiting Bologna when I was there.

As a community ambassador for Denver, I held run camps for kids, represented the team at various functions, and met and chatted with season ticket holders. I helped fundraise for local charities and conducted anti-drug lectures, too. Putting me in this role was especially powerful, I thought, because to many I was the poster child for drug abuse and failure. Now, after finding my redemption, I was the poster child for overcoming addiction. It was a rewarding job and something I could have done for many years. But my heart continued to pine for coaching. I wanted to give it a shot, either as an assistant or a head guy somewhere.

* * *

Around this time, in early 2005, my old friend Isiah Thomas invited me to speak with his New York Knicks team. Thomas, who used to own the entire CBA, was now the team president of the Knicks after coaching the Indiana Pacers. I was conducting a basketball clinic and he asked me to come in and talk to the team, which included the likes of Vin Baker, Jamal Crawford, Penny Hardaway, Allan Houston, and Stephon Marbury. I talked with them about attitude and mentality, explaining how winning and losing can be contagious. The team wasn't playing great that year, having just lost 18 of 21 games, and needed a spark.

But talking to the team got *my* fires going, too. It made me want to be in that environment more and more. I'd been clean for about fifteen years and was ready to prove to the league I wasn't the same person I was when I'd left it. But a bad reputation can be hard to shake. When I talked to the Knicks, I talked to them about how losing leads to more losing. And I knew in my heart that I could bring wins to a group like them. I told the *New York Times*, "There's always a way that you can come out of this thing." Penny, another big guard, said to the paper, "He's been through the losing, he's been through the bad media, he's been through everything." Yup.

* * *

After asking around and talking to people I knew in the league, getting a coaching job in the NBA seemed like a pipe dream. So I began to look elsewhere. When I was banned from the league in the late eighties, I found new places to play. Now, I looked in some of those same places for a coaching job. That's when one of my old teams, the Albany Patroons, entered the picture. After Isiah Thomas's CBA ownership experiment failed, the league went under in 2001. He had hoped for it to become the official NBA developmental league. But that turned out to be the G League.

In 2005, though, the CBA was back and so was one of its signature teams, the Albany Patroons. Yes, on December 14, 2004, just ahead of the new season, I was named head coach of the Patroons, my former team that I'd won a championship with under coach Bill Musselman. Now I was a CBA coach (living in another snowy city!). The team's president, Jim Coyne, had hired me. As a former player and trophy winner, my name was good publicity for the team. But while my well-publicized career scared some people in the NBA, it didn't scare off Coyne. Why? Because he'd been there, too. Coyne had his own downfall, of sorts.

In 1992, Coyne was working for Albany County when he was convicted of bribery, conspiracy, extortion, and mail fraud. He'd accepted a $30,000 bribe from an architect for a job, and went to prison as a result. Coyne said that while in jail he'd seen a lot of ruined lives and people who had lost hope and their futures. With that life experience, he had sympathy for me. He'd seen a newspaper article about me that said I wanted to get into coaching, so he'd reached out and soon made me the next in a long line of Patroons head coaches that included Phil Jackson. Now, though, the league was quite different.

As I soon found out, the CBA wasn't nearly as popular as it had been when I was playing. Even then, it wasn't no great shakes. But now, it was held together with chewing gum and duct tape. Since it was the 2000s, the NBA was more readily available on television. Because of this, people weren't going to CBA games nearly as much and attendance was way down. Also, the reputation of the league suffered in the wake of Isiah's controversial stewardship. But I made my fair share of headlines. Even surprising some of my old friends, including Otis Birdsong, who was shocked I'd taken a job as a coach (since I got into so many shouting matches with my past ones!).

* * *

In my first year with the Albany Patroons, we went 20–28, finishing in third place in the Eastern Conference. We snuck into the playoffs, but lost in the first round. I was loud on the sidelines, waving my hands, barking at refs, shouting at my players. It was quite the display. I got more technical fouls than I should have. And sometimes I wouldn't shake the opposing coach's hand. I gave my team a simple playbook, stressed practice, and we did better than anyone expected. But it would be even better next season.

My lead assistant with the Patroons was Derrick Rowland, who was also the Patroons' career scoring leader. Rowland was also one of my former teammates on the Patroons when I was playing for the team. We'd gone 65–10 together, and I knew that Rowland was a good guy and a hard worker. As for me, I was like a young Bill Musselman on the sidelines. Loud, energetic, and I only cared about winning. Watching Bill, I'd learned a few things. Number one, you have to have good players. Number two, you have to have their respect.

In my first year with Albany, we had all young guys and I learned during the season that plan just wasn't going to work. Young guys don't like to listen. You need vets to win. In the CBA, you were allowed nine roster moves per year. I used all nine in the first month. I had to get rid of my young guys! The game of basketball is a simple one. It's the coaches and the players that make it difficult on themselves by not doing the right thing. Human error and all that. As a coach, I tried to keep it simple for everyone. I'd learned that in Jersey under Stan Albeck.

* * *

With my French wife still in Europe, the 2006–07 season would prove to be another strange one for me. I was encouraged by what we had done the year prior. The team gelled at times, and I was confident we could play better and go farther in the playoffs. And I was right—well, up until a point. In the CBA, I wanted to continue to show my skills as a coach so that I could maybe get a job in the NBA like former CBA coaches Phil Jackson, George Karl, or Bill Musselman had, or perhaps get one overseas. But both were proving difficult. Instead of letting those distractions get to me, I threw myself into the Albany team.

As it turned out, I did a pretty darn good job. I recruited a new roster, and I understood my players. I knew the pressures and what it took for them to succeed. One of my guys, Jamario Moon, even signed an NBA contract later with the Toronto Raptors. I was like Coach Prime even before Deion Sanders! All of my energy and efforts proved positive until the day it fell apart.

We finished the season first in the American Eastern division and were heading for the playoffs once again. We won our bracket, the American Conference championship, and advanced all the way to the CBA Finals. I could smell the championship.

In the best-of-five finals, we matched up against the Pacific Northwest's Yakima Sun Kings. And in the first game, I started a shitstorm—though not on purpose.

In that game, we lost at home in Albany's Washington Avenue Armory Arena. But the day after that opening loss, I found out

I'd been suspended for the rest of the championship series. In the closing minutes of the first game, fans began to heckle me. I was used to it for the most part by now, but sometimes the camel's back gets broken by a single straw. And though I shouldn't have let it happen and though I regret it today, I shouted an anti-gay slur at some heckling fans.

To this day, I know I shouldn't have done that. And after the game, things only got worse, though not at all intentionally, when the *Albany Times Union* published an interview with me in which I said that Jewish people are "crafty [because] they are hated worldwide." With that one-two punch, Coyne suspended me for the rest of the season and the Patroons lost the next two games of the finals. The Sun Kings took home what should have been our championship, their second in a row. But if I hadn't said what I'd said, we could have taken it back to Albany. After the championship, I left the Patroons, replaced by Vincent Askew.

* * *

Even though I enjoyed learning the coaching ropes in the CBA, I had plenty of issues in Albany. It was unfortunate. Coyne brought me in, said he wanted to help me, knew what I could do, but then undercut me left and right. Maybe I wasn't the person he *thought* I was, but I was winning. I was getting interviewed by the *New York Times* about how well me and the team were doing my second season. Still, though, he fought me on roster moves and didn't excuse me when I needed to take a few days off to do an event with the NBA (the league he knew I wanted to get back into). Of course, I left anyway and did what I needed to do.

I didn't help my case all the time, though. At one point, I even kicked Coyne's wife out of Patroons practice. She was babying the players, and I didn't want her around anymore. Jim and his wife were too close to the players. They were missing the forest for the trees. And it caused Jim and I to have a falling out. It came to a head when I wanted to trade one of our guys, this 6-foot-10 guy who wasn't getting any rebounds and wasn't playing well. I told Jim I wanted to deal him, but Jim wanted to keep him around. He said he was good for the community. The community? *Winning is good for the community*, I thought.

So when Jim and his wife went on vacation, I traded the big guy and got who I wanted back, a 6-foot-7 beast named Marvin Phillips, who could jump out the gym, rebound, and defend his ass off. Marvin was so good that I would bring him to two other teams I'd coach later in life. Jim wasn't happy about that. But part of my recovery at the time was to tell the truth, even if it was difficult. So that's what I did, and it sure got me into trouble. I didn't think Coyne would fire me since I was doing so well, the team was winning, and butts were in the seats. But that's when I shot myself in the foot.

To this day, I know I shouldn't have yelled the anti-gay slur into the stands. That just was stupid. I wasn't thinking. But what I said about Jewish people wasn't a slur. Throughout my life, I have had many close Jewish friends, including David Stern. And I have a child with a Jewish woman, too, Leah, who was raising our Tamara in the faith. I also lived in Israel for a year and had first-hand experience of the country. After the first game of the finals, Coyne didn't reprimand me. He told reporters I should have known better. But when pressure intensified, he acted.

I got myself into more hot water in that interview with the *Times Union*. We'd talked about my contract negotiations, and I said I wasn't worried because "I've got big-time lawyers. I've got big time Jew lawyers." People immediately said that I was a racist. The Anti-Defamation League issued a response, saying I was wrong. Realizing what had happened, I sent out a response, too. Coyne suspended me. Thankfully, some of my closest friends came to my defense. I even filed a lawsuit for defamation, which was later dropped. David Stern said that a suspension for my "inappropriate and insensitive" anti-gay slur was worthy. And he was right. (And just to be clear: I don't have anything against anyone's lifestyle.)

And as for the so-called racist comments about Jewish people, Stern said, "I have no doubt that Michael Ray is not antisemitic. I know that he's not." Writer Christopher Isenberg from the *Village Voice* looked at what I said and understood what I'd intended to mean. That I was in fact praising Jewish people, even if I didn't deliver it eloquently. Author Ze'ev Chafets said I was being complementary. My old friend Peter Vecsey defended me, too. I was so grateful for each of them. The thing was, at the time, I didn't understand how what I'd said had rubbed people the wrong way. It felt like I had said the equivalent of "the NBA is made up of Black people."

It's a *stereotype*, yes. But was it *hateful?* No. As I look back on all of this with a few decades distance, though, I realize I could have been clearer with my praise. In the end, my contract with the Patroons wasn't renewed and I was let go. The team also accused me of conducting contract negotiations with other teams. I wasn't doing that—not seriously. But even if I had, lots of coaches do that, especially in the CBA. The idea that people aren't trying to find the best deals for themselves in a minor league is silly. After all, the team clearly didn't even want me around, so I was glad to say goodbye. I'd wanted things to end better there. But *C'est la vie!*

* * *

Two weeks after I left the Albany Patroons, the CBA board of directors cleared my name of any wrongdoing. Now I was officially free to keep coaching in the league, even if I wasn't totally comfortable there anymore. But I had to keep going.

I got a job next with the Oklahoma Cavalry, which was returning to the city since winning the 1997 title. Located in Lawton, a town I would call home for many more years, I was ready to be the head guy in the Dust Bowl minor leagues. My first call was to my old buddy Otis Birdsong, who had been the president and GM of the Arkansas RimRockers. Otis saw how serious I was and came onboard. Time to kick some butt.

Memory Lane: Michael Amir Richardson

My father is my example, we share the same passion for high-level sports. We have the same mentality and, despite the distance, we stay in touch everyday thanks to FaceTime. When I was little, I used to go to the United States with him to basketball camps, and as soon as he can, he tries to come to France to see my games these days even if he doesn't have much time. We maintain a strong bond. He's an admirable person and a good man in everyday life. I'm proud of the sporting and human values he's passed on to me.

18

FIVE CHAMPIONSHIPS

WINNING feels incredible. Ultimately, it's the reason for all sports—and that's because it's a natural high. I'd experienced a fair amount of winning in my life as an athlete, both in the NBA and Europe, but I hadn't yet coached a team to a championship. I'd gotten the Patroons to the CBA Finals, but then all that crap happened and I wasn't able to finish the job. Now, in Oklahoma, teamed up again with my old running mate Otis Birdsong, I was ready to take that next professional step. And win.

On May 24, 2007, I was named the new head coach for the new edition of the CBA's Oklahoma Cavalry. There was something about being in the West. Of course, it's not much like the *Wild West* of the 1800s, with all the houses and shopping malls. But today, it does still have that same sense of untamed land that it's always had. It's not New York, nor Los Angeles. That's for sure. Hell, a hamburger in Lawton cost about two bucks and a good home is less than $200,000. There was something both new and old about the region.

Oklahoma wanted pro basketball. The area had tasted it when the New Orleans NBA team had to relocate to Oklahoma City after Hurricane Katrina. That's why the owners, led by Brian Hopgood, brought the CBA team back. Soon, Oklahoma City would get the Seattle pro team, the SuperSonics (now the Thunder). But for a little while, the Cavalry were the only game in town. And I was the head coach. We played in the Great Plains Coliseum, which held about 3,500 people. We had big crowds. Lots of families came to see us play. It was a good tight-knit community, and the games were rocking. In fact, I got so comfortable there, I've lived in Lawton ever since.

The town is less than ninety minutes south of Oklahoma City, along Route 44. We packed the gym because we were winners. While most things are pretty laid back, our gyms were like rock concerts—especially when we played teams like the Puerto Rico Capitanes (there is a large Puerto Rican population in Lawton). Our cowboy mascot and our cheerleaders made sure everyone got engaged in the games, and Otis was a great GM. He and I worked seamlessly together, and we've actually continued to work together to this day in various other businesses. But with the Cavalry, we got things going as soon as we arrived.

We both had NBA experience, so we ran it like an NBA team. Run and gun. The problem was that the Cavalry wasn't rich like an NBA team. At one point the team's checks started bouncing and I got into it with ownership. It got so bad that ownership fired me on December 16, 2007. I wasn't going to let my guys get duped out of money due to bad ownership. If I did, they wouldn't respect me and follow what I said in the games. I had to stick up for them. That's when the axe fell. It seemed like my coaching career might be over before it began in Oklahoma. But just then something great happened.

The 2007–08 season was the first for the Oklahoma Cavalry in about a decade. The franchise had been in the CBA previously from 1990–97, but it and the entire league folded after that. The Cavalry came back in 2007 with new ownership. But like their checks, they didn't stick around for very long. Then when new-new ownership came in, I was rehired and I went back to work. The new sheriff in town was a guy named John Zelbst, a prestigious lawyer and rancher from the area. Along with a few other co-owners, John was the head honcho with the team and a tremendous guy to work for. We both wanted to win at all costs.

Zelbst, a big sports fan, had bought some front row seats to our games next to the coaches. He was a big supporter of the Cavalry but, in many ways, he *was* the cavalry when we needed him. He was our reinforcement. One day before he owned the squad, we met for lunch and he asked if he could come in one day to watch the team practice. I told him sure, no problem. So when he came to practice the next day, I introduced him to the players as our next owner—you know, I was being a little sly, *hoping* he'd buy the team. "No, no, no," he said, "I don't want to be part of that!" But two weeks later, he bought the franchise—along with three other investors—to keep the team in town. John said he didn't want anyone to coach the team but me—that's how I stayed on.

We finished that first season with a 30–18 record. The second seed in the CBA's Western Conference, we made the playoffs and upset the reigning West champs, the Yakima Sun Kings, which had beaten my Patroons team the year before. It was sweet revenge. We played the Minot SkyRockets in the finals, winning the series in five games. If I was like a puma as a player, sleek and fast, then I was like an explosion of fireworks as a coach. I was wild, trying to help will our team to win. In the minor leagues, most teams are filled with talented guys who just haven't put it all together. I could relate to them and I knew, most of all, they needed motivation. I brought it like a wild man. And with the Cavalry, it worked! The final score of the fifth game in the finals that season was 96–86, and it might have been my favorite 10-point win in my career. I was a championship CBA coach. In the finals that year, Zelbst announced the change of the team's name, too. The Oklahoma Cavalry were now known as the Lawton-Fort Sill Cavalry to represent our fan base. Giddyup!

* * *

Some of my favorite players I coached in Oklahoma stayed with me for years. Guys like Shawn Daniels, who I had on the Cavalry for the 2008–09 season. He was a big guy, 6-foot-7 and about 260 pounds. Shawn could jump like a kangaroo, but he also knew how to use his body to rebound and hold off defenders. He was smart and could pass the ball but, more than anything, he knew how to win, and did the little things that led to success. We also had two great guards, DeAnthony Bowden, a quick slasher from Creighton who could really score, and Brandon Dean, who had a knack for getting steals in big moments.

The 2008–09 season was a rough one for the CBA, which lost about six teams. The season was cut by six weeks, and the championship was shortened from five games to three. But wouldn't you know who was in the finals? That's right, the Cavalry.

There's more.

Our opponents? The Albany Patroons.

An author couldn't have written a better script. What made the whole thing even crazier was that, due to financial issues the CBA was facing, all three games were to be played in New York State *in* Albany, some 1,600 miles from Lawton. Given the location, I knew there would be people talking about me, but I made sure not to pay a lick of attention.

I had a single goal in mind. In the finals, I was a wild man, shouting and moving my hands, barking at bad calls, telling my players what to do. Normal coach stuff, but on steroids. I was known for getting tossed early in games at times, but I didn't care now. There was no way I would let our team lose. No way the Patroons were getting another ring at my expense. Turned out, though, all my tactics worked. We won the series in three games, with every card stacked against us. In front of about six hundred fans, we won the third game in overtime, no less, by two points, 109–107. Bye-bye, Jim Coyne! Better luck next time!

* * *

Days after we won it all, the CBA folded again, citing the 2000s recession. But that wasn't the end of the Cavalry. John Zelbst and his co-owners weren't going to let the team go, even if it was losing money (upwards of $300,000 a year). To avoid this, the team joined the Premier Basketball League, which originated in 2008, for the 2009–10 season. In our first PBL season, we went 19–2 and went into the playoffs as the top seed. We beat the Halifax Rainmen in a two-game sweep. Next up were the Rochester Razorsharks. We lost the first game to them in Rochester, 110–106. In that game, one of my players, Oliver

Miller, a former NBA star, went into the stands to shut up some hecklers.

The three-hundred-plus-pound Miller, who was supposed to be one of our even-keeled veterans, went into the stands to protect me. Some loudmouth Rochester fans had thrown a bottle at my head after I was ejected from the game in the final minutes for arguing a call. Then people started fighting in the stands. After the game, Oliver was suspended and never played pro ball again. I'll always love Oliver for doing that.

But it wouldn't be the last of us. In game two and three of the PBL Finals, we crushed Rochester. We were on a mission. No one was going to mess with us after what happened to me and Oliver in game one. Fuck that. Bye, Rochester! That made three titles for me in three years with Lawton and John Zelbst. And each year, I won Coach of the Year. Nothing sweeter than that!

* * *

The following season, we finished 17–2 and were headed back to the playoffs, where we would face (and beat) the Halifax Rainmen again. Going into the first game—which was the only one that we lost in the three-game series—we had a 33-game home winning streak, but that snapped. In the PBL Finals, we again played the Rochester Razorsharks. But the owner of the team was also the owner of the entire league, so you knew there would be some chicanery. Just how much, though, surprised even me. This series had some horrible officiating and was incredibly frustrating. The team's owner brought in his own refs and at one point, the refs changed a block-charge call to a charge, which went against us. It took everything I had not to level the guy who changed the call. In all my years, I'd never seen such dishonest referees. We ended up losing that game by a single point. I was so mad after the game that I ran after the referees, who went to hide in their locker room. There was police there and they told me, "Coach, we can't let you in there." So, I just screamed and screamed, "You cheated! You cheated!" When I went back to the team locker rooms, I saw many of the players fighting outside in the hallway. It was a mess.

We lost the series, 2–1, in the middle of spring. Seemingly hours later, on April 19, Zelbst said that we wouldn't be returning to the PBL for a third year. Without a league, there was no more Cavalry. And still there were no calls for me from the NBA, college, or overseas to coach. I didn't understand it. I'd won three minor-league titles in a row and had nothing to show for it. But that's life; you have to push forward. My next stop was London, Ontario. Way up in the snow belt, some two-and-a-half hours outside of Toronto. Cold country. John joined that team as a minority owner.

A few of my Oklahoma players came with me up north (though Otis Birdsong didn't), including Shawn, DeAnthony, and Brandon Dean. I also brought guard Tim Ellis, a former player for the Kansas State Wildcats who also played for the Yakima Sun Kings in the CBA. I had Rodney Buford, who had played for Marquette in college and the Miami Heat and a few other teams in the pros. I brought Buford along with me to Canada as well. My team was stacked—I was a heck of a recruiter—and I was ready to make another run at some championships.

* * *

A question I get a lot these days is why I didn't end up coaching in Europe. The answer is that I thought about it, but the leagues over there make it difficult for a person to become one. It's easier to be a player over there—a team can just pick you up if they need you. But if you want to coach a team, they put you through language tests. And while I could speak a little French and Italian, I certainly wasn't fluent. If you've had NBA head coaching experience, those tests quickly disappear. But I didn't have that, so I was kept out of the ranks, still thought of as a foreigner. It was too bad, as I felt like I could have done some good things overseas as a coach.

Still, I was excited for another international adventure in Ontario. Another question I got around this time was if I would ever like to put on a uniform again. The answer to that was *hell no*. I'd played until I was forty-six and I got all my basketball playing out of me by then. Besides, I don't know if I could have played up there in London—it was so cold! You had to have young legs to handle the freezing temperatures. It snowed during most of the year and the snowbanks would be up to your car doors. Thank goodness the city was prepared for it. The city was also prepared for basketball.

The fans of the team up there liked me for many reasons, but perhaps first among them was how I dressed. I was known as the best-dressed coach in the league and people would come up to me and take pictures because I had on a nice suit and to see what kind of shoes I was wearing. Truth be told, I've always been a shoe freak. I probably own five hundred pairs—the ones I've long liked the best are beaded shoes from Las Vegas shoe man Donald Pliner. When I was a kid my brother used to tell me, "You're not complete until your feet is neat." I guess I've always taken that to heart.

Even in the NBA, shoes were a big deal to me. When I was with the Nets, I had a Nike contract. But back then, Nike wasn't *Nike*. Michael Jordan hadn't yet blown up the business with his signature kicks. At the time, Dawkins also had a contract with Nike. But then this new company came into the mix from New Jersey, called Pony. The rep for the company came into Nets practice one day and was throwing around big money. And I saw Darryl get a shoe deal from Pony, so I wanted one, too.

Shit, I thought, if he can do it, so can I. If they're paying Darryl that kind of money, why not pay me? Other guys on the team followed suit. At the time, there was no one telling us we couldn't wear Nikes and Ponys. So we did just that. I even wore one Nike shoe and one Pony shoe in a game. Let's see Steph Curry or LeBron do that today! Later in my career, I was the last player to ever wear Converse in the NBA, too. While Tree Rollins was the last to wear the canvas Chuck Taylors, I was the last player to wear any kind of Converse All-Stars (though I did so with orthotics). If that's not impressive, I don't know what is!

Back in London, we averaged more than 5,000 fans per game, and probably closer to 5,500. It was unbelievable. Founded in 2011, the Lightning was an original team in the National Basketball League (NBL). The area is normally hockey country, but the London Lightning gave the residents their first taste of real professional hoops and a reason to use the arenas during off days. It was the minor leagues, but the fans loved it. I ended up setting records in London, going on long winning streaks. I won Coach of the Year twice as well, and the team is still going to this day.

I was announced as the team's first head coach on August 17, 2011. That first season, I won the league's first-ever Coach of the

Month Award (one I'd win multiple times). For the first year, we finished 28–6 and went on to win the 2011–12 NBL championship, beating the Halifax Rainmen (my old foes), 116–92, in the fifth and deciding game of the series. The next season, we finished 33–7 and won the 2012–13 championship, beating the Summerside Storm. We were destroying teams and I was feeling good. I'd just won my fifth minor-league championship, doing it in three different leagues no less. So I decided to coach one more year in London.

That 2013–14 season, we didn't win it all. We finished the season 23–17 and lost in the playoffs during the conference semifinals (our starting point guard was injured, which hurt us). It was still a great run. After that, I wanted to try to coach in the US again. By now I'd won five rings and been to the finals seven times since I'd started coaching. I didn't know what more I had to do in order to get a job at the next level. Every year I had a different roster, and had to get them to play together and do so consistently. I took a lot of joy in making everything work so well and winning so often. Now I had to figure out what would be next for me.

* * *

If you ask my old friend Otis Birdsong, he'll tell you that I was a great minor-league coach—and I was. He'd wanted to hire me when he was running his own team. And when I got to Oklahoma, we linked up and worked well together. But during my minor-league coaching days, Otis tried to help me get a job with a new team bubbling up in my home state. He talked to me about what a great story of redemption it would be if I could come home to Colorado and lead the team to a championship. After getting banned from the NBA, wouldn't that have been great? Otis even reached out to David Stern to see if he could help me get an interview for the job.

Stern was able to connect me with the team, but the interview they gave me was short and only over the phone. It lasted about ten minutes, from what I remember. They wouldn't even bring me in for a face-to-face meeting. Otis and David had done all they could. Sometimes you can't outlive your past no matter how many championship trophies you bring home. Otis told me there are still people who ask him why we're still friends, wondering why we work together, asking if the parents of the kids we coach wonder what my influence might be? Hearing that, I just sigh and keep myself moving forward.

Memory Lane: John Zelbst

I started out as just a fan with the Cavalry. I purchased some courtside seats close to the bench. I would go with my wife, Cindy, and we'd invite some friends. Well, it turned out they started struggling financially. So another man here in town, Mike Brown, put a group together and came to me for legal advice. Before long, I became involved in the team and we obtained ownership of the Cavalry. But the CBA did not want us to hire Michael. One of the fellas who owned the team in Albany was the president of the CBA and Michael had coached for him the year before.

They'd went sideways and Albany let Michael go. So when our group came in, the CBA said we could purchase the team, but that Michael couldn't be the coach. I said, "Well, that's a deal-breaker then." If they wanted us to buy in, we were going to pick whatever coach we wanted. Any other option was a nonstarter for us. Finally, of course, they were desperate to keep the number of teams up in the league and we got our way. Well, with Michael as coach, we blew through that league and won championship after championship. If you're a sports fan of any sort, you couldn't help but know about Michael Ray. He's such a dynamic guy.

In fact, I think half the fans came to see Michael on the sidelines. It was quite a show! He was very involved, knowledgeable. I've been around athletics all my life, as a collegiate football player, and I'll tell you what I found out about him. Michael read the court better than anyone I've ever seen. It's still just amazing to me how he'd do it. I remember we had this player, DeAnthony Bowden, who set the all-time scoring record in New York in the playoffs with 61 points. I remember Michael saying to the team in the huddle then, "If anybody else shoots the ball, just come sit down here next to me."

Michael had a great understanding and feel for the game. He liked to have veteran players, too, particularly late in game. Guys who don't turn the ball over when we needed a score. In the minor leagues, you're only allowed so many moves and trades during the season. Well, it was like a revolving door a lot of times in our gym. He'd bring guys in, and they'd go out almost as quick as they came in sometimes. He was hard to play for in that sense. I remember we had one guy come in from Yakima, who told me he was a little scared to play for Michael. But he learned that if you played hard and did what he said, there were no problems.

Michael and I started off with an employer-employee relationship, but we ended up becoming best friends. We've shared a lot of ups and downs. Michael married a local girl and stayed here in Lawton. I stayed with him as a partner when the team went up to Canada after the CBA and PBL broke up. He won me five championships! He was just a terrific coach, a terrific spokesman, and had great messages for the youth and anyone else who'd listen about life and what happens after basketball. These days, my wife and I have had courtside tickets to the Oklahoma City Thunder for about sixteen years. And Sugar comes to games with us.

Everyone knows him in the NBA, too. What's amazing is that we'll see NBA referees after the game, and they'll wave us over to get their picture taken with him. If you know anything about the NBA, you know Michael was a superstar when he was in the league. And I remember last year, Chauncey Billups was in town with Portland. Of course, Chauncey is a Denver guy, and he knew Michael from growing up there. So he invited Michael to come back into the locker room and all the players there wanted to get a picture with him. He has such an engaging personality, and he just knows everybody!

Michael introduced me to David Stern, and I have photographs with him, too. I've always wondered, it's almost like Jack Kennedy, when Michael left the NBA, he was at the height of his prowess. So no one saw his skills diminish. When people meet him today, in their mind they remember the monster that he was on the basketball court. You just couldn't stop him; you couldn't control or contain him. Today, as everyone knows who meets him, Mike has a stutter. So, I asked him one time, "When you were a kid, did that create problems for you?" And he said his mother gave him some of the best advice.

She said, "When other kids laugh at you, son, just laugh with them." That's kind of like his whole attitude about life now. Just laugh about it, then go home and make something of it. Michael is truly phenomenal. And what a great citizen he's been here in our community in Lawton. Me and him, his wife and my wife, we travel all over the place together. My wife and I have a place in the Caribbean, and he's well known down there, too. I get calls from people, "When's he coming to St. Martin?" And he'll go and he'll put a clinic on for the kids. We've had a lot of fun together. My life has very much been enriched by our friendship.

19

THE NEXT GENERATION

SPEAKING of Otis Birdsong, he and I have continued to work together since teaming up in Oklahoma. These days, we have become business partners, running camps and workshops for kids. I love teaching and I really love helping kids. (I've even done some substitute teaching in Oklahoma.) Today, Otis and I run free camps in New Jersey, Florida, Texas, Colorado, and other cities. We work with former New Jersey Nets owner Joe Taub's foundation, and we serve kids who are underprivileged. It's about teaching life skills. About eating right, taking care of themselves, about the dangers of drugs and alcohol and bullying. We also provide meals and school supplies.

Otis and I talk every day, whether it's about the camps and our work or just to see how each other are doing. When everything happened with me in the mid-eighties, a lot of people who I thought were friends chose to have nothing to do with me, wouldn't return my calls, or wouldn't want to work with me. But not Otis. He's a true friend. He knows what it's like, too. A few of his family members have had trouble with drugs. Otis has done everything in sports, from playing in the NBA to starting a management firm to working with former Dallas Cowboys quarterback Roger Staubach, to working in the minor leagues. He's as loyal as they get.

Together, we wanted to teach the kids about being a professional. As friends, Otis and I are always honest with each other. We understand one another. And I always tell him, if I have a nickel, half of it's his. There is a foundational quality to our friendship, which I think is important. It's why we're so good at teaching the fundamentals of the game, too, because we care about them a great deal at this point in our lives. I've seen what can happen to a person if they lose track of their roots, their base. In the game of basketball, I think the current AAU system is at fault for not teaching young kids the fundamentals. Dribbling, passing, shooting, movement.

The game is supposed to be fun, but the AAU system today puts too much pressure on them. The reality is kids have a better chance of winning the lottery than making the NBA. But we wonder why they take the wrong path if it doesn't work out. That's why Otis and I use basketball to teach them about life. Because of the game, I've traveled all over the world and seen how it benefits others. From my camps with Otis and the hundred-plus campers they draw to even going to places like India and Africa with the NBA Academy, it's about believing there is more to life than what's around you now. That's what our Ball Stars Youth Camp has done the past dozen years.

Regarding the next generation, my hope is that today's players continue to do their homework and learn about the greats who came before them. Bill Russell and his peers paved the way for my generation, and my generation helped pave the way for today's players who make hundreds of millions of dollars, and today's owners, who can sell their teams for billions. It's a lineage, and if you don't honor and respect the past, it's going to up and bite you. Same goes for styles of play. It shouldn't just be threes all day with no defense. Make sure to do your research, kids! Learn about the guys and gals who came before today's social media athletes. You'll be glad you did.

* * *

Today, family is the most important thing in my life. My wife Kim and I own a salon in Lawton. And I'm proud to say I have eleven grandchildren (and counting). During my life, I had five kids. My oldest, Tosha, is a stay-at-home mom who lives in Denver; my son Corey, who I had with my former girlfriend Brenda, is a fireman who lives in New Jersey; my daughter Tamara (who we all call Nikki) is a pediatrician in New York City; my son Michael Amir lives in France, where he is a pro soccer player there in the first division; and his sister Kimberly is a skilled translator and a sweetheart. Their mother is named Ilham. I also adopted Leah's lovely daughter Naomi.

While no one has lived a perfect life, I'm proud of what I've been able to do in mine, thanks largely to my family. Kim, who I married a few years after splitting from Ilham (she still lives in Europe), has three kids of her own, too. Yes, we have one BIG family. And it just makes me so happy to be involved in all of their lives. I can't wait to be a great-grandfather one day, and I try to visit my kids whenever I can. I'm always flying to some place or other to check on them and their children—I get to see their little rooms, watch them play with Legos and other toys. Even Otis has noticed it. As he says it, I'm just a family man. What a gift!

BANNED

Memory Lane: Kimberly Richardson

My father is someone who has been very present for his children, despite the distance for me and my younger brother, because we live in France. My dad likes to have fun, laugh, and is very affectionate and generous. Those are his biggest qualities. He's always here for us, always takes the time to make phone calls to us every day.

I remember when I was little and he was playing basketball. I was really impressed and proud of my dad. I was very proud of the person that he was because of his humbleness while also being very talented. For me, he was my hero. Like, "Wow, I have a dad that is a professional athlete!" As a young kid, you're always impressed when someone in your family is famous.

A few years ago, I was in Cannes, and I was talking with this guy who was there with his son and sports came up. I mentioned that my dad was a famous basketball player and he asked me his name because he said he used to watch basketball. Well I told him my dad's name and the guy said, "Oh, I know him! How is it possible I'm talking with his daughter?"

Then I called my dad to FaceTime him. I don't know if my dad will remember this now, but I FaceTimed with him and this guy, and he was really happy just to say hello. He said to my father, "I've been a big fan of yours for a long time!" It was very nice. And these days French basketball is getting huge.

When my dad was in Antibes, they played in the Pro A league. There were very good teams then and I know that he had a big impact. In the gym, there is still a big sign for when they won the championship. I remember going to that gym when I was younger when they won, and I remember my dad being part of everything for the victory, which makes me so proud.

CONCLUSION

ONE of the hardest things I've had to deal with in my later years is the death of my mother, Luddie Hicks. She was a saint, and my biggest regret in life is ever letting her down. She died about ten years ago, and I've thought about her every day since. John Zelbst even flew in for her funeral and sat with us at the family table. That's love. When my mother was alive, I could always pick up the phone and talk with her. Even today, it feels like I'm empty when I think about her. She always called just me Michael Ray. My dad's mother also died not too long ago. And when she passed, my brother brought my father up to Denver. When I visited, I would see him here and there.

It was strange, but he was my dad and I just told myself, "It is what it is." My father fought in the Vietnam War and when he came back from battle, he'd lost some of his mind. When I was a kid, he'd sit with me and tell me how he saw people get their heads cut off and their eyes gassed out. How people stuck knives in other people's faces. It's safe to say that Vietnam was something he never got over. He left for war after I was born, and when he came back he was no longer dealing with a full deck. I remember one time when I went to go visit him in Texas when he was living there with his mother. He had an apartment out back behind her old café. Dad never locked his door, but he had knives hanging over the doorway. When I went to visit him, he always told me to whistle or knock or send him a signal before I came inside. But one time I forgot. I just opened the door and a giant knife fell to the floor, slicing down the side of my head, just missing my ear. All my dad said was, "I told you, boy! Announce yourself when you're coming in here." I was about nine or ten years old. Well, dad died about three years ago now. I guess I miss him. More, I just wonder what happened to him. War and life will get even the best of us. Even without him, my mother made a strong family for us in Denver.

* * *

It's hard, to be honest. Sometimes doing so can affect a lot of people, especially those you don't want to hurt. After I was banned, I could have taken down players, even hurt the NBA. But I didn't want to do any of that. I'd thought about writing a book then, but it wasn't the right time, and it wouldn't have been about my life so much. If I had written a book then, it would have been about my banishment from the NBA, which I think is only a small part of my life's story. And there would have been pressures to name those who might have gotten involved in drugs but who weren't caught like I was. But ratting on people is not my game.

I've always been willing to talk about myself. To tell my story. And here it is, in these pages. I'm not ashamed of anything that I did, at least not in the way that it makes me hide from the world with the covers over my head. I've made mistakes and I've paid for them. I'm not proud of what I did, the lifestyle that got me banned from the NBA for two seasons before my reinstatement. But if I don't talk about it, how could anyone learn from my mistakes? I've been clean for thirty-five years now and have dealt with a lot and seen much of the world. I have my peace of mind.

Recently, though, there was another book that came out about me, which I had nothing to do with. I won't mention the title or author, but there are many errors and many innuendos that I bristled at. The author seemed to imply—or desperately want to imply—that I may have fixed games while with the Knicks, shaving points. But it's all false. The idea of fixing a game never crossed my mind. Not once. When I played, all we wanted to do was win and beat the next guy.

In the very same book, he also said that I showed my *bare ass* to Coach Stan Albeck during a Nets practice one afternoon, which is also blatantly wrong. I loved Stan and never did that to him, or anyone else in the NBA. That guy's book is a joke.

Yet another book, *Larceny Games*, mentions the Knicks possibly being involved in point shaving in the mid-seventies, some five years before I arrived. The book also mentions me and my teammates in another incident later on. But again, this is false. Just because I had a cocaine problem in the early eighties doesn't mean I was fixing games to satisfy it in the NBA. And to imply that or even get in the ballpark of that implication is wrong and sloppy. It's disingenuous.

Let's move on.

* * *

Lately, I've been setting up meetings and counseling recovering addicts. While going to rehabs can work, I've found that many of the centers just want to take people's cash. It's big business. Once the insurance money runs out, so does the care. So for me, the biggest thing about being sober is not being around the drugs. Don't put yourself in places where you might come across them. Whether that be cocaine or alcohol or whatever. The other thing is to find people who support you, who you can talk to. Addiction is a lifelong battle. You need to vent about it at times. With those two things in place, you're more than halfway home.

If you listen to people in recovery, they often share the same story. It was gradual, just a weekend thing at first. And then everything snowballed quickly and their lives were changed forever. Once you enter recovery you have to understand that you aren't going to be able to please everyone and not everyone is going to support you and your healing. But the question is, can you please yourself and know that you are doing the right thing? Are your kids happy with you? Is your wife happy with you? Is your mother happy with you? Your siblings? Nothing else really matters beyond you and the people you care about most.

* * *

America is a country of addiction. If it's not drugs or alcohol, it's fast food or guns or gambling. It's whatever is the easy way out. Guys want to make fast money. People don't want to work—not until they learn the real value of it, anyway. And that value is not just in the dollars you can amass, but in the character it can build internally. Rome wasn't built in a day, and neither was the human spirit. When I got hooked, I was just passing the time. Not thinking I'd get into drugs. Today, I commiserate with plenty of users and even for NBA players. We wonder, how did we get involved in all this even when we knew it was crazy? And how did we manage to even survive?

If there is a moral to my story, it's that I've examined myself and am confident in who I am today. I'm not scared of myself. I'm not scared of death, nor of the truth. It's a feeling I hope I can impart onto others. To feel the same way. While it's a shame that my career may never be remembered for its heights, or that I was never able to battle Michael Jordan or Magic Johnson in the playoffs, I've come to terms with that. I've lived my life as best as I could. And lots of players before and since me have done way worse things than I ever did! Let the chips fall where they may. Life isn't about holding grudges. I just treat people with the respect I feel I also deserve.

* * *

There are many things I'm proud of today that I was able to accomplish on the basketball floor. Like four NBA All-Star appearances (all voted in by the coaches), leading the league in assists in 1980 and steals three seasons, earning Comeback Player of the Year in 1985 and being on the All-Defensive team twice. Also winning two Italian League championships overseas and a European League Cup are also up there, too. (I was the top scorer the year we won the European Cup in 1990.) I also won a French Basketball Cup and was an All-Star overseas seven times. That's a lot of hardware.

As a coach, I won five minor league championships and two Coach of the Year Awards. And I wouldn't mind getting back into coaching. But at the very top of my list of accomplishments is getting my life back on track and becoming a family man. My hope now is that people judge me on my entire life, not just a few bad years. If it hadn't been for my drug use, I may

have made nine or ten All-Star teams in the league and I may
be a Hall of Fame player. Maybe on the Top 75 team! Heck, I
made the University of Montana Hall of Fame and was named
a Top-50 player in Big Sky Conference after being a three-time
all-conference player.

But wondering about what-ifs now is like wondering what
the world would be like if JFK or MLK weren't assassinated.
It's impossible to know. But I believe I am right where the Man
Upstairs always wanted me. Young people often ask me what
kind of player I was when in the league. To me, I was a lot
like Russell Westbrook. I was a fast triple-double machine who
played both ends with intensity. Imagine if Westbrook was out
of the league after eight or nine years and had a big gap in the
middle of those years due to personal problems. The world
would have lost a lot and so would he have, too.

Not to mention the eighties get overlooked at times when
people consider the history of the NBA. The decade is reduced
to Boston and LA, Bird and Magic. But there were so many great
guys in the league then, from Julius Erving to Moses Malone,
Otis Birdsong, me, and many others. Studying history is important. It's worth exploring when you can. It was the decade that
forged Michael Jordan. He was a giant, yes, but he also stood on
the shoulders of other giants. Today, there are many fans who
saw me in the eighties who would say I was the second-best
guard of the decade behind Magic. But, of course, there was also
Isiah, Jordan, and many other greats.

I'm happy to report, though, that several publications have
put me on the Nets all-time team of the eighties, even though I
was only there for a few seasons. Yes, basketball has always been
very good to me. Financially, mentally, and physically. I have

seen the entire world thanks to the game and met people I'd only dream of meeting without the sport. The other day I read a few more stats about my career, lesser-known ones. I had one of the biggest differences between being the top assist leader compared to No. 2 (Tiny Archibald) in league history. I was also one of the few players to lead the league in assists on a losing team. And no one but me and the logo, Jerry West, have ever averaged more than 6 assists and 2.5 steals for a career.

Today, I'm No. 30 all-time in assists per game (7.0) and I have the fourth-most steals in a single season (265). I also played the second-fewest games of anyone who nabbed 1,000 steals. And while I don't think I'll ever make the Basketball Hall of Fame, there is certainly a case to be made, given the ups and downs of my life. You can't tell the story of pro basketball without mentioning my name. And I even got my number retired overseas in Italy! I went back to my old stomping grounds in 2023, and my Bologna team celebrated me by retiring my number.

Before I arrived, I figured there would be a few fans in attendance, but there were thousands on hand. When I walked into the gym, there was a standing ovation for me for something like fifteen minutes. It had been nearly thirty years since my playing days in Bologna, but the fans were reminding me of Sugarmania all over again. I couldn't help but shed a tear or three. It was unbelievable. A lifetime of experiences rushed back to me. Game-winning shots, trash talking, and competing with players all over the world. People may say I didn't deserve the pain and punishment I got, but who's to say I deserved any of the glory and adoration, either? Believe me, I was a lucky man.

* * *

I'm now sixty-nine years old. I have no patience for golf, but I do like to play cards, chess, and backgammon. Occasionally, I'll fly out to someone's charity golf event, but I can't play the game much at all. A few years ago, I was diagnosed with prostate cancer. I've since undergone surgery for it. The problem has come back here and there, and I've even received radiation therapy. It's been a process, but I stay on top of it. I'm one of those guys who likes to know what's going on with his body and I'm not scared to talk straight with doctors. Every year, I fly out to Las Vegas for the NBA Retired Players Association meetings, but I never go to summer league—it's just too hot for me to watch basketball in Vegas in the summer!

Some nights, I try and catch my son playing soccer on television. Morocco against Egypt was on the other day, the two teams playing for the African Cup and Michael's Moroccan team won! It was the first time in over fifty years that they'd made the finals, and they won. His team just competed in the Paris Olympics and they won a bronze medal—I couldn't be happier for him and all he's been able to accomplish. Michael, whose mother is Moroccan, is a midfielder, he's the guy that controls the game— just like his dad. Michael can pass the ball, he's got vision, and manages the tempo of a game. I've gotten better at understanding soccer because of him. I used to think it was too low scoring, but now I understand the field position strategies. It's a hard sport!

These days, I realize that getting older is a wild thing. It's hard to accept at times and it causes you to reflect, which is one of the many reasons why I wanted to write this book. But one of the great outcomes of doing so was coming across an old scrapbook. In it are letters from fans, including one from 1982 written in cursive by a young Marc Taylor, which said, "The Garden won't be the same without you. Everyone always got on your case about trying to take situations into your own hands but I understand that you was just trying to get the team rolling." There are newspaper clippings about my banishment and reinstatement, old photos, programs in Italian and English, box scores, college stats and much more.

You know, when something bad happens to you, when people say you've done wrong in your life or career, it can be easy to take that on or believe you're less than you really are. But leafing through the hundreds of pages of delicate newsprint and memorabilia, I remember even more fully who I am and always have been. Michael Ray Richardson.

* * *

At home in Lawton now, I cut the grass, cook, and do my husbandly duties. My wife and I have a nice clientele with our salon. During the summers, I do my camps with Otis.

The world is changing but, as you get older, you learn to deal with things differently. That's the value of gaining experience. You learn to accept what your life has in store for you. Yes, you were there every step of the way, and your decisions were your own. But in another way, everything was all set out for you from the moment you were born into the world. Everything that I saw and did, all that I went through along the way, that was just part of my scripture. I've found clarity in that thought. And I laugh more these days than I ever did in my entire life. How could I not? I'm just so grateful.

Memory Lane: Kim Richardson

Michael is amazing. He's just everything to me. He's what my children and I needed when we first met. The perfect person to find when you're done with all the BS of life. We first met at a party in Oklahoma in 2007. He was just getting out of basketball practice and stopped in for a minute. I knew who he was because my little brother, Malcolm Johnson, played for him on the Cavalry. At the party, Michael didn't know if I was there with somebody or not. I didn't know him other than that he was the basketball coach.

But he sent a lady over to ask me if I was there alone. And I was there alone. I didn't know what she wanted with me at first but then she said, "I have a friend that wants to meet you." I said, "Okay, send him over, I know he can talk for himself." So I gave him my number. Our first date was at an Applebee's, and it's been great ever since. He is really good with me and my three children. When Michael met, my daughter was fifteen, my son was thirteen, and I had an eight-year-old. He gave his attention to all of us. Michael is just a great father and a great husband.

After we got together, he started making me breakfast every morning. And in the summers, we travel all the time now. We go to the beach, every year we go to Saint Martin in the Caribbean with John Zelbst and his wife, Cindy. John is a tremendous friend; you couldn't ask for a better friend than John and his wife. As far as Michael's past, I already knew about it once we started dating. Anytime you can Google a person; there's nothing to hide. But it didn't stop anything because I saw that he was not that person anymore.

Michael is an all-around good man. He will do anything for you. He's a genuine person—not just with me, but with my family. He couldn't be a better person, and I'm not just saying that because he's my husband. Michael just has a big heart. I love that about him. He's a crybaby, too! Last year I got really sick and I just noticed that every little thing touched his heart. He took really good care of me. Michael just does what a husband is supposed to do. If you ever look up the word *husband* in the dictionary, you'll see Michael Ray's name under it.

INDEX